You've Got to Have a Dream

You've Got to Have a Dream

The Message of the Musical

Ian Bradley

WESTMINSTER
JOHN KNOX PRESS
LOUISVILLE · KENTUCKY

Published in the United States in 2005 by Westminster John Knox Press, Louisville, Kentucky.

Published in Great Britain by SCM Press.

Cover design by Eric Handel, LMNOP

This book is printed on acid-free paper that meets the American National Standards Institute Z39.48 standard. ♾

PRINTED IN THE UNITED STATES OF AMERICA

05 06 07 08 09 10 11 12 13 14 — 10 9 8 7 6 5 4 3 2 1

Library of Congress Cataloging-in-Publication Data

Bradley, Ian C.
    You've got to have a dream : the message of the musical / Ian Bradley.
        p. cm.
    ISBN 0-664-22854-2 (alk. paper)
    1. Musicals—Religious aspects.   I. Title

ML2054.B73 2005
782.1'4—dc22

2004061234

For Lucy, Mary and Andrew who have endured
and to varying degrees even encouraged this
somewhat bizarre fixation in the family.

Contents

Acknowledgements

It was the Divinity students at Aberdeen University who got me going on this topic when, knowing my love of musicals, they presented me with Michael Walsh's lavish critical biography of Andrew Lloyd Webber in March 1999 as a leaving present after six very happy years there. In the five years since then, my burgeoning interest and research in this subject has been aided by a large number of people. First and foremost, I must single out the students doing my 'Theology of the Musical' module at St Andrews University, and especially Elaine Pardoe, Sandy Tedford, Rebecca Howard, Emma Tee, Philip Corbett and Joshua Edelman who have all supplied me with cuttings, CDs, videos and other material.

I have gained a great deal from the participants at two courses on the topic of the theology of the musical which I led at St Deiniol's Library, Hawarden – the first under the title 'Any Dream Will Do' in May 2001 and the second 'You've Got to Have a Dream' in February 2003. I would particularly like to thank Peter Francis, the warden of St Deiniol's, for his help and encouragement in this venture.

I have also shared my thoughts on this theme with an audience at Pepperdine University in January 1999, with members of the Methodist Church Music Association at their millennium conference at Swanwick in August 2000, with postgraduates in a seminar of the Institute for Theology and the Arts at the Divinity School, St Andrews University, and at the general assembly of the Unitarian Church in Edinburgh in April 2003. The material in Chapter 2 was first developed in talks to the conferences of the Arthur Sullivan Society, and I am grateful to its secretary, Stephen Turnbull, for all his support and friendship. Several congregations have been inflicted with my singing from the pulpit – among them St Paul's Cathedral, Dundee, Sedbergh and Glenalmond school chapels, St Andrews University Chapel and sundry parish churches.

Articles representing 'research in progress' have appeared over the last five years in the *Church Times*, *Life and Work* and *The Tablet*, and I am grateful to the editors of those periodicals for letting me air my views. I am also particularly grateful to my good friend Stephen Shipley, senior worship producer for BBC religious broadcasting, for allowing me to present a musicals-based Sunday Worship on Radio 4 in February 2003 under the title 'To Dream the Impossible Dream'. Although I had feared Radio 4 listeners might object to show songs being used as hymns, the reaction to this programme was very positive and further convinced me of the importance of this subject.

Those who have answered my specific queries and supplied me with helpful information include Stephen Schwartz, Stuart Watson, John Bush Jones, Robert Saunders and Corey Spence. I am particularly grateful to Stephen Schwartz, Tim Rice, Tom Jones, Darrah Cloud, Jim Steinman, Ben Elton, Sheldon Harnick, Willy Holtzman and Dale Wasserman for their generosity in allowing me to quote from their work, and to Alan Honig, David Robinson of the Really Useful Group, Kate Bullock of International Music Publications, Kara Darling of the Rodgers and Hammerstein organization, Nadia Karnouche of Universal Music Publishing, Terry Whittaker of Carlin Music, Sharon O'Neill of EMI Music Publishing, and Sue Coombes of Alain Boublil Overseas Ltd, for help over copyright issues.

This book was originally commissioned for SCM Press by John Bowden, whose initial support and enthusiasm was an important spur to getting me started on it. I have since received consistent support and encouragement from the staff at SCM-Canterbury Press and especially from Barbara Laing, Jenny Willis and Christine Smith.

A Research Leave grant from the Arts and Humanities Research Board and a grant from the Cameron Mackintosh Foundation enabled me to complete the research for this study. I am very grateful to both these benefactors, without whom this book would not have appeared.

Introduction

The musical is surely the most ubiquitous and dominant cultural icon of our age. It has a commanding position in the theatrical life of both London and New York. Over the last 25 years there have consistently been more musicals than straight plays running in the West End at any one time – the ratio has averaged around 8 to 7. On Broadway, the supremacy of the musical is much greater. As I write this there are just six non-musicals playing in Broadway's 26 main active theatres. Provincial theatres and amateur companies on both sides of the Atlantic are even more thralled to and enthralled by musicals. The programme of productions in the Bristol Hippodrome, one of the United Kingdom's biggest provincial theatres, for 2003 reveals that apart from two weeks of opera, one of ballet and a Christmas pantomime, the entire year is given over to musicals. Local theatres across the United States rely on touring versions of Broadway shows to fill houses and subsidize other less profitable productions. Schools have increasingly embraced *Guys and Dolls*, *Grease* and a handful of other musical evergreens for their major annual productions.

The triumph of the musical has broken theatrical records and produced mind-boggling statistics for both audience attendance and box office receipts. For long popular in English-speaking countries, the musical has now become a truly global phenomenon and is indeed one of the most striking and successful examples of globalization. *Jesus Christ Superstar* has been translated into eleven languages and performed in forty countries. *Cats* has so far been seen by over 50 million people and grossed well in excess of two billion dollars worldwide. *Les Misérables*, having taken much of the western world by storm, has been translated into Chinese and performed in Beijing. A student recently returned from Tokyo bearing a poster advertising the Japanese version of *The Lion King*. Although overwhelmingly British or American in origin, musicals are hugely popular in much of Continental Europe. On a recent visit to Budapest I could have taken in, within the space of one week, performances in Hungarian of *West Side Story, Cats, Godspell, Man of La Mancha, Funny Girl, Chicago* and *The Sound of Music.*

There is a very significant difference of attitude towards musicals on the two sides of the Atlantic. In the United States they are taken seriously as an art form and lauded as the country's distinctive contribution to culture. In the Yale University book store musical theatre is shelved next to Shakespeare. In the United Kingdom, by contrast, the huge popularity and commercial success of the genre damns it in the eyes of much of the cultural and artistic establishment. For their detractors, musicals are not an art form so much as a commercial product, manufactured in a cynical and calculated way, ruthlessly hyped and marketed to make a particularly vulgar form of mass entertainment. Ever more elaborate in their scenery and special effects, possessing what one critic has called 'that sense of the scenic overkill whereby you leave humming the sets', they are castigated for depending for their effect on technological gimmickry and careful packaging.[1] In the words of the journalist Veronica Lee there is 'a very British ambivalence to musicals – we flock to see them, but we don't regard them as "proper" theatre'.[2] The dramatist David Hare accuses musicals of having seriously dumbed down the whole nature of theatrical performance and fundamentally changed the audience's relationship with drama by making spectacle, accessibility and tunes to hum the standard definition of what theatre should be. Similar sentiments were voiced in a letter in *The Times* following the announcement that both of the United Kingdom's main subsidized theatres would be staging musicals in their 2000–01 season (the National Theatre with *Singin' in the Rain* and the Royal Shakespeare Company with *The Secret Garden*):

> It was a bad day for the English theatre when the galumphing pretentiousness of *Les Misérables* became a popular success, and our two major companies decided that a good way to eke out their meagre subsidies was to put on money-making musicals. . . . Valuable stage time is being taken up by these 'pop' productions while many classics of world theatre languish unperformed.[3]

The commitment of Britain's two main publicly subsidized and 'classical' theatre companies to staging musicals stands in marked contrast to the general dismissal of the genre by the cultured classes. The National Theatre has given musicals a prominent place in its repertoire since presenting *Guys and Dolls* in 1982 and the Royal Shakespeare Company was responsible for the first UK production of *Les Misérables* in 1985. The fact is that for both companies the receipts from musicals provide essential subsidy for their more 'serious' productions in the field of spoken classical and contemporary theatre.

Most academics, including academic theologians, share this disdain for a cultural form which, on the face of it, seems the epitome of blatant commercialism and materialism. In fact, my thesis in this book is that the musical, and especially the modern musical, has a significant theological content and spiritual dimension and provides for many people an experience which can genuinely be described as religious as well as entertaining.

Where is the connection between the highly commercial world of musical theatre and the realms of theology and spiritual experience? Let me begin my attempt to answer this apparent conundrum by posing ten *Trivial Pursuits*-style questions that I ask the students embarking on my 'Theology of the Musical' class at St Andrews University. In case readers of this book want to play the game properly, I have reserved the answers for a footnote:

1 Which recent musical has a scene in which a Unitarian Church is blown up?
2 Which musical brought together the sons of two leading biblical scholars as collaborators?
3 Which classic musical features the Save-a-Soul mission with its march song 'Follow the fold and stray no more'?
4 Which musical features the Rhythm of Life Church and has a scene set in a YMCA hostel?
5 Which musical has a first act song that mentions an obscure figure from the Old Testament and a second act scene during which a hymn is played reverently on a piano accordion? (Bonus points for identifying the character and the hymn.)
6 Which song from a Christian musical reached No. 1 in the British charts in 1999, despite being dubbed 'vile' by George Michael and boycotted by BBC Radio 1 and Radio 2?
7 According to Garrison Keiller's imaginary Father Wilmer, Roman Catholic priest of Our Lady of Perpetual Responsibility at Lake Wobegon, which denomination meets for worship in order to say the pledge of allegiance, talk about sharing and sing 'Climb every mountain'?

8 Which song from a Rodgers and Hammerstein musical is now found in several hymnbooks, sandwiched between 'What a friend we have in Jesus' and 'While shepherds watched their flocks by night'?

9 Which song from another Rodgers and Hammerstein musical has been turned into a doxology in many American churches but does not appear in any hymnal because the composer's executors will not allow it to be used for religious/liturgical purposes?

10 Which song from a recent musical was sung as an anthem at the inaugural gala for President George W. Bush and at the inter-faith service held at 'Ground Zero' after the terrorist attack on the World Trade Center with the composer at the piano in both cases?[4]

As a bonus question, I generally ask my students which show songs have featured in recent years in the very popular programme of communal hymn singing, *Songs of Praise*, which is broadcast every Sunday evening on BBC television. The answer, which in this case I will not keep readers in suspense over, is 'more than you might think'. The list includes 'Can you feel the love tonight?' from the *Lion King*, sung by Welsh male voice choirs in the Albert Hall in November 2000; Harold Arlen and Johnny Mercer's 'Accentuate the positive', sung by Marion Montgomery and Laurie Holloway in their Berkshire drawing room in May 2001; 'I don't know how to love him' from *Jesus Christ Superstar*, sung in the Tower of London in a programme to celebrate the spiritual dimension of monarchy in November 2001; 'Loving you is not a choice' from Sondheim's *Passion* on Mothering Sunday 2002; 'When you walk through a storm' from *Carousel*, sung by Lesley Garrett and Daniel O'Donnell from Belfast's Waterfront Centre in November 2002; 'There's a place for us' from *West Side Story*, sung by Charlotte Church in January 2003; and 'The rhythm of life' from *Sweet Charity*, which featured in the first *Songs of Praise* Festival of School Choirs in March 2003.

There has, indeed, been a whole edition of *Songs of Praise* devoted entirely to songs from musicals, all of them written by the same composer. A special tribute to Andrew Lloyd Webber on the occasion of his fiftieth birthday in 1998 featured numbers from *Joseph*, *Evita*, *Jesus Christ Superstar*, *Cats* and *Whistle Down the Wind*. At first sight, such treatment for the leading figure in British musical theatre seems astonishing. No one from the world of Christian music has ever received a similar accolade, not even Graham Kendrick or Cliff Richard. Yet it was not just the BBC that turned Lloyd Webber's fiftieth birthday into a quasi-religious event. A journalist attending the celebratory birthday concert in the Albert Hall, in which the performers included the London Community Gospel Choir, noted that 'the first half of the evening, with songs from *Jesus Christ Superstar*, *Joseph*, *Evita* and the *Requiem* seemed almost like an evangelist's meeting'.[5] A more intimate gathering at the composer's home in Sydenham included a church service where the preacher, Canon Don Lewis, took as his text 2 Kings 3.15: 'The prophet Elisha commanded, "Send me a minstrel!" And when the minstrel played, the power of the Lord came upon him.' He went on to make clear that in his view Lloyd Webber was, indeed, a minstrel sent from God:

> His great works *Joseph* and *Jesus Christ Superstar* have introduced Biblical themes to a Biblically illiterate age with bountiful effect. And Andrew's proclamation of the gospel is far broader and more infectious than are our efforts in the church!
>
> Andrew's tunes are irresistibly hummable. They are a powerful vehicle for carrying themes of the spirit of God through the world. 'Love changes everything' – hailed by the secular young and Mothers' Union members alike – will remain a classic for all time. And it proclaims beyond the millennium, and in idiom we all understand, the centrality of love, which sober-minded St Paul could but hammer into the Church of Corinth.
>
> Lloyd Webber musicals carry a message. A message of faith, a message of caring for each other, a message of the gospel. And they carry that message infectiously. It takes courage as well as genius to attempt what Andrew does. Creativity takes you into unchartered waters. Takes you into the very workshop of God!
>
> Send me a minstrel, and you will know power from God![6]

A further stage in the beatification, or maybe even the sanctification, of Lloyd Webber was reached in the spectacular edition of *Songs of Praise*, which as far as BBC religious broadcasting was concerned launched the third Christian millennium. Staged at the Cardiff Millennium Stadium on the first Sunday of the year 2000 and attended by over 60,000 people, including the Prince of Wales and his two sons, the programme was a classic of popular folk religion. Bryn Terfil led the company in a medley of Welsh hymns. Cliff Richard sang the setting of the Lord's Prayer to the tune of *Auld Lang Syne*, which had been written as a finale of the musical *Hopes and Dreams* by Stephen Deal and Paul Field. Daniel O'Donnell crooned 'Light a candle in the darkness'. The climax of the programme came when Andrew Lloyd Webber walked into the middle of the stadium to introduce a three-way mix involving two of the hit songs from his West End show, *Whistle Down the Wind*, and his setting of lines written by Anna Crompton, a 14-year-old Ipswich schoolgirl and winner of a national competition initiated by his Open Churches Trust to find the best new prayer for the millennium. As the show's star, Laura Michelle Kelly, sang its title song, a Welsh male voice choir interjected with extracts from its biggest hit number, 'No matter what', and a somewhat truncated version of Miss Crompton's prayer which was shorn of its opening line 'Dear Lord our Heavenly Father' and of its second half which asked: 'Give us courage to face the challenges of feeding the hungry, clothing the naked, housing the homeless, and healing the sick. Give us the power to make a difference in your world, and to protect your creation. Through Jesus Christ our Lord, Amen.'

What was left of the prayer was a fairly bland set of humanist aspirations with no distinctive Christian focus or challenge. Lloyd Webber's setting of the millennium prayer was in marked contrast to the approach of John Taverner, the austere composer who has embraced Eastern Orthodoxy, when asked to set Britain's all-purpose, multi-faith millennium resolution for performance at the Greenwich Millennium Dome on New Year's Eve 1999. He insisted on inserting the words 'O Lord' at the end of every line. Unlike Taverner's effort to create a genuine spiritual moment at the heart of what would otherwise have been an almost wholly secular celebration, the Lloyd Webber medley which formed the centrepiece of the *Songs of Praise* millennium special seemed on the face of it to belong more to the world of show business hype. For those of us who have watched in horror as *Songs of Praise* has progressively abandoned its long-standing commitment to straightforward hymns and 'ordinary' people talking about their often very extraordinary lives and faith and become increasingly obsessed with celebrities and soft-focus schmaltz, this episode seemed to provide final confirmation of the programme's irretrievable drift into the light entertainment camp. Or could it be that by giving Lloyd Webber so prominent a place in their flagship programme for the start of the new millennium, the BBC religious broadcasting department was acknowledging, maybe fortuitously and subconsciously, the theological and spiritual power and significance of contemporary musical theatre and recognizing that it is perhaps now a more influential source of popular theology and spirituality than the churches?

In increasingly incorporating songs from shows in *Songs of Praise* the programme's makers have, indeed, identified the new hymns of our post-modern spiritual supermarket. Michael Wakelin, since 2001 the series producer, has defended the programme's increasing use of songs like Bette Middler's 'The Rose', and 'My heart will go on' from the film *Titanic*: 'These crossover songs have a part to play as people with a knowledge of hymns become fewer. We need to play them the music that they know with lyrics that make sense for them in both a sacred and secular context.' He has even suggested that the programme can 'sanctify secular music'.[7] In fact, the divide between 'secular' and 'sacred' songs is becoming more and more blurred as lyrics and tunes from shows increasingly find their way into hymnbooks and services of worship. 'You'll never walk alone' from *Carousel* is now to be found in a number of British and American hymnals. 'Oh Lord, I'm on my way' from *Porgy and Bess* has featured in compilations of 'My Favourite Hymns'. Show songs regularly turn up on worship albums recorded by church choirs and music groups. A CD produced by St Richard's Church, Hanworth, under the title 'Now That's What I Call Worship' includes 'Gethsemane' from *Jesus Christ Superstar* sandwiched between 'Be thou my vision' and 'Amazing Grace'. A compilation of 'hymns, worship songs and anthems' recorded by the Northallerton Methodist Choir features 'The Rhythm of Life' from *Sweet Charity* bracketed between the hymns 'Lord, thy church on earth is seeking' and 'When in our music God is glorified'. The sleeve note comments: 'You may be surprised to find included the Broadway showstopper but as you listen to the words we hope that you will agree that this "secular" piece carries a challenging message. It certainly enhances our theme at Northallerton of "Building for God".'[8]

Churches in the United States in particular are now using songs from shows to enhance and reinvigorate their worship. In California a Methodist church has pulled itself back from the brink of extinction by introducing songs from musicals into its services. Average attendance at Sunday worship at the church in Crescent Heights, West Hollywood, was down to four people when the pastor, John Griffin, decided to start a sing-along service using show songs rather than hymns. The congregation has increased more than tenfold as a result. For ten successive Sundays in 2001 the Cathedral of Hope in Dallas, Texas, the largest metropolitan community church in the world, based both its main morning services on specific musicals in a programme described as 'Odyssey Down Broadway' (see page 205). On a recent visit to Lubbock, Texas, I was delighted to find that the town's First United Methodist Church has put on a musical for the last 25 years. The 2004 offering, taking its place in the annual church calendar between a concert by the King's Singers and an organ recital, was *The Music Man.*

One of the most striking examples of the 'crossover' effect whereby 'secular' songs are taking on a spiritual and pastoral function is the growing use of music from films and stage shows at funerals and memorial services. This seems as yet to be much more prevalent in the United Kingdom than in the United States. Data collected by the Co-operative Funeral Service, the largest providers of funerals in the United Kingdom, suggest that such songs are coming to challenge the primacy of traditional crematorium favourites like 'Abide with me' and the 23rd Psalm. The top ten most requested pieces of music at funerals in Britain over recent years have included 'My heart will go on' from *Titanic*, 'Bring him home' from *Les Misérables*, 'Wishing you were somehow here again' from *Phantom of the Opera*, 'You'll never walk alone' from *Carousel* and 'Memories' from *Cats*. These songs clearly speak pastorally to mourners and represent their feelings of grief and loss in a way that traditional and even modern hymns and worship songs often seem unable to do.

On both sides of the Atlantic musicals are also increasingly supplying uplifting communal anthems for significant national occasions. The song 'Let us love in peace' from Lloyd Webber's moving musical about sectarianism in Northern Ireland, *The Beautiful Game*, was chosen for both George Bush's inaugural gala and the main inter-faith memorial service at Ground Zero in Manhattan on 28 October 2001. When the hundreds of thousands of people gathered in the Mall in London at the climax of the celebrations of the Queen's Golden Jubilee in June 2002 broke into singing as they waited for the royal appearance on the balcony of Buckingham Palace, it was not to the strains of 'Rule Britannia', 'Land of hope and glory' or even 'All you need is love', the Beatles' repetitive chant which had been brought out earlier in the day to do duty as a suitably bland and politically correct jubilee national anthem. No, what the crowds roared out to express their sense of the quasi-spiritual nature of this great act of communal celebration was 'You'll never walk alone' from *Carousel*.

There has, of course, been a long tradition of enlisting songs and tunes from the musical stage for inspirational purposes. 'Rule Britannia' came originally from Thomas Arne's 1740 masque *Alfred*. The majestic tune *Helmsley* for Charles Wesley's 'Lo, he comes with clouds descending' may have been based on a tune from another of Arne's works, *Thomas and Sally*. The Salvation Army famously adapted late nineteenth and early twentieth-century music hall songs, turning such classics as 'Champagne Charlie is my name' and 'The daring young man on the flying trapeze' into evangelistic choruses. 'Edelweiss' from *The Sound of Music* has been turned into an unofficial doxology, 'May the Lord, mighty God, bless and keep thee for ever' in many North American churches. In 1969 the Mormon Tabernacle Choir issued an album of show songs entitled 'Climb Every Mountain'. The sleeve note pointed out that 'although these songs may not be considered religious songs, they are in the highest sense of the word, inspirational'. It went on to point up the spiritual message of individual songs:

> The title-song *Climb Ev'ry Mountain*, exhorts us to search until we find our dream, while *Born Free*, a hymn to the harmony of man and nature, asks us to follow our hearts in the search for the good and the beautiful. *You'll Never Walk Alone*, one of the most inspirational songs ever written, admonishes us to live always with hope in our hearts and to look beyond our trials and tribulations. The sad and wistful nature of man is the subject of the gentle *Lost in the Stars*, which speaks so movingly of loneliness and vastness in God's creation, and the haunting *Over the Rainbow*, a song of gentle longing for the pure and innocent way of life. *Somewhere* is an affirmation that someday, somehow, we will find the way of life we desire, while *Sunrise, Sunset* poignantly reminds us how swiftly life, with its happiness and tears, flows by. *The Impossible Dream* urges us to fight courageously for our dreams against all the odds.[9]

A further album of 'inspirational and optimistic tunes from Broadway shows and motion pictures' recorded by the Mormon Tabernacle Choir in 1979 and entitled 'A Grand Night for Singing' included 'The Heather on the Hill' and 'There but for you I go' from *Brigadoon*, 'If I loved you' from *Carousel* and 'Welcome home' from Harold Rome's

1954 show, *Fanny*. Welsh male voice choirs regularly include items from musicals in selections which are primarily 'inspirational' and otherwise drawn from a more conventional sacred music repertoire. On one album recorded by the Treorchy Male Voice Choir, 'I don't know how to love him' from *Jesus Christ Superstar* comes between 'Onward, Christian soldiers' and 'Laudamus', a Welsh chorale based on the hymn *Bryn Calvaria*. On another, 'Memory' from *Cats* takes its place alongside 'Jesu lover of my soul' and 'Be still my soul'. I was fascinated that the inaugural concert of the student gospel choir in the university where I teach, held in St Andrews Baptist Church in May 2002, included 'Someone to watch over me' from Ira Gershwin's *Oh, Kay!*, 'The Lion Sleeps Tonight' from *The Lion King* and 'Singin' in the Rain' alongside Gospel standards like 'Amazing Grace' and 'We are marching in the light of God', sacred songs from the Moody and Sankey stable and modern pop songs like 'Say a little prayer for me' and 'Reach for the stars'.

The fact is that songs from musicals are increasingly taking on the role of communal chants and folk songs as well as hymns. It was, indeed, significant that the Millennium *Songs of Praise* took place in a football stadium, the one place outside churches where communal singing still regularly takes place. Commercially manufactured as they may be, there is a vulgarity about songs from musicals in the best sense of the word – they unite people across age groups, social backgrounds and increasingly across national boundaries in a way that is now true of few other songs. To that extent they are heirs to the music hall songs that were sung in the trenches during the First World War. Some of the best and most popular also have something of the hymnodic about them, both in melodic structure and in the style of their language. While this is particularly true of the great anthem-like solos and choruses like 'You'll never walk alone' and 'Do you hear the people sing', it is discernable in many other numbers as well. They have something of the quality that a 1967 *Times* leader noted in the music of the Beatles, belonging to a tradition 'hidden from the unobservant by electronic impediment which goes back through *Hymns Ancient and Modern* to pastoral pentatonic tunes and other revitalized archaisms'.[10]

There is, of course, a deep and even primal relationship between music and the spiritual dimension of life. At root it perhaps derives from the sounds that brought the world into being. Scientists have recently recorded what might be described as the music of creation –

the harmonic notes which rang out like a bell in the first fraction of a second after the Big Bang. Cosmologists believe that these minute ripples of sound became the seed of matter, eventually leading to the formation of stars, galaxies and planets. The phenomenon known as cosmic background radiation suggests that the whole universe started with sound waves compressing and rarefying matter and light. It seems to be the case that in the beginning was not so much the word as the hum. Findings from the so-called boomerang experiment confirm what has long been held by mystics in both eastern and western spiritual traditions. Attempting to answer the question 'why does music appeal so much to humanity?', Hazrat Inayat Khan, a Chishti sufi, professional performer of classical Indian music and founder of the modern Sufi movement in Britain and USA, has written:

> The whole of manifestation has its origin in vibration, in sound. This sound, which is called nada in the Vedanta, was the first manifestation of the universe. Consequently the human body was made in tone and rhythm. The most important thing in the physical body is breath, and the breath is audible; it is most audible in the form of the voice. This shows that the principal signs of life in the physical body are tone and rhythm, which together make music.[11]

Recent research has also made us aware of the beneficial effect of music on human health, creativity and well-being. Listening to Mozart has been shown to improve children's spatial-temporal reasoning skills and reduce tension in over-crowded urban areas. The 'Mozart effect' seems to extend to the non-human world. Among its results, according to Don Campbell's 1997 book on the subject, have been an increase in the density of the yeast in a sake rice wine brewery in Ohara, Japan, by a factor of ten after exposure to Mozart's *Magic Flute* and improvement in the maze-negotiating skills of rats after being played the same composer's string quartets. Music therapy is increasingly being used to stimulate the victims of strokes and of degenerative conditions like Alzheimer's disease and dementia and there is growing interest in the therapeutic effects of music on babies while still in their mothers' wombs. In a world of seemingly ever-increasing levels of stress and tension, the calming and healing benefits of melodic and ordered music are becoming more and more evident and valued. Raymond Barr, director of the Coronary Care Unit at St Agnes Hospital, Baltimore, has recently confirmed the claims of the silver-tongued presenters of the 'smooth classics' programmes on the Classic FM radio station by proving scientifically that half an hour listening to classical music can produce the same effect as 10 mg of Valium. Others find relaxation and release through listening to Gregorian chant or CDs featuring the singing of whales.[12]

In fact, there is nothing new in the realization of music's therapeutic and mood-changing properties. In primal societies shamans used repetitive rhythmic drum beats to induce altered states of consciousness. Martin Luther noted that 'nothing on earth is so well suited to make the sad merry, the merry sad, to give courage to the despairing, to make the proud humble, to lessen envy and hate, as music'.[13] Many writers and philosophers have pointed to the particular ability of music to touch the emotions rather than the intellect and to create atmosphere. As Honoré de Balzac observed, 'music appeals to the heart, whereas writing is addressed to the intellect; it communicates ideas directly, like perfume'.[14]

The particular ability of music to communicate not just ideas but atmosphere has long made it a key component of religious ritual and worship. Song and dance seem to have been central to the earliest primal religious ceremonies. The use of chant in early Jewish temple and synagogue worship and of chorus and sacred dance in classical Greek drama have both been regarded as major influences on the development of Christian liturgy. In his book *The Heaven Singing* Richard Rastall has written fascinatingly about the key role of music in medieval religious drama, arguing that in the biblical, saint and morality plays performed in the streets of Britain's towns in the Middle Ages music was especially important for its representational role. He notes that it was particularly used to symbolize Heaven but also as a tool of the Devil, to mark a change of location or the passage of time, to facilitate stage business and to suggest a major shift of mood or significant development in the plot.[15]

The Church has always had a somewhat ambivalent feeling about this essentially theatrical element to the power and potential of music. It is significant that the popular manual *Teach Yourself about Musicals* begins its history of musical theatre with a consideration of the role of the Church. It points out that 'the Church was one of the first bodies to recognize the communication potential of music and song' but goes on to suggest that 'by driving out the more adventurous performers and composers, the Church helped inadvertently to promote the development of secular music' and specifically to pave the way for the secular masques and comic operas which were the ancestors of modern musical theatre.[16]

In fact, there has long been a thin dividing line between the worlds of secular and sacred music. There is nothing new about the crossover between the musical theatre stage and the sanctuary. In revitalizing his Methodist Church in West Hollywood through introducing show songs, pastor John Griffin is following the lead of William Booth, the founder of the Salvation Army who set Gospel songs to the popular music hall numbers of his day. The 'weekend job' of Paul Bateman, the first musical director of *Phantom of the Opera*, as organist at Palmers' Green United Reformed Church parallels the dual career of Arthur Sullivan who was equally at home in the church organ loft and the theatre pit and who composed hymn tunes and sacred oratorios as melodious and appealing as his comic operas. Andrew Lloyd Webber is by no means the first 'secular' composer of music for the theatre to have turned his hand with some success to writing a Requiem. Verdi's *Requiem*, famously dubbed by Hans von Bulow 'an opera dressed up in a cassock' is an essentially theatrical work. Appropriately, it was performed in 2000 by English National Opera in a staged version which explored the themes of bereavement, fear and consolation and included a scene where forty couples danced very slowly in a 'ballroom of sorrow'. Mozart's *Coronation Mass* and Berlioz's *Grande Messe des Morts*, with its requirement of a minimum of 210 performers, are other works that belong as much to the opera house as to the sanctuary. Mozart's *Requiem* has been turned by Brigit Scherzer into a ballet that explores death's hold over all of us, the life and loves of the composer and the destructive effect of modern society on humans. Several works that set liturgical texts have been written for stage performance, notable examples being John Taverner's *Celtic Requiem* and Leonard Bernstein's *Mass* (discussed below on pages 213–17).

If some of the great religious works in the classical music canon have an essentially theatrical feel, then the opposite is also true and some of the best music written for theatrical performance has a spiritual quality and focus. This is particularly true in the world of opera. It is highly appropriate that alongside the selections of favourite marches, love duets and choruses from opera, there should also be a CD devoted to operatic prayers. In the words of its sleeve note, 'at certain crucial moments in opera leading characters fall to their knees in prayer, and it is these moments which have inspired composers to produce some of their most uplifting and deeply felt music'.[17] Arias from opera feature alongside items from the oratorio and sacred song repertoire and the world of musicals on several of the popular 'crossover' compilation albums of inspirational music. Kiri Te Kanawa's collection, *Songs of Inspiration*, for example, includes the nuns' chorus from Johann Strauss' *Casanova*, Gounod's *Ave Maria*, and 'You'll never walk alone' from *Carousel*.

If classical music and opera provide many people with spiritual solace and inspiration, and perhaps even an encounter with God, then so does a visit to the theatre. This has been well observed by Paul Glass, for ten years chaplain of the West Yorkshire Playhouse:

Imagine a place where people gather to worship so fervently that they often clap their hands together in eager anticipation. Imagine a place where people are confronted with the deep, perplexing issues of what it means to be human. Imagine a place where people are helped to face up to issues within themselves that they had long buried or ignored and find themselves brought to a point of healing. Imagine a communal experience where people are lifted to the heights of joy and excitement and leave the building lighter, happier, better able to face their lives and the questions they are daily confronted with. Where is this church that is doing everything right? Where is this tiny paradise on earth? At your local theatre.

Audiences in theatre come – in a sense – to worship. To worship particular actors, or favourite authors, or directors or even design teams. Audiences come to have their spirits lifted or their hearts moved. They also come to be entertained (and can we say that was never true of a congregation with a high profile, grand-standing preacher?). If a theatre audience is helped to understand the human condition more completely or aided in their ability to love others more completely because they have a greater understanding of what it means to be alive, then I believe the theatre has performed a fundamentally Christian task.[18]

Paul Glass's observations seem to me to apply particularly to musicals. People approach a musical much as they approach a service of worship in a church. They dress up, they come from a whole variety of places and backgrounds to congregate together in rows of seats that are not unlike church pews in their fixed settings and close proximity. There is a sense of awe and expectancy as people wait for the orchestra to strike up and the curtain to rise. The level of audience participation is generally much greater in musicals than it is in so-called 'straight' plays, something that is missed by critics of the genre who characterize it as a form of massage which induces a wholly passive response where all that is required is for the audience to 'lie back and absorb' and be willing 'to be momentarily amazed and to ooh! and aaah!'.[19] There is often an element of singing or clapping along with the performers on stage. Sometimes there is more direct participation, as when members of the cast emerge from the auditorium as they do in *Cats*, come down off stage as in *Joseph*, or mingle with the audience in the interval and offer them a glass of grape juice as in *Godspell*.

Musicals also provide their audiences with a spiritual experience of some depth, which can move people to tears and engage their emotions in a way that is more than mere entertainment or escapism. I first became conscious of this dimension during a matinée performance of *Les Misérables* in the Edinburgh Playhouse. I was surrounded in the front stalls by secondary school students. Their awed silence throughout the performance and utter absorption in the great drama of redemption being enacted before them reinforced the cathedral-like atmosphere of the theatre's cavernous auditorium. Even more striking was the number of these teenagers, whose clothes and pre-show conversation proclaimed them to be dedicated exponents of 'cool' and cynicism, moved to tears by the show's message of the power of forgiveness and sacrificial love. While peer group pressure is obviously a factor in inducing mass emotion, these were not crocodile tears, nor were they the kind of hysterical reaction similarly whipped up by pop singers and certain kinds of evangelists. These young people were clearly genuinely moved and uplifted by what they had seen and heard on stage. They were both involved and to some extent, however briefly, changed by it. The performance had taken them out of themselves and put them in touch with deeper metaphysical values.

Now *Les Misérables* is a musical particularly packed with spiritual and theological content. It is about big religious themes – redemption, judgement, the extraordinary power of forgiveness and sacrificial love. *Les Misérables* the musical is, in fact, more explicitly Christian in both its language and message than either Victor Hugo's novel or the original concept album from which it was developed (see page 146). This is not an isolated phenomenon. Andrew Lloyd Webber and Jim Steinman's *Whistle Down the Wind* is more overtly religious, and overtly Christian, than Mary Haley Bell's short story on which it is based. I first saw it at a matinée performance at the Aldwych Theatre in London where my companions in the dress circle were a coach party of middle-aged ladies from Wales. They could well have been church-goers, indeed they may well have been on a Mothers' Union outing. From the very first bars of the opening song about the keys to the vaults of heaven which could have come straight out of the early twentieth-century Welsh revival, there was a rapt attention and involvement in the unfolding story about the naivety and ambiguity of religious faith which I could not help comparing to the half-hearted response which greets the average Sunday morning sermon.

Neither *Les Misérables* nor *Whistle Down the Wind* could be described as easy listening or escapist fantasies. They exemplify a fundamental shift which has taken musicals away from the optimistic, folksy atmosphere of the golden age of Broadway to what have been described by one critic as the 'doomy-gloomy, through-sung block-busters' of the closing decades of the twentieth century.[20]

Not that we should dismiss the great Broadway musicals of the mid-twentieth century as having no philosophical or theological depth. In my book, *The Power of Sacrifice*, I quote from a song in *The Sound Of Music*:

> A bell is no bell till you ring it,
> A song is no song till you sing it,
> And love in your heart wasn't put there to stay,
> Love isn't love till you give it away.[21]

I suspect that this may well have been the first time that the lyrics of Oscar Hammerstein have been cited in a work of academic theology but I very much hope that it will not be the last. For me these four lines, which precede the reprise of 'You are Sixteen Going on Seven-teen' in the stage version of the show but are sadly and unaccountably missing from the film version, provide one of the simplest and clearest expressions of the doctrine of *kenosis*, the self-emptying, outpouring nature of Christian love.

Some of the theological and spiritual resonances in other Broadway musicals from the early and mid-twentieth century will be explored in Chapter two following an investigation of what might seem the even more unlikely topic of the theological dimension in the works of Gilbert and Sullivan. The bulk of this book, however, will be con-cerned with themes found in more recent and predominantly British and European musicals from the last four decades of the twentieth century. Some historians of musical theatre see a decisive shift in the genre occurring with the appearance of *West Side Story* in 1957. It is often portrayed as the first major musical to deal with the downside of life, set in the slums and backstreets of New York with warring immigrant gangs as its central characters, and in the words of a classic work on the subject as 'American musical theatre's only great tragedy'.[22] Yet the real change, I think, came rather later – in the early 1970s – and was a British movement in almost conscious opposition to the naïve optimism and cosy folksiness of the American musical. *Jesus Christ Superstar* (1971) was the first of the intense, unremitting, angst-ridden, through-sung opera-like musicals which have dominated the worldwide musical stage for the last 30 years. It is no coincidence that it should have had a religious theme. So did its near contemporaries, *Joseph and The Amazing Technicolor Dreamcoat* (1968–72) and *Godspell* (1971). Not surprisingly, this trinity of biblically inspired musicals occupy a central place in this book.

As well as introducing spiritual and theological themes into the world of musical theatre, *Jesus Christ Superstar* also pushed back the frontiers of the genre and transformed it into a more serious medium, in some ways more akin to opera but in others perhaps more similar to the television documentary. Recent stagings have, indeed, emphasized this latter similarity with their use of hand-held video cameras to record in harrowing close-up the agonizing final hours of Jesus' life and project them on to large screens. Perhaps more even than *West Side Story*, *Jesus Christ Superstar* shifted the subject matter of musicals from stylized fantasy to gritty and brutal reality. Increasingly through the 1980s and 1990s the subjects being tackled by musicals have been those that one might rather have expected to encounter on earnest, late-night television documentaries – the nature of depressive illness and the ramifications of the British class system in *Blood Brothers* (1983), the impact of the AIDS virus in *Rent* (1996) and the mentality of the terrorist and the horror of religious bigotry and sectarianism in *The Beautiful Game* (2000). These and other hit shows, set in tough working-class communities and dealing with major contemporary social issues without glitzy gloss or romantic escapism, suggest that lyricists and composers of musicals are increasingly the social commentators and chroniclers as well as the bards and ovates of our times, presenting and interpreting life as it is, not just as it might be.

There is, indeed, a growing realization that the musical is now 'where it is at' and that this particular medium is perhaps the most powerful and effective one to use today to make a particular point. Where formerly propagandists and others with a strong message to convey might have turned to the straight theatre or to television, they are now harnessing the huge dramatic and emotional power of musical theatre. *King Stephen*, a musical about the ousting of Hungarian culture and nationalism in the early middle ages, which was seen by more than ten per cent of Hungary's population in the 1980s, played a significant role in turning people against communism and Soviet domination. In the latter years of Saddam Hussein's dictatorial rule over Iraq, his novel *Zabibah and the King* was turned into a musical which became the largest production in modern Iraqi theatre. Its plot revolves around a love triangle made up of a cruel husband, representing the United States of America, a brave wife, representing the Iraqi people, and an insecure king worried about who will succeed him, representing Saddam. Western intelligence officials were reported to have studied the text 'for clues about the despotic president's megalomania as well as any thoughts he may have about handing over power one day'.[23] A 'Bollywood' film musical released in 2003 has as its subject the Taliban terror in Afghanistan. *Escape from Taliban* is based on the true story of an Indian woman who married an Afghan Muslim and was forced to flee the country when the Taliban issued a death sentence against her for refusing to convert to Islam.

It is significant that opera has also recently gone in a similar direction and adopted both the subject matter and the style of television docudrama. This is noticeably the case in the work of John Adams, composer of *Nixon in China* (1987), based on the encounter between Richard Nixon and Mao Tse-tung in 1972, and *The Death of Klinghoffer* (1991) about an American tourist kidnapped by Palestinian terrorists on a Mediterranean cruise ship. Adams, who has also composed *El Nino*, an oratorio on Christ's nativity, which he describes as 'my own version of the *Messiah*', shares with Andrew Lloyd Webber a fascination with religious themes and a boyhood love of musicals, which greatly influenced and shaped his composing career. Put off opera for years after being taken to *Aida* at the age of ten, he developed a sense of how music and theatre could work together when he took part with his mother in a local amateur production of *South Pacific*.[24]

As well as becoming noticeably more serious and realistic, modern musicals have also taken up more explicitly religious and spiritual themes. I suspect that the reasons for this are complex. In part, it may be a response, conscious or unconscious, to the new market for up-front spirituality and in part a reflection of the fact that lyricists and composers are themselves caught up in the contemporary search for meaning, moral values and meta-narrative in the reductionist jungle of post-modern relativism. It is not just songs from shows which seem to have increasingly espoused religious imagery. So do many pop songs. When Madonna was asked what was the most overriding inspiration for her songs, she had no hesitation in replying 'the crucifix and the suffering of Christ'.[25] As establishment religion and conventional church-going decline, perhaps it is not surprising that religious imagery and themes are surfacing more and more in the anti-establishment worlds of arts and entertainment. Musicals, with their cross-cultural appeal and strange mixture of commercial calculation and creative genius, are at the very heart of the new touchy-feely, up-front spirituality of post-modern society with its search for values, its quest for experience and sensation and its openness to a whole range of visual and aural stimuli.

All this makes it even more curious that musicals are so little regarded by academics and serious commentators. At root is the artistic snobbery so well described by Patrick Boyle:

> It has long been fashionable among the arts-loving intelligentsia to be snooty about them, particularly if the music is composed by Andrew Lloyd Webber. They are regarded as inconsequential, middlebrow entertainment, popular with Radio 2 listeners and coach parties from Birmingham, confections designed to please the gay community, New York Jews and Women's Institute members from the shires. In music shops, songs from the musicals come under the heading of 'Easy Listening'.[25]

As I have already noted, this snobbery is much more rooted in the United Kingdom than in the United States. There is, in fact, a substantial body of recent North American academic writing on musical theatre just as there is a long tradition of US opera companies performing musicals. It includes Ethan Mordden's quintet of studies of the Broadway musical in the 1920s, 40s, 50s, 60s and 70s, *Make Believe* (1997), *Beautiful Mornin'* (1999), *Coming Up Roses* (1998), *Open a New Window* (2002) and *One More Kiss* (2003) and Geoffrey

Block's *Enchanted Evenings* (1997), all published by Oxford University Press, and John Bush Jones' superb study of the social and political context of American musicals, *Our Musicals, Ourselves* (Brandeis University Press, 2003).

There are some signs that attitudes are at last beginning to change in Britain. The BBC's classical music station, Radio 3, now devotes a weekly programme to the music of stage and screen and the network also gave serious consideration to Richard Rodgers when he was featured as composer of the week as part of the celebrations for the centenary of his birth in 2002. The Rodgers centenary also produced the first full-length staging of a musical at the Promenade Concerts, with *Oklahoma!* being performed in London's Albert Hall fifty-nine years after its New York opening. In December 2003 the Royal Opera House put on Stephen Sondheim's *Sweeney Todd*, the first musical ever to be performed on the main stage at Covent Garden. Musical theatre courses are gradually being introduced into the curriculum of the academies and colleges of music in the United Kingdom.

However, in terms of academic interest and study in the United Kingdom, musicals are still a no-go area. On both sides of the Atlantic, moreover, they have failed to arouse any interest among those engaged in the disciplines of theology and religious studies. There is very considerable contemporary interest in the interface between theology and music, as evidenced by such major recent works as Albert Blackwell's *The Sacred in Music* (Lutterworth Press, 2000) and Jeremy Begbie's *Theology, Music and Time* (Cambridge, 2000), and between theology and the theatre, explored among others by Shimon Levy in *Here, There and Everywhere* (Sussex Academic Press, 1996), *Theatre and Holy Script* (Sussex, 1999) and *The Bible as Theatre* (Sussex Academic Press, 2000). Yet none of these works makes any mention of musicals.

There are references to musicals in several of the books that have come out in recent years on the subject of the theology of film, notably in Bernard Scott's *Holywood Dreams and Biblical Stories* (Fortress Press, Minneapolis, 1994), Clive Marsh and Gaye Ortiz's *Explorations in Film and Theology* (Blackwell, 2000), Andrew Greeley and Andrew Bergesen's *God in the Movies* (Transaction, 2000) and W. Barnes Tatum's *Jesus at the Movies* (Polebridge Press, 1998). The distinctive Jewish contribution to Hollywood musicals is touched on in J. Hoberman and Jeffrey Shandler's *Entertaining America: Jews, Movies and Broadcasting* (Princeton University Press, 2003). One musical film has attracted particular attention for its theological message. Bob Fosse's *All That Jazz* (1979), which focuses on the heart attack and death of showbusiness impresario Joe Gideon, is widely taken to be an interpretation of the world and ethos of the Broadway musical. For Carey Wall it is no coincidence that the film's leading character is given a name associated with the Bible since 'show business is the Bible to this man and in making shows he preaches the show business gospel to others'.[26] At the heart of this gospel is the idea of life as performance and the imperative to get on with the show, symbolized by Ethel Merman's singing of 'There's no business like show business' at the end of the film as Gideon's dead body is zipped into a bag. For Andrew Greeley *All That Jazz* evokes more powerfully than any other artistic creation the female side of God. He finds in the characterization of Jessica Lange and the ambiguous figure of Angelique, the Angel of Death, a suggestion that God is not just love but passionate sexual love. Carey Wall is also struck by Gideon's encounter with the beautiful woman in white which for her 'symbolizes the transformative power that, unexhausted, converts Gideon's death from further heart attacks into a last performance on the stage of life that lies in the redemptive, communitas plane of earlier musicals'.[27] Greeley writes:

> If one defines religion as the quest to understand the meaning of life, the nature of death, and identity of God, then *All That Jazz is* profoundly religious – perhaps the most religious film ever made. It is all the more religious precisely because the film-maker was anything but a religious man before he encountered the Angel of Death.[28]

These, however, are relatively rare testimonies to the theological significance of musical films. In general, the booming new academic discipline of theology and film has only paid attention to screen musicals when they treat the life of Christ. It has not, so far as I am aware, encompassed such theologically loaded and religiously charged movies as *The Sound of Music* and *Fiddler on the Roof*.

The almost total neglect of musicals on the part of theologians stands in marked contrast to their enthusiastic engagement with other aspects of popular culture and mass entertainment. The last few years have seen books published on the theological dimension of science fiction, perhaps the most notable being Mike Alsford's *What If? Religious Themes in Science Fiction* (Darton, Longman & Todd,

2000). The spirituality of the *Star Wars* films has been explored by David Wilkinson in *The Power of the Force* (Lion, 2000). Mark Pinsky's *The Gospel According to the Simpsons* (Westminster John Knox Press, 2001) has superbly and exhaustively analysed the implicit and explicit theology expressed in the characterization, attitudes and exploits of Homer, Marge, Bart, Ned Flanders, Reverend Lovejoy and other figures in the Springfield community. There are at least four recent books on the theology and spirituality of *The Lord of the Rings* and *Harry Potter*. Yet musicals have somehow escaped the attention of that growing band of theologians who are interested in interacting with contemporary popular culture.

The reason for this neglect, I am sure, is the snobbish disdain for the genre which has already been noted. There was a good example of this in a recent article in the *Church Times* by David Self which accused professional theatre of shunning Christian themes in favour of pagan and classical drama. Pointing to the Royal Shakespeare Company's epic production of *Tantalus*, based on the mythology of the Greek gods, Self asked why professional theatre engages with 'the myths of discredited gods at the expense of the epic stories of the Bible'. While acknowledging that in its 1960s heyday the BBC did engage with Christian themes in such dramas as *Paul of Tarsus* and Dennis Potter's *Son of Man*, he complained that 'the professional stage had to make do with the populist *Godspell* and *Jesus Christ Superstar* – neither of them exactly profound'.[29]

That is precisely the kind of dismissive comment that has moved me to write this book. Perhaps I may be permitted to quote here from the letter I wrote in response to it:

> David Self in his article on professional theatre's neglect of the Christian story is being rather hard in dismissing *Godspell* and *Jesus Christ Superstar* as populist and 'not exactly profound'.
>
> Popular both these musicals have certainly been, and maybe vulgar too, but as the students taking my 'Theology of the Musical' module would testify, they contain significant theological nuances and raise a host of significant and profound questions about the nature and character of Jesus.
>
> *Godspell* was written by a student seriously considering ordination, John Michael Tebelak, and arose directly from his feeling after attending the Easter vigil service at the Episcopal Cathedral in Pittsburgh that the church's approach to putting across the Gospel

story in worship was fundamentally dull and that, in his words, 'instead of rolling the rock away from the tomb they were piling more on'. *Jesus Christ Superstar* is a highly original and almost unbearably powerful treatment of the last week in Jesus' life, which has provoked many discussions to my knowledge among young people especially about Jesus' mission and purpose.

The RSC's *Tantalus* is, I am sure, a fine and significant production but I suspect that it is only likely to be seen by a relatively small number of the theatre-going classes. *Godspell* and *Jesus Christ Superstar* – like other modern block-buster musicals which deal with the 'big' themes of redemption, sacrifice, loss and identity – have been seen by millions of people who would not normally go to serious drama, nor, indeed, to church. They are also regularly performed by schools and colleges. There is a snobbish prejudice against musicals in the artistic and academic establishments. I hope that is not going to extend to the churches as well.

Appreciation of music is perhaps more riddled with snobbery than that of any other art form. It is the kind of snobbery that regards Bach as infinitely superior to Mozart. I draw some comfort from Karl Barth's observation:

> I am not absolutely sure whether the angels, when they are engaged in the praise of God, play just Bach; I am sure, however, that when they are among themselves they play Mozart, and that then, indeed, the dear God also listens to them with special pleasure.[30]

I appreciate that the composers whose work forms the subject of this book come a notch or two below Mozart but they share much of that composer's zest for life and melodic gifts. They also share the vulgarity and popularity which made him so disliked by many in the musical and cultural establishment of his own day. Richard Rodgers and Andrew Lloyd Webber seem to me in many ways the modern heirs of Mozart. There is more in this book about their musicals than about the work of the more 'serious' and academically respectable George Gershwin and Stephen Sondheim. This is not just because their work is more popular but also because it is, I believe, considerably more spiritual.

The contrasting critical and popular acclaim accorded to Sondheim and Lloyd Webber has been well explored by Stephen Citron in his book *Sondheim and Lloyd Webber: The New Musical* (OUP, 2001). The former is loved by the critics but it is the latter who is loved by the public. Stephen Sondheim is, indeed, the one figure in contemporary musical theatre whose work is taken seriously by academics and the cultural establishment, perhaps because, in Mark Steyn's words, 'he makes musicals for people who don't like musicals'.[31] He is the subject of a number of major academic monographs. He is also, to my mind at least, the most secular of all the major contemporary practitioners in the genre. These two features may well go together. Sondheim's lyrics and tunes are clever, witty, cynical and sophisticated. Their intellectual appeal is undoubted but they are almost wholly without any spiritual dimension. They lack either the communal warmth of Rodgers and Hammerstein or the agonized yearning of Lloyd Webber. Their essentially secular quality was well described by the critic Charles Spencer, writing about the review *Putting It Together*, based on Sondheim's show songs, which opened in London a few days after the terrorist bombing of the World Trade Center in New York:

> Sondheim's solipsistic characters, witty rhymes and jagged dissonance quickly begin to seem intolerable. Instead of his clever-cleverness, one longs instead for the communality, the big-heartedness and even the sentimentality of Rodgers and Hammerstein. A song such as 'You'll Never Walk Alone' suddenly seems preferable to Sondheim's detached irony and self-advertising wit.[32]

The secularism of Sondheim was brought home to me in a rather different way by observing the make-up of two recent student productions at St Andrews University. The shows performed were Gilbert and Sullivan's *Iolanthe* and Sondheim's *Company*. While there was a considerable overlap in those taking part in the two musicals, there was one striking difference. The *Company* cast was largely missing the Christian students and members of the Chapel Choir who had been in *Iolanthe*. It clearly did not appeal to them in the way that Gilbert and Sullivan did. It was not wholly in jest that I described the Chapel Choir as 'the spiritual arm of the Gilbert and Sullivan Society' in a subsequent University sermon.

So what is my justification for devoting a book to the theology of the musical? Let me match the ten questions that I posed at the beginning of this introduction with ten answers at its conclusion.

1. Incarnational theology demands it. I take my stand with Gareth Jones on the proper locus of theology:

> Speaking of God is an open activity, rather than one closed off except to certain expert practitioners. It is then quite legitimate to speak of theology occurring in churches, schools, universities, even on street corners – indeed, anywhere that people come together and, one way or another, start to speak about God in terms of the revelation which is believed to have occurred in Jesus Christ. Theology, on this model, is about communication . . . and (it) can occur via a number of different media. It can certainly occur as written or spoken text, as in a popular or an academic book, or a sermon or address. But it can also occur as a poem, a piece of music, an action, a relationship, a sacrament, a film, a play, an opera – in fact almost anything can communicate theological meaning.[33]

Significantly, among recent examples of this model of theology, understood as 'communicating something of the meaning of God's revelation in Christ, and its significance for human existence, whether from the perspective of faith or a thorough questioning of faith', Jones lists *Jesus Christ Superstar* in a rare academic endorsement of the theological importance of this work.

In their important book, *Explorations in Theology and Film*, Clive Marsh and Gaye Ortiz, building on the classic work of Richard Niebuhr and Paul Tillich, make a powerful apologia for finding theology in popular culture.

> Millions of people watch films, Christians are among them. The thinking of Christians (their theology) is thus in part informed by their cinema-going and video-viewing. And the theological/religious/ideological viewpoints of those who would not wish to call themselves Christians are likewise in part influenced by movie-watching.[34]

These remarks seem to me to apply equally to musicals, as do Marsh's five specific reasons for 'doing' theology through the medium of film:

> First, using film in theology is a key way in which Christian theology can work out what is going to be possible to say in our contemporary climate about any of theology's major themes.

Second, using film in theology reminds us of the importance of the public dimension of any Christian theology.

Third, films enable Christian theology to be reminded that it is a discipline which seeks to do justice to the emotional and aesthetic aspects of human life, as it deals with life's issues.

Fourth, films are 'vulgar' in the sense of being 'of/for the people'; i.e. they constitute arguably one of the most influential cultural media of the moment in the West today.

Fifth, and finally, theology comes much closer to journalism than it may ever care to admit. Theology that takes film seriously reminds itself of its own ephemeral character.[35]

If anything, I would argue that musicals conform even more closely to these definitions than films, especially in respect of their pull on the emotions and sentiment, their concern with life issues, their vulgarity and the range and power of their appeal. Marsh and Ortiz suggest that films are embedded in a matrix whose horizontal axis runs from art at one end to entertainment at the other. Most musicals are firmly at the entertainment end of the matrix. That is why they are despised and shunned by academics and why they are so worthy of study by all concerned with theology and contemporary culture.

2. Musicals have a powerful representative role. They manifestly express for many people emotions and feelings which are otherwise inchoate or bottled up. This is why songs from shows are increasingly being requested at funerals and weddings. At one level, musicals perform the two great roles of myth as characterized by Claude Levi-Strauss – they mediate the fundamental problems of life and they think for us without our being aware of it. The song 'I am what I am' in *La Cage aux Folles* has helped many people to feel more liberated and easy about their sexuality. Snatches from *Les Misérables* have to my knowledge helped several individuals in difficult personal situations. There are people who rely on lyrics from musicals to give direction to their lives. One such is Rosie O'Donnell, whose syndicated daytime talk show on American television has been described as 'a virtual worship service for the theatre'. Having lost her mother when she was young, she found that musical theatre provided 'a world of projected sensation, filling in the gaps of a child overcome with longing. It was a way to express emotions and feel emotions.' She writes: 'Something emotional will happen to me, and a lyric will come up to define my

life.' In the aftermath of the shootings at Columbine High School in Colorado in 1999, it was Jean Valjean's line from *Les Misérables* 'If I speak, I am condemned. If I stay silent, I am damned' that moved her to use her talk show to preach her belief in gun control. The *New York Times* analysed her condition thus:

> To a fellow theatre lover, the diagnosis is plain. Ms. O'Donnell suffers from show-tune-itis. It is a lifetime affliction, and there is no hope of a cure. It is particularly rampant among a certain subset of baby boomers for whom cast albums, in the heyday of musical comedy, provided the emotional underscoring of their childhoods. Ms. O'Donnell was one of these, a little girl from Commack whose mother passed on to her a devotion to the theater in the form of an LP that contained what might be the slogan of a world seen through rose-coloured glasses: 'Don't Rain on My Parade'. One session with 'Funny Girl' and Barbara Streisand, and Ms. O'Donnell had found her hymnal.[36]

Songs from shows are, indeed, taking over from hymns as triggers for releasing pent-up emotions and spiritual feelings. With the growing seriousness and religious slant of musicals, they are increasingly conforming to Erik Routley's classic definition of a hymn as 'a song of a serious kind making use of poetry and music in a way which tends to exalt the mind of the singer and listener towards lofty subjects – whatever subject may be recognized by that particular community as lofty'.[37] They are also taking over more broadly the function of folk song as defined by Routley:

> Secular folk song goes with words concerned with the things that mean most to a community. Basically these are love, work and death. Folk song universalizes these experiences; it objectifies them . . . A folk song can handle everything from high humour to high tragedy but when it does that, it makes life's incongruities and anomalies entertaining by transforming them into humour, and life's griefs less oppressive by allowing the singer to stand away from them, and obscurely no doubt but none the less assuredly, to feel that the burden is shared by humanity.[38]

So we find 'Empty chairs at empty tables' being taken up as a universal folk anthem and lament for those suffering from HIV/Aids and 'Give peace a chance' from *The Beautiful Game* being used to express the yearning for peace after the terrorist outrage of September 11 2001. These songs from commercial musicals are now fulfilling a similar function to the radical protest songs of Bob Dylan and Joan Baez in the 1960s.

3. Musicals have a pastoral and therapeutic role. This is really an extension of the representative role mentioned above and of the ability of musicals to universalize and articulate human experience. It is why so many show songs are being requested at funerals. They are speaking to people in their grief in a way that the more conventional hymns and songs of the church are not. When grieving parents in Essex wanted to put on their daughter's gravestone the line from the Abba musical *Mama Mia* 'I believe in angels – something good in everything I see', they were refused a faculty by the Chelmsford diocese of the Church of England on the grounds that this was not appropriate language for a church graveyard. Yet it was clearly speaking words of hope to them in their grief. The therapeutic properties of *Mama Mia* were further illustrated when it opened on Broadway with advance ticket sales of £19 million within a month of the World Trade Center attacks. The show, which already had the nickname from its producers of 'the Lourdes of musicals' for its curative effect on audiences who cast aside walking sticks, crutches and inhibitions to dance along to its catchy tunes, was hailed by the *New York Times* critic as 'just what the city needed and the unlikeliest hit ever to win over cynical sentiment-shy New Yorkers'.[39]

4. Musicals shape our understanding of the Bible and the central Christian drama of creation and redemption. According to Gyles Brandreth's irreverent send-up of the whole world of musical theatre, *Zipp!*, sixteen musicals have been based on the Bible. Only Shakespeare has been a more popular source, inspiring nineteen musicals, with Dickens coming in third as the inspiration for twelve. The tradition of basing musicals on biblical themes goes back a long way. An 1874 American musical pageant, *The Deluge*, which lasted five hours and featured 500 singers and dancers, related the Genesis story from the creation to the flood with 'a large, imposing English lady' playing the part of Satan. More recent shows include Richard Rodgers' *Two by Two* (1970) and Stephen Schwartz's *Children of Eden* (1991), both discussed later in this book, *The Apple Tree* (1966), which featured

just three characters – Adam, Eve and the Serpent, *Hard Job Being God* (1972), which ranged through the Old Testament and the Apocrypha from Sarah and Abraham to David and Susanna and folded after six performances, and *Your Arms Too Short to Box with God* (1976), a re-telling of St Matthew's Gospel through gospel singing at a black Pentecostal revival meeting.

The best-known biblically based musicals are the mighty trinity of *Joseph*, *Godspell* and *Jesus Christ Superstar* which continue to play to packed houses thirty years after they were written and have been hugely influential in forming the biblical and theological consciousness of several generations. Tim Rice and Andrew Lloyd Webber have arguably done more than most priests and preachers in the last 30 years to promote biblical knowledge and awareness. There may well be serious distortions from the Christian point of view in their handling of biblical stories, as Terence Copley has argued in respect of *Joseph* (see page 119), but they have at the very least introduced scriptural characters and themes to thousands of young people who might otherwise have been largely unaware of them.

It is worth noting in parenthesis that alongside the many biblically based shows, there is also at least one musical which gives serious treatment to the early history of the Christian church. *Philemon* (1975) with music by Harvey Schmidt and words by Tom Jones, the team responsible for *The Fantasticks*, is set in Antioch in 287 AD during a period of intense persecution of Christians. Its central character, Cockian, is an amoral street clown who is hired by the Romans to impersonate Philemon, a Christian leader, and gain information about the Christian community in the area. Moved and converted by his new associates, Cockian goes to his death rather than betray his new-found Christian friends. *Philemon* is rarely performed, partly because it requires the on-stage torture of Cockian as he has a transcendent vision of love and compassion, but Tom Jones tells me that he has a dream 'of doing it in a church or cathedral one of these days'. [40]

5. Musicals influence liturgy. As already noted, show songs are finding their way into hymnbooks and into church services. I have been relieved to discover during research for this book that I am not the only preacher who regularly sings show songs from the pulpit. Innovative ways of linking liturgy to the growing appeal of musicals are described and discussed in the final chapter of this book. There are

questions to be asked about what the churches might learn from the huge success of musicals in putting over often quite complex spiritual themes. There is also what I have elsewhere called the 'Lloyd Webber effect' on church music and the fascinating way in which many new churches are being built to look and feel like theatres. This is what one of my students wrote about entering Carrubers Christian Centre in Edinburgh:

> Walking in, a great sense of extravagance hit me – lovely chairs, expensive carpet, a modern stained-glass picture as opposed to a window and most of all, a sound desk. The miracle of modern technology now allows technicians to sit and control not only the sound and lighting, but also which pages are to be displayed on the projector screens at the front of the church. Hymns are no longer read from hymn books, but projected so all can see. I really thought that I was in a theatre, watching a play, or even more a musical.[41]

6. Musicals display many of the classic qualities of ritual. They are performed, embodied, enacted and gestural (not merely said). They are formalized, elevated, stylized and differentiated (not ordinary, unadorned, or undifferentiated). They are repetitive, redundant and rhythmic (not singular and once for all). They are collective, institutionalized and consensual (not personal or private). They are patterned, invariant, standardized, stereotyped, ordered and rehearsed (not improvised, idiosyncratic or spontaneous). They are valued highly, deeply felt, sentiment-laden, meaningful and serious (not trivial or shallow). They are symbolic, referential and dramatic (not primarily discursive or explanatory) and, increasingly, they are also mythical, transcendent, religious and cosmic (not secular or merely empirical).[42]

Are audiences in musicals taking part in a new form of ritual behaviour? Certainly that is how the response to one particular musical has been interpreted by several academic observers. *The Rocky Horror Show*, especially the film version but also on stage, encourages an extraordinary level of audience participation which involves dressing like characters in the show and bringing 'props' to use at appropriate moments, such as rice to throw during the opening wedding scene, water pistols to simulate a rain storm, candles or torches to shine when Brad and Janet sing they can 'see a light' and even pieces of toast to throw up in the air when Fran proposes a toast during dinner. The audience also maintain a lively dialogue with the performers and interject comments. The audience reaction to *The Rocky Horror Show* is, in fact, just about the only aspect of musical theatre that I am aware of which has been the subject of significant academic attention. Anmittai Aviram, writing in the *Journal of Popular Culture*, has proposed that the term 'cult' should be applied to the show and its following 'not in its banal media-hype sense but rather in its classical sense, the celebration of mystic rites pertaining to a divine being or divine beings and to the appropriate secret lore'. John Kilgore sees the musical as involving a controlled eruption of disorder and sexual excess and the restoration of calm and order. Susan Purdie, who reads it as a kind of secular ritual of 'otherness' and doubling against solemn piety and liturgy, describes the behaviour of the audience as 'a ceremony'. Sal Piro, who acted as master-of ceremonies during many early shows and edited a newsletter for devotees, recalls having seen 'many, many people handle this as a religion in the early days'.[43]

The frenetic and highly stylized reaction engendered by performances of *The Rocky Horror Show* is atypical but other musicals have engendered a not altogether dissimilar response. The huge success in the United Kingdom of the sing-along *Sound of Music*, and more recently the sing-along *Joseph* and *Wizard of Oz*, shows the extent to which audiences enjoy identifying with the characters on stage or film, dressing up like them and singing along with their songs. Reviewing the 2003 revival of *Joseph* at the New London Theatre with Stephen Gately in the title role, Lyn Gardner identifies both the vulgarity and the sense of community fostered by musicals in general and by this one in particular:

> This is an evening entirely without the snobbery that so often affects theatre: you can eat fruit gums all the way through, and nobody minds if the kids sing along with the songs they know. In fact, part of the success of the evening is its assumption of familiarity; of something shared between actors and audience.[44]

7. Musical theatre has to some extent become a kind of para-church or new religious movement. There are increasing numbers of people who, even more than Rosie O'Donnell quoted above, live out their lives according to precepts and principles gained from show songs and for whom musicals have more than a virtual reality and provide a framework for living. At one level, musicals provide an immediate,

immanent, upfront, soft spirituality which washes over you and which is very undemanding and unthreatening. They also inspire an extraordinary level of devotion from fans like the *Starlight Express* addict who spent over £30,000 in seeing the show more than 800 times because 'watching it always makes me feel better and cheers me up'. Musicals undoubtedly play a very central role in some people's lives which is not dissimilar from that played by the church. This almost idolatrous aspect was brilliantly conveyed in Gyles Brandreth's *Zipp!* when a shrine to Andrew Lloyd Webber was brought on stage towards the end of the show. His photograph was garlanded with flowers in the manner of a Hindu deity with a casket, presumably containing some relic, resting in black velvet drapes below. There is room for a thesis on the extent to which musical theatre does, in fact, now constitute a para-church. Maybe somewhere someone is already writing one.

8. Musicals point to changing cultural movements and perspectives, not least in the area of philosophical and religious values. It would be quite possible to write a cultural history of the United States and the United Kingdom over the last sixty years based on an analysis of the dominant musicals of successive decades. In the 1940s and 1950s the emphasis in Broadway shows was on the American dream – promoting community values and a sense that anyone could make it by following their dream. Musicals of the 1960s had a similarly optimistic perspective. One particular show, *Camelot*, came to symbolize the thousand days of John Kennedy's presidency. The 1970s and 1980s brought a much more angst-ridden and intense style of musical full of gritty reality. Charles Spencer has written of 'the doomy portentousness and po-faced lack of humour that so often afflicted blockbuster musicals in the Thatcher years'.[45] The end of the twentieth century was widely hailed by critics as marking the end of the big blockbuster musical and, indeed, possibly the end of the whole genre. It may be that the twenty-first century will spawn a very different cultural icon.

9. Musicals are an important hermeneutic tool and give a point of reference for theological observation and comment. Rowan Williams chose to deliver his first televised New Year message as Archbishop of Canterbury standing in the front of the set of *Chitty Chitty Bang Bang* at the Palladium Theatre, London and reflecting on the world of

theatrical make-believe and commercial make-over. It is striking how often Christian columnists and commentators grab their readers' attention with a quote from a musical. As I write this, I have in front of me three recent examples from across the theological spectrum. From the evangelical camp there is an article by Lon Allison, Director of the Billy Graham Center at Wheaton College, Illinois, which begins ' "It's a hard-luck world". Do you recognize that tag line from the musical *Annie*? I've been singing that line and the melody in my head all morning.'[46] From the liberal stable a piece on the failure of the post-war dream of the National Health Service and the Welfare State in the Iona Community's magazine *Coracle* begins by quoting 'I dreamed a dream' from *Les Misérables*.[47] For a more catholic perspective, *New Directions*, the magazine of the Forward in Faith movement in the Church of England provides appropriate labels for different styles of churchmanship: *The King and I* for Evangelicals, *Higher and Higher* (a 1933 musical), for Anglo-Catholics, *Anything Goes* for liberals and *Half a Sixpence* for the Church Commissioners.

10. There is a surprising amount of theology or 'God-talk' in musicals. Let me just give one example here. A word count that I have made of the English language version of *Les Misérables* reveals 31 references to God, often in the context of prayer, eight mentions of heaven, six of Jesus, three of the soul and explicit allusions to the passion and blood of Christ, the witness of the martyrs, the way of the Lord, sacrifice, salvation and sainthood – altogether a more comprehensive and orthodox catalogue of Christian images and themes than one would find in many contemporary liturgical texts. Theological references and resonances abound in many other musicals, as the following chapters will reveal.

There is one particular message that resounds through the whole canon of twentieth-century musical theatre. It is summed up in the title that I have chosen for this book – 'You've got to have a dream'. I strongly suspect that if one were to do a computer word count among the lyrics of musicals the word 'dream' would come up more frequently than any other noun or verb with the exception of love. Music has, of course, long been used to signify dreaming and dream states – one only needs to think of its significance in Shakespeare's *A Midsummer Night's Dream*. It has had a particular association with dreams and intimations of the other world – a theme that has recently been explored in both pre-Christian and Christian Irish literature in

Karen Ralls-MacLeod's book *Music and the Celtic Otherworld* (Polygon at Edinburgh, 2000). As already noted, Richard Rastall has pointed out how music was particularly used in medieval religious drama to symbolize heaven. That association persists in contemporary musical theatre, albeit in a secularized form. The Pet Shop Boys chose *Closer to Heaven* as the title for their musical about a bisexual love triangle between a young barman, an ambitious club manager's daughter and a streetwise drug dealer.

Dreams are enormously important in the Bible. They are both symbolic and prophetic messages from God. Personal to the dreamer, they speak in symbol and image and sometimes require interpretation. If dreams are portrayed in the Old Testament especially as a key method of God's revelation to humans, they are also represented as a wonderful fruit of the spirit, as in Joel's prophecy which is picked up in the Book of Acts that in the last days God will pour out his spirit on all flesh and 'your old men shall dream dreams' (Joel 2.28–32, Acts 2.17). This biblical injunction to 'dream dreams' has been taken up enthusiastically by Christians of a catholic and mystical bent. For the Celtic enthusiast, Noel O'Donoghue, 'the region of dreams has within it pathways along which the Holy Spirit can reach us', while for Sister Mary Magdalen: 'we need to listen to them, for they are one of God's languages; vehicles of truth far too significant to be washed away in the flood of daily busy-ness'.[48]

There is another more Protestant Christian tradition which is deeply suspicious of dreams and dreamers. It is well articulated in Dietrich Bonhoeffer's remark that 'by sheer grace God will not permit us to live even for a brief period in a dream world. He does not abandon us to those rapturous experiences and lofty moods that come over us like a dream. God is not a God of the emotions but the God of truth . . . God hates visionary dreaming; it makes the dreamer proud and pretentious.'[49] In this understanding, the Christian calling is to face the reality of life and to change and repent rather than live in an idle and self-indulgent dream world.

Part of the reason for these very different perspectives is the difficulty in distinguishing between the dream as message from God and the dream as escapist fantasy and wishful thinking. It has to be said that many of the dreams sung about in musicals, especially in the heyday of Broadway in the 1940s and 1950s, seem to come into the latter category. They have their own ambiguity, however. Those two great quasi-religious anthems from Rodgers and Hammerstein,

'Climb Ev'ry Mountain' with its injunction to 'follow every pathway till you find your dream' and 'You'll never walk alone' with its message to 'walk on, walk on though your dreams are tattered and torn', combine the message that you should follow your dreams and translate them into reality with more than a hint that those dreams may come from God. While there is a strong Pelagian streak in the philosophy, or theology, underlying these songs, a sense that it is all up to the individual and that 'you can do it if you try', there is also a deeper spiritual undercurrent, just as there is in the song from *South Pacific* which gives this book its title, 'You gotta have a dream – if you don't have a dream, how you gonna have a dream come true?' and in Don Quixote's quest 'to dream the impossible dream' in *Man of La Mancha*. This is not just a message to be found in musicals, of course. After successfully circumnavigating the globe single-handed, yachtswoman Ellen MacArthur, said, 'If I have any message from this then it is that if you really have a dream and you want to achieve it then you can and it really is possible.'[50]

This kind of dreaming has been especially prominent in American musicals. It is, indeed, part of that bigger collective American consciousness known as 'the American dream', which resonates in the compositions of Bruce Springstein and in thousands of other popular songs. It is significant that the first really popular American musical of the twentieth century, George M. Cohan's *Little Johnny Jones* is a classic encapsulation of the American dream. This theme continued to dominate American musical theatre through the first half of the century, reaching its apogee in the works of Rodgers and Hammerstein. Although much of the dreaming in classic Broadway musicals is about personal ambition and is essentially individualistic, there is also a wider social dimension. It is no coincidence that Martin Luther King should have introduced his call for a racially integrated, socially just America with the words 'I have a dream'.

Europeans, and perhaps the British in particular, have been more ambivalent and cynical about dreaming and more conscious of how dreams can turn sour and be overtaken by reality. One of the most significant changes of emphasis brought into musical theatre by the British takeover of the 1970s and 1980s was, I think, in the attitude to dreams. It is exemplified in the great song from *Les Misérables*, Fantine's 'I dreamed a dream' which tells of a dream being shattered by the tigers in the night and of life killing the dream. The narrator in *Blood Brothers* reflects how wonderful it would be 'if only we didn't live in life as well as in dreams'. Stephen Sondheim characteristically sides with the ambiguity and cynicism of the British on the subject of dreams. The opening song from *Assassins*, 'Everybody's got a right to their dreams', is given to the shooting arcade proprietor and turns into a meditation on dangerous fantasies. In the context of this show, the message 'aim for what you want a lot' is not about reaching for the stars or climbing every mountain but gunning down a president and taking out an opponent.

There is a counter-theme to this dominant motif about having and following your dream. This is the incitement to live for the present as expressed in 'I'm going to do this before the parade passes by' in *Hello, Dolly*, 'The best of times is now' in *La Cage Aux Folles* and 'Today is the day of our life' in *Rent*. But for each of these incitements to stop dreaming and get on with living in the here and now, there are a dozen songs from musicals expressing wistful hope, dreaming and pointing to another day, another world, another way. Sometimes the dominant motif seems a post-modern secular relativism that 'Any dream will do' but more often there is a kind of spiritual yearning and hankering expressed in the dream songs. Abba's 'I dreamed a dream' leads into a statement of belief in angels and the goodness latent in all things. The Belfast teenagers' almost unbearably moving anthem to peace in *The Beautiful Game* begins as a 'dream about a day when we'll be calm, serene, completely carefree' and ends as a prayer 'for that one ordinary day when all the pain will finally cease'. Two of the show songs most requested for funerals, 'My heart will go on' from *Titanic* (which begins 'Every night in my dreams') and 'Wishing you were somehow here again' from *Phantom of the Opera*, both have this yearning quality. It is significant that musical theatre's most significant attempt to tell the biblical story of creation, *Children of Eden*, portrays God creating the world not *per verbum* but through dreaming it into existence.

There is almost a sense here of dreams having a sacramental quality, mediating grace, signifying the sacred and conveying spiritual effects. No one has articulated this dimension of popular song better than Dennis Potter, the brilliant British television dramatist who took up the craft of writing as a direct result of his childhood fascination with the language of the sacred songs of Moody and Sankey and who was convinced that 'cheap' songs 'have something in them of the Psalms of David'. Explaining their central role in his classic 1978 BBC television drama serial *Pennies from Heaven*, he observed:

Their sweetness, their banality, their sugariness – you can almost lick them they are so sweet, and yet they have this tremendous evocative power – a power which is much more than nostalgia.

Those songs stood together as a package in that they seemed to represent the same kinds of things that the psalms and fairy-tales represented: that is, the most generalized human dreams, that the world should be perfect, beautiful and loving and all of those things. A lot of the music is drivel, in that it's commercial and never too difficult, but it does possess an almost religious image of the world as a perfect place.[51]

Set during the great depression of the 1930s, *Pennies from Heaven* contrasts the seedy reality of the life and world of Arthur Parker, a travelling salesman, with the lofty and optimistic dreams expressed in the popular songs of the day to which he mimes. Potter wrote the television dramas while he was recovering in hospital from a particularly nasty illness and during a period of religious enthusiasm. He said of them 'I wanted to write something about the resilience of human dreams . . . I believe that there is a sort of religious yearning that the world shall be whole, and what I want people to recognize by the end of the plays is that the songs are only diminished versions of the oldest myth of all in the Garden of Eden.'[52]

Many of the songs in *Pennies From Heaven* have a dream-like quality. Alongside their escapist message they articulate a sense that behind the immediate misery and evil in the world there is an ultimate goodness. It is through them that Arthur finds his faith. Potter remarks that Arthur, 'lacking any sense of God or faith, literally believes in those cheap songs to the depths of his tawdry, adulterous little lying soul'.[53] They are the agents of his redemption. There is a scene in the second episode where Arthur is sitting in the lounge of a cheap hotel listening to his fellow salesmen airing their woes of life in the Depression. He tries to articulate the feeling that comes to him through the songs: 'There's things that is too big and too important and too bleed'n simple to put in all that lah-di-dah, toffee-nosed poetry and stuff, books and that – but everybody feels 'em.' He goes on to reflect on his experience in the trenches in the First World War:

Worth more than a dry blanket, they was – them songs. Blimey, I CAN ALMOST TASTE IT! It's looking for the blue, ennit, and the gold. The patch of sky. The gold of the, of the bleed'n dawn, or

the light in somebody's eyes – Pennies from Heaven, that's what it is
. . . Somewhere the sun is shining – And do you know where? Inside
yourself! Inside your own head! Puts the real meaning into them
songs'.[54]

His cynical colleagues are quick to remind him that the songs of Tin
Pan Alley were 'just a business . . . dreamed up in a back-office by a
couple of Jew-boys with green eyeshades' but for Arthur, as for Dennis
Potter, they represent the human dream for perfection, for Zion, Eden
or the shining city of gold, a dream which expresses a basic religious
impulse. In Potter's case they carry him back to his childhood upbringing on Sankey's *Sacred Songs and Solos* with their message of being
bound for a land that is pure and holy and marching to Zion, the
beautiful city of God. In his last work for television before his death,
Cold Lazarus, there is a scene set in a chapel in the Forest of Dean, just
like the one he attended as a boy. The children are singing:

> I am thinking today of that beautiful land
> I shall reach when the sun goeth down;
> When through wonderful grace by my Saviour I stand,
> Will there be any stars in my crown?

Potter was well aware of the closeness of popular songs to hymns, and
particularly of their similarity to the Psalms. In a scene in *Pennies from
Heaven* the head teacher of a junior school asks the female teacher,
Eileen Everson, with whom Arthur is besotted, to read Psalm 35 at
morning assembly. She immediately breaks into an Elsie Carlisle
number 'You've got me crying again' which for Potter was 'a straight
translation of that particular psalm'.[55]

In the final scene of *Pennies*, Arthur makes a strange resurrection-
like appearance on Hammersmith Bridge after being hanged for a
murder that he did not commit. He is then joined by Eileen in a mimed
performance of the song 'The Glory of Love'. These closing moments
confirm the transformative redemptive power of the popular songs,
which along with dreams have punctuated the depressing realism of
the story. Potter's biographer, J. B. Cook, who describes *Pennies* as 'an
avowedly religious work, written from a Christian standpoint', has
observed that it is the message of the cheap songs with their spiritual
yearning and wild optimism which is ultimately triumphant: 'As with
the Hollywood musical, the power of music is finally shown to win

through. Resurrecting Arthur, it defies and disrupts the "realist" narrative that had portrayed his execution.'[56] Cook characterizes *Pennies* as 'a drama in which the viewer is invited to choose between "predictable" pessimism (depression and repression, culminating in Arthur's legalised murder) and "improbable" optimism (faith in the songs which leads to his miraculous resurrection)'.[57] The songs belong not to the realistic naturalistic world but to a world of the spirit where individuals retain the freedom to dream of other possibilities and perhaps gain the power to shape their own destiny.

> It is therefore the songs which, standing in opposition to the pessimism and repression of the central narrative, constitute the optimism in *Pennies* – part of a simple assertion of belief that 'the world shall be whole'; the triumph of hope over experience. In this light, *Pennies* can be seen to abound with Christian symbolism. The trial and persecution of the innocent Arthur, his hanging and subsequent inexplicable appearance on Hammersmith Bridge, all carry echoes of Christ's Crucifixion and Resurrection. At the moment of extreme pessimism, when it seems brutality and death have triumphed, the 'miracle' happens . . . It does so through the power of an instinctive faith. Arthur believes in something. In the face of others' cynicism and all the evidence of experience, he clings to his conviction that the songs (the 'psalms') are true and it is this which sees him through, even to the bitter end. His reward for his trials is salvation through God: that is, through the God-like 'Author' who, in deciding he should live, expresses his own instinctive belief, the gut reaction or emotional choice of 'Says My Heart'.[58]

Alongside their evident escapism and idle fantasizing, the dream songs which are so central to musicals on both stage and screen can also have that transformative, redemptive, even sacramental role that the hits of the thirties had for Arthur Parker. They express spiritual yearning, unlock spiritual truths and often carry substantial theological meaning. It is this understanding of their significance and potential which lies at the heart of this book. I want to take issue with those who dismiss musicals as theatrical junk food, providing a highly spiced and highly hyped experience, which has no depth, or lasting impact. They are vulgar. They are experiential. They do play on emotions and rely on spectacle and colour and boldly drawn character as much as on subtle argument and abstract proposition. So did the medieval mystery plays. I began this introduction by claiming that musicals are the dominant cultural icon of our age. I want to argue that they may be iconic in a deeper sense, with an almost sacramental, hymnodic, transforming power to point beyond themselves to the realm of the spiritual and the divine.

So ends my dream –

the theology of Gilbert and Sullivan

Students taking my Theology of the Musical class are regularly confronted with an examination question which asks 'Is there a discernible theology in the works of Gilbert and Sullivan?' On the face of it, this might seem an extraordinary topic for an essay, more absurd even than the far-fetched plots of the Savoy operas themselves or the perverse Gilbertian topsy-turvydom which has given this first chapter a title about the ending rather than the beginning of a dream. Surely theology is just about the last thing that one would expect to find in the works of Gilbert and Sullivan. It is certainly true that, unlike more recent lyricists and composers, they eschew biblical stories and big metaphysical themes. Yet as I hope to show in this chapter, the Savoy operas are not without an underlying theological and philosophical perspective and this perspective in many ways sets both the parameters and the tone for the development of musical theatre in both the United Kingdom and the United States.

Gilbert and Sullivan demand consideration at the start of any investigation into musical theatre because they really establish and define the genre. Virtually every book on the subject of musicals takes the Savoy operas as their starting point. Writing about the development of the British stage musical, for example, Sheridan Morley notes 'there can be no doubt that it was Gilbert and Sullivan who had made it possible'. For him, their key achievement lay 'in writing the first modern hit songs, and in writing them exclusively and specifically for the theatre'.[1] The influence of Gilbert and Sullivan on the birth and development of the American musical was, if anything, even more important. *HMS Pinafore* really opened the American stage to musical theatre as a respectable family entertainment.

W. S. Gilbert and Arthur Sullivan were radical and daring innovators who effectively created the new genre of musical theatre by taking and transforming elements of both music hall and grand opera. Because of their largely conservative and traditional appeal now, we tend to overlook just how radically innovative they were. Perhaps their most revolutionary achievement was to transform the theatre from the haunt of the dissolute working and drinking classes to a wholesome place of entertainment to which middle-class families could safely go without a blush or whiff of shame. When they started out the theatre was essentially a rackety and coarse institution, dominated by the music hall ethos of drinking, spitting on the sawdust floor and baying from the gallery and denounced by religious leaders on both sides of the Atlantic as a sink of iniquity and vice. In the words of the historian David Cannadine, 'they created a new form of entertainment, precisely pitched between the music hall and the concert hall, which was intelligent but not intellectual, tasteful but not pretentious, tuneful but not cloying'. ² It is almost entirely thanks to Gilbert and Sullivan that we owe the modern idea of musicals as a perfect form of all-age family entertainment.

As well as transforming the conventions of music hall to make musical theatre respectable, Gilbert and Sullivan also changed the conventions of opera to make it accessible. They achieved this first and foremost by establishing a parity between words and music. It is no coincidence that their names are inseparable. With opera it is only the composer who is remembered and credited. We think of Bizet's *Carmen*, Mozart's *The Marriage of Figaro* and Beethoven's *Fidelio*. The same is true of operetta – we think of Offenbach's *Orpheus in the Underworld* and Strauss's *Fledermaus*. But we don't think of Sullivan's *Mikado*, any more than we think of Rodgers's *Sound of Music* or Lloyd Webber's *Evita*. The Savoy operas introduced the parity and partnership between lyricist and composer that was to be one of the hallmarks of the twentieth-century musical. In that respect, as in others, Rodgers and Hammerstein, Lerner and Loewe, Rice and Lloyd Webber are the direct heirs of Gilbert and Sullivan.

As far as Sullivan was concerned, of course, the music in the Savoy operas was, in reality, led and dictated by the words. He famously complained that he had to subordinate his music to Gilbert's lyrics. Gilbert for his part refused to collaborate with Sullivan on a grand opera because 'the librettist of a grand opera is always swamped by the composer'. On the whole, later twentieth-century musicals have been similarly word-led, as exemplified by the fact that the usual mode of working is for the lyrics to be written first and then set to music.

Andrew Lloyd Webber's works are unusual in being music-led with the tunes generally preceding the words. It is noticeable that among the creators of modern musicals who have openly acknowledged the influence of the Savoy operas on their own work, librettists predominate over composers. Sullivan establishes a paradigm for the role of the composer in musical theatre which might be said to be that of the sacrificial calling of the music man as the one who basically subordinates himself and his melodies to the lyricist/librettist and to the words. One aspect of this is the way his melodies generally follow the cadences of speech, a technique followed by most composers in musical theatre. In his important study of the musical, *Broadway Babies Say Goodnight*, Mark Steyn notes the extent to which lyricists generally dictate the form of melodies in Broadway musicals: 'They like songs to follow the cadences of speech, a note per syllable and long notes for important syllables.' This is very different from both pop music and operetta where there are frequent melismas 'permitting insignificant monosyllables to twitter across two notes'.[3]

I wonder if this emphasis on the primacy of the word, which distinguishes both the Savoy operas and the twentieth-century musical, is in fact a very Protestant phenomenon and gives us a clue as to why musicals have flourished in particular geographical and cultural milieux. It is, of course, possible to trace it back to classical times – Plato laid down that harmony and rhythm must follow words and not vice versa – and it was also an aspect of the Renaissance humanist tradition. But it was the Protestant reformers, especially Calvin, who particularly insisted that music be subordinate to words. Could this lingering Protestant legacy provide one reason why the musical has been very largely an Anglo-Saxon phenomenon? The great majority of musicals have been written in English either in the United States or the United Kingdom. They have also been notably more successful in the Protestant countries of northern Europe than in the traditionally Catholic lands in the southern part of the continent.

While the British and Americans were flocking to see the Savoy operas, the distinctly different genre of operetta was winning audiences in France, Austria and Hungary. Operetta, as its name implies, and as the French appellation of *opera comique* makes clear, is closer to opera than is the twentieth-century musical which traces its lineage back to Gilbert and Sullivan. It gives the music greater priority and is less concerned with story and with the nuances and subtleties of language. It is also fundamentally lighter and less didactic in purpose.

It seems to me highly significant that operetta belongs predominantly to Catholic Continental Europe. It does not have that preachy, moralizing quality which has been particularly identified in the work of Rodgers and Hammerstein but which, as we shall see, is also found in a surprising number of the most successful later twentieth-century musicals.

This quality is present in the works of Gilbert and Sullivan although it is subordinated to the wit and cleverness of Gilbert's lyrics and softened by the lightness and lyricism of Sullivan's music. The Savoy operas are not concept musicals which set out to ram a big message with a capital 'M' down their audiences' throats. They do, however, demonstrate an underlying philosophy of life and, if not a distinct theology (God is hardly ever alluded to and is almost entirely absent as a presence), an overarching sense of moral order. Gilbert and Sullivan may have been out primarily to entertain and amuse their bourgeois audiences but Gilbert, in particular, was not without his didactic and moralizing side. To that extent, he establishes an important paradigm for the development of the twentieth century word-led musical. John Bush Jones, like most historians of American musical theatre, sees Gilbert and Sullivan as 'the primary progenitors of the twentieth century American musical'. He goes further than others, however, in identifying their crucial contribution not just in providing the model for the integrated musical in which book, music and lyrics combine to form an integrated whole but also in 'demonstrating that musicals can address contemporary social and political issues without sacrificing entertainment value'. [4] I would add that they also establish the moral and ordered dimension of musical theatre which is so marked a feature of its subsequent development, especially in its mid-twentieth-century Broadway golden age.

There was, of course, a significant stream of early twentieth-century Anglo-American musicals which were closer to operetta than they were to Gilbert and Sullivan. They were the creation of composers who came from operetta's central European heartland, pre-eminently the Hungarian-born Sigmund Romberg who composed *The Student Prince*, *The Desert Song* and *The New Moon*. Those responsible for these shows were not themselves Catholic but rather Jews. In this respect, they were following in a strong operetta tradition. Jacques Offenbach, the creator of the French *opera comique* and great rival to Gilbert and Sullivan, was himself the son of the cantor in the Strasbourg synagogue. Operetta was at least as much a Jewish as a

Catholic phenomenon. The American musical in the first half of the twentieth century was emphatically much more of a Jewish than a Protestant phenomenon. Virtually all the major librettists and composers of American musicals until the 1960s were Jewish, or of Jewish extraction. There is room for a detailed study on the influence that Jewish ideas and influences have played on the development of the musical. In musical terms, the Jewish emphasis on melody rather than harmony, the cantor rather than the choir, has almost certainly played an important part in developing the soaring memorable melodies of show songs. I suspect that the word-led, preachy aspect of musicals owes at least as much to Jewish as to Protestant influences and reflects the similar traditions of a people brought up on the reading of sacred Scriptures with a sense of the importance of book and text and of the subtlety and power of words. Indeed, the musical seems to me to stand as a significant shared symbol and product of Jewish–Protestant values and emphases over and against operetta's embodiment of more Catholic themes.

It is interesting to note in passing that W. S. Gilbert had a particular fondness for the historical books of the Old Testament, believing that no work in literature surpassed them for 'simplicity, directness and perspicuity' and for sheer narrative power. This attachment to Bible stories is shared by Tim Rice, one of a number of leading twentieth-century lyricists who have acknowledged the influence of Gilbert and Sullivan on their work (others include Lorenz Hart, Ira Gershwin, Alan J. Lerner and Sheldon Harnick). It is also surely not without significance that in the United States especially, Gilbert and Sullivan has long had a very substantial Jewish following and fan club. This Jewish appeal has perhaps reached its apogee in the Yiddish versions of *HMS Pinafore*, *The Mikado* and *The Pirates of Penzance* produced by the Gilbert and Sullivan Yiddish Light Opera Company since the early 1980s. More generally, there is a deep appreciation of the 'Jewishness' of Gilbert's humour in terms of its subtle irony, clever wordplay and delight in paradox.

As well as giving importance to the words, the Savoy operas broke with the traditions of both music hall and opera in giving prominence to costumes, scenery and props. Huge care was lavished on these areas by Gilbert. He was also excited by the dramatic possibilities of special effects and *trompe l'œils* like the ghosts stepping down from their picture frames in *Ruddigore* and the incantation scene in *The Sorcerer*. The Savoy operas did not just sound good, they looked good. They were spectacular as well as tuneful and witty. This was another area in which they created new standards and expectations which were taken up by the musical. Audiences may not have left *Iolanthe*, as the more dismissive critics were later to suggest they left some of the more extravagant Lloyd Webber shows, humming the sets but they did thrill to the sumptuous colours of the peers' robes and the fairytale effect created by the fairies' shimmering wings. Gilbert was keen to exploit new technology in the theatre. I suspect he would have thrilled to the crashing chandelier in *Phantom of the Opera* and the helicopter landing in *Miss Saigon*. In a real sense he prepared the way for them.

Perhaps the most important innovation of the Savoy operas was the key role which they give to the chorus. This gives them a communal dimension, a characteristic shared by the musicals of Rodgers and Hammerstein and by many British musicals of the 1960s and 1970s which are often as much about communities as individuals and have a strong social dimension. It is also crucial to their popularity with amateur societies and their role in building and strengthening community among those who perform them. It is not just the principals who have the fun and the limelight in G & S. The chorus in Gilbert and Sullivan opera has its own strong character and its key role in the story and the spectacle. Its roots lie less, I suspect, in the classical Greek chorus acting as narrator and voice of public opinion, although there are elements of that, than in the British tradition of church choirs singing hymns and anthems in four-part harmony – we are back to Protestantism again. It is no coincidence that the Savoy operas emerge on the back of the great choral revival in mid-Victorian Britain which saw thousands of people attending classes in tonic sol-fa and part-singing and the emergence of hundreds of choral societies up and down the country whose repertoire centred around such works as Mendelssohn's *Elijah* and Stainer's *Crucifixion*. Sullivan himself was steeped in this world and wrote for his stage choruses as if he was writing for church choirs.

The 'churchy' feel of Sullivan's choral music and the community-building experience of putting on a Savoy opera perhaps at least partly explain why Gilbert and Sullivan has always been so popular with church members. Many of the British amateur G & S performing societies started as offshoots of churches and chapels and a surprising number still retain their ecclesiastical links, especially those tied to Methodist and Congregationalist chapels. Of the four active G & S performing groups in Sheffield, for example, three are linked to

Methodist churches, as is the main society in nearby Derby. Here is another aspect of the Protestantism of the Savoy operas. There are in fact two distinct Protestant cultures which supply many of Gilbert and Sullivan's most devoted fans and performers – the predominantly male world of upper-middle-class Anglicanism in which boys progress from being sisters, cousins and aunts at prep school to peers and policemen at public school and the provincial Nonconformists who, like Captain Corcoran, occupy a station in the lower middle class and are the mainstay of many local amateur societies. Although as far as I know it has never been scientifically measured, personal observation over many years leaves me in no doubt that there is a significant statistical correlation between churchgoing and enthusiasm for Gilbert and Sullivan. Maybe it is because both pastimes involve engaging in what Mad Margaret in *Ruddigore* identifies as the ultimate sign of madness, singing choruses in public. Perhaps there are even closer parallels. David Cannadine notes that 'for all their gaiety and laughter, it was once remarked that the performance of a Gilbert and Sullivan opera at the Savoy, with a rapt audience following every word in their programme, and turning the same page at the same time, was reminiscent of a prayer meeting in a church or chapel'.[5]

Matters ecclesiastical, if not exactly theological, have a higher profile in the Savoy operas than might at first seem to be the case. The Church takes its place alongside the army, the navy and the stage in the quartet of professions lauded by the Lord Chancellor in *Iolanthe*. Following the precedent established in the introduction, let me try readers out on another briefer set of Trivial Pursuits-style questions about ecclesiastical references in Gilbert and Sullivan:

1 In which of the Savoy operas is reference made to a Wesleyan Methodist of the most bigoted and persecuting type?
2 Where do they scarcely suffer Dr Watts's hymns?
3 In which song is mention made of the leading scholastic theologian of the Middle Ages?[6]
4 How many clergymen appear in the Savoy operas?

The answer to this last question, like the one about the number of songs from musicals that have been featured on *Songs of Praise*, is more than you might think. First and most obviously there is Dr Daly, the endearing Vicar of Ploverleigh in *The Sorcerer*, once a pale young curate beloved by all the maidens in the village but now reconciled to dying a bachelor and burying his sorrow in the congenial gloom of a colonial bishopric. Then there is the bishop who appears among the ghostly Murgatroyd ancestors in the second act of *Ruddigore* and whose sole contribution to the story is when he raises his hand to show his opposition to the idea that Robin Oakapple should carry off a maiden as his daily crime. Pooh-Bah in *The Mikado* holds the archbishopric of Titipu among his many offices and Don Alhambra del Bolero must be a Catholic priest in order to fulfil his office as Grand Inquisitor of Spain in *The Gondoliers*.

Gilbert originally conceived of two clergymen occupying the central roles in *Patience*. In his first draft, the opera was a satire on the Tractarian movement and its two leading characters were rival clerics, one rejoicing in the name of the Reverend Lawn Tennison, who vied with one another in mildness and insipidity until one was persuaded to dance, smoke, play croquet and adopt a more jocular attitude to life. On reflection, Gilbert felt that this subject might be deemed inappropriate and he turned the leading characters into rival poets. The line 'I am not accustomed to uttering platitudes in stained glass attitudes' is one of the survivals from the original version. Given how many clerical fans the Savoy operas have, it is a pity that the rival clergymen plot was abandoned. It is by no means unknown for G & S to be quoted from the pulpit. At the service in which I was licensed as a minister in the Church of Scotland, the sermon was entirely based on Jack Point's song 'O a private buffoon is a light-hearted loon'. As the preacher, Ian Taylor, author of *The Gilbert and Sullivan Quiz Book*, longtime producer of the Edinburgh Gilbert and Sullivan Society and Church of Scotland parish minister, pointed out, it contains a very apposite warning for every aspiring minister: 'What is all right for B would quite scandalize C, for C is so very particular. And D may be dull, and E's very thick skull is as empty of brains as a ladle, while F is F sharp, and will cry with a carp, that he's known your best joke from his cradle.'

Gilbert himself seems to have been only a very occasional churchgoer and to have had no very strong religious faith. He was, on the face of it, a straightforward, uncomplicated British gentleman, sharing with Tim Rice a passion for cricket and a brief flirtation with a legal career. In fact, there was a deeper and more complex side to his background. His father, as well as being a naval surgeon, was a prolific amateur novelist with a fascination for the supernatural and abnormal psychic phenomena. Gilbert senior had a strong social conscience and is intriguingly described by his son's biographer, Jane Stedman, as being 'anti-Catholic, anti-Church of England, anti-vivisection, and pro-Semitic'.[7] His conviction that poverty rather than malevolence lay at the root of much crime and his sense that life was absurd and full of injustice both transmitted themselves strongly to his dramatist son. Its legacy is perhaps clearest in the song 'Fold your flapping wings' written for Strephon in *Iolanthe* but cut from early performances after reviewers claimed that its heavy social message was out of place in a comic opera:

Take a wretched thief
Through the city sneaking,
Pocket handkerchief
Ever, ever seeking:
What is he but I
Robbed of all my chances –
Picking pockets by
Force of circumstances?
I might be as bad –
As unlucky, rather –
If I'd only had
Fagin for a father.

Like many of his contemporaries, W. S. Gilbert was undoubtedly much struck by Darwinism with its theory of natural selection and the survival of the fittest. He caricatured 'Darwinian man' in a song in *Princess Ida* about the lady who was loved by an ape. In order to impress his love, the ape grew moustaches, joined a toilet club and generally became human but the lady was not impressed, reflecting that 'man, however well behaved, at best is only a monkey shaved'. In a more profound way Darwin's theories almost certainly confirmed Gilbert's sense of the arbitrariness and unfairness of life. Virtue, he had the Mikado reflect, is triumphant only in theatrical performances. In real life, as the glee in the second act of *The Mikado* observes, the fates allot their gifts in an arbitrary way with the result that 'A is happy, B is not' though 'B is worthy, I dare say, of more prosperity than A'.

Gilbert's post-Darwinian emphasis on the arbitrariness of fate rather than on the providential dispensations of a just and merciful God has been well documented and explored by Alan Fischler in his study of the comedy in the Savoy operas.

Christian Providence is conspicuously absent from the world of the high Savoy operas and from the consciousness of the characters who dwell therein. Rather, we find Josephine polytheistically invoking both the god of love and the god of reason in *HMS Pinafore*, Grosvenor appealing to Chronos in *Patience*, and Princess Ida praying to Minerva for help in educating her students. Even when he created an entirely serious dramatic situation, in which stage prayer could not have been constructed as blasphemy, and set in the Protestant context of Tudor England, Gilbert refused to allow Elsie to call upon the God of Christianity, having her rather apostrophize Mercy as she waits for Fairfax to be led to the block in the *Yeomen of the Guard*. Nor are the earlier operas any more orthodox: it is the demonic Ahrimanes whose unseen presence dominates *The Sorcerer*, while the gods and goddesses of *Thespis* are borrowed (and burlesqued) from Roman mythology.[8]

Fischler points out that in Gilbert's libretti, the divine is displaced by the human. The reversals in fortunes that come in his operas are always presented as the result of distinctly human causes – the resolution of an earlier state of confusion through a human confession or the reinterpretation or amendment of some existing law. It is through human ingenuity and obedience to and fulfilment of the law rather than through divine grace or intervention that the characters achieve their salvation. He points out that this substitution of human law and ingenuity for divine providence perfectly fitted the duty-based morality and post-Darwinian religious anxieties of the Victorian middle classes.

At one level, there is a deep pessimism in Gilbert's outlook as reflected in the trio in *Princess Ida*:

The world is but a broken toy,
Its pleasures hollow – false its joy,
Its pains alone are true, alas!

A similar sentiment is expressed by the train of little ladies as they make their entrance in *The Mikado*:

Is it but a world of trouble –
Sadness set to song?
Is its beauty but a bubble
Bound to break ere long?

Because Sullivan set these songs to such exquisitely lyrical melodies, we are apt to miss this vein of pessimism in Gilbert. This is another way in which the Savoy operas anticipate what happens in many musicals where profoundly sad words are often set to highly melodic tunes which are easy on the ear. 'I dreamed a dream' in *Les Misérables* is a classic case (see page 155). Whether this mitigates their effect and they would have more power matched with a more dissonant and less catchy melody is a debatable point. In Sullivan's case, it was not just his passion for soaring melodies that perhaps led him to turn an essentially depressing set of lyrics into something inspiring and ultimately life-enhancing. His own outlook on life was fundamentally different from Gilbert's. He was much more in love with the world and with life, much less preoccupied by its arbitrariness, absurdity and unfairness. Sullivan emphatically did not believe that the world was a broken toy, its pleasures hollow and its joys false. In setting these and similar sentiments, he could not suppress his own love of life and worldliness. This tendency to soften harsh and melancholy observations, which could be seen almost as a redemptive gift, was to be shared by the composers of many twentieth-century musicals. In twentieth-century opera, by contrast, there has been much more readiness to use dissonance, unresolved progressions and even atonal melodies to express such emotions.

There is a parallel redemptive-like quality about Gilbert's portrayal of human character. For all his sense of the absurdity of the human condition, he is not ultimately a cynic. He sees humanity as absurd rather than contemptible. Very few of the 'baddies' in the Savoy operas remain totally unredeemed and untouched by human warmth and affection – Dick Deadeye is about the only one I can think of who is as twisted and misanthropic at the end as he was at the beginning. Katisha is softened by Ko-Ko, Sir Despard Murgatroyd repents of his wicked ways and gives up all his wild proceedings under the gentle tutelage of Mad Margaret, who is herself tamed by invocation of the magic word 'Basingstoke'. There is a strong emphasis in Gilbert's plots on sincerity and faithfulness, even self-sacrifice. John Wellington Wells in *The Sorcerer* does the decent thing and takes his own life as the only way of undoing the unfortunate effects of the love potion that has been unleashed on the inhabitants of Ploverleigh. Jack Point, the only really tragic figure in the Savoy operas, literally seems to die for the love of a lady and is shown caring about something other than his terrible old jokes. Dame Hannah remains loyal to Sir Roderic

Murgatroyd in *Ruddigore* despite all the snubs she has received from him, Hebe stays with Sir Joseph Porter to soothe and comfort his declining days in *HMS Pinafore*, the Heavy Dragoons become aesthetes for the sake of their lady loves in *Patience*, Frederic displays unflinching loyalty to his overpowering sense of duty throughout *The Pirates of Penzance*. There is perhaps almost even a spark of the divine in these characters. They deserve Sullivan's soaring anthem-like settings for their songs.

For all Gilbert's concern to point up the ambiguity, contradictions and even absurdity in the human condition, there is also a strong sense of overarching order in the plots of the Savoy operas. With the notable exception of *The Yeomen of the Guard*, all comes out right in the end – the conundrums, mistakes and misunderstandings are sorted out. Everything may seem topsy-turvy but order does almost always prevail. There are clear elements here of the convention from the world of fairy stories that all live happily ever after, and of the pantomime tradition of unexpected transformations which see evil thwarted and good prevail. The moral order is reasserted and re-established. So, too, is the established social and political order. For all Gilbert's gentle satirical digs at institutions like the peerage and the army and his sense that crime owed more to social circumstance than moral depravity, the Savoy operas have a fundamentally conservative message. Love does not level all ranks in *HMS Pinafore*; the Venetian monarchy is not overthrown by republican egalitarianism in *The Gondoliers*; the pirates yield to the policemen when the name of the Queen is invoked in *The Pirates of Penzance*. A similar framework of overarching moral order and a resolution of potentially disruptive and disturbing elements to create a basically happy ending characterizes most musicals throughout the first three quarters of the twentieth century until the angst-ridden words and music of *Jesus Christ Superstar* break the mould. Indeed this overall sense of order and optimism is crucial to both the identity and appeal of the musical. In his director's guide to musicals, Scott Miller observes that 'for many people, the appeal of a musical is its simplicity, its innocence . . . For others, its beauty is in its ability to make order out of chaos, to sort through the craziness of our lives and make sense of it all.'[9] Peter Stone, writing about the slightly more restricted genre of musical comedy, notes that the word 'comedy' is very important to musical comedy, because the form is basically optimistic. When it ceases to be a happy-ending show, you are looking at opera . . . Musical comedy is an optimistic form and must end optimistically, offering some sort of pleasure at the end.[10]

The optimism in the Savoy operas is not an easy, escapist kind of fantasy. It is most characteristically expressed as a determined resignation to get on with life. In so far as there is a basic philosophical message underlying the works of Gilbert and Sullivan it is surely that of *carpe diem*, taking each day as it comes and making the most of every moment. It is superbly expressed in the quintet from *The Gondoliers* which begins 'Try we lifelong we can never straighten out life's tangled skein' and is introduced by Don Alhambra's recitative which perhaps gets as close as anything Gilbert wrote to a metaphysical statement in its reflection that we might as well submit to fate since 'life is one closely complicated tangle' and 'death is the only true unraveller'. In the gospel according to Gilbert, the conviction that only in death will things be sorted out does not prompt thoughts of divine judgement and accountability but rather a determination to 'string the lyre and fill the cup, lest on sorrow we should sup'. Care is 'a canker that benumbs'. Life, in contrast, is 'a pudding full of plums' and a 'pleasant institution' which we should take as it comes:

> Hop and skip to Fancy's fiddle,
> Hands across and down the middle –
> Life's perhaps the only riddle
> That we shrink from giving up.

There is not much theology here – certainly not much room for God – but this basically humanist creed is accompanied by a profound and persistent concern with death and whether it should be viewed as friend or foe. This is the theme of Fairfax's song 'Is life a boon?' in *The Yeomen of the Guard* with its speculation about whether it is always true 'that Death, whene'er he call, must call too soon'. A similar ambivalence about death underlies Hilarion's Act 3 aria in *Princess Ida* 'Whom thou hast chained must wear his chain' with its closing couplet 'If kindly death will set me free, Why should I fear to die?'

No song in the entire Savoy canon better expresses this ambivalence about death and fundamental philosophy that life is to be lived than the one which gives this chapter its title. Julia Jellicoe sings 'So ends my dream' towards the end of *The Grand Duke* as she comes to terms with the shattering of her cherished dream of marrying the Grand Duke. She begins in the depths of despair, a mood which is heightened by one of Sullivan's most brooding and heart-rending melodies:

> All is darksome – all is dreary.
> Broken every promise plighted –
> Sad and sorry – weak and weary!
> Every new-born hope is blighted!

Next comes the familiar Gilbertian tussle over whether death is to be welcomed or resisted in such a state of despair:

> Death the Friend or Death the Foe,
> Shall I call upon thee? No!
> I will go on living, living though
> Sad and sorry – weak and weary!

Then, with a dazzling display of coloratura bravado, the song completely changes gear both musically and emotionally as Julia resolves to go on living and enthusiastically expresses the dominant philosophy of the Savoy operas:

> No, no! Let the bygones go by!
> For no good ever came of repining:
> If today there are clouds o'er the sky,
> Tomorrow the sun may be shining!
>> Tomorrow be kind,
>> Tomorrow to me!
>> With loyalty blind
>> I curtsey to thee!
> Today is a day of illusion and sorrow,
> So *Viva* tomorrow!

This song is much closer in sentiment and sympathy to the way the dream theme is treated in the musicals of the late twentieth century than to the way it is handled in shows from the heyday of Broadway. In beginning with and acknowledging the reality of shattered dreams, it anticipates 'I dreamed a dream' in *Les Misérables*. In its affirmation of the importance of going on living and embracing tomorrow it anticipates 'The best of times' in *La Cage aux Folles* and 'La Vie

Boheme' in *Rent*. It has that striking note of realism which distinguishes Gilbert and Sullivan's operas from most of the musicals written in the first half of the twentieth century where the dream theme is much more aspirational and escapist. For Gilbert and Sullivan, musical theatre fulfils the function that the picaresque novel does for Dickens. It is a vehicle through which to reflect the durability and vitality of the human condition which rises above its essential absurdity. Amidst all their shattered dreams and unfulfilled expectations people go on living and hoping. In their treatment of life the Savoy operas adopt a nuanced realism that was not fully picked up again in the world of musical theatre until the closing decades of the twentieth century, notably by British lyricists and composers who turned their back on Hollywood's more romantic and idealized approach, albeit in a much more angst-ridden and tortured way than their Victorian progenitors.

While much of this realism and ambiguity about the human condition which is displayed in the Savoy operas undoubtedly comes from Gilbert, it also owes something to the character of Arthur Sullivan. He was a much more complex figure than his collaborator, being at once more spiritual and more worldly. Plagued by painful illness through much of his adult life, he must have wrestled like Fairfax, Hilarion and Julia with the question as to whether death could be friend or foe. At the same time he had a zest for life in the fast lane, whether in the casinos of Monte Carlo or the salons of fashionable London society. Regarded by the musical establishment as the potential English Brahms or Mendelssohn who would give Victorian Britain its great classical composer, he never fulfilled his promise and was derided for devoting himself to comic operas and parlour ballads. His motives for staying predominantly in these popular and lucrative realms were partly pecunicary. He had seen his own father struggle on a pittance as a musician and he wanted to have money not just to indulge his tastes for gambling and the good life but also to shower on his impoverished relations and live out the generosity and warm humanity that were at the heart of his make-up. When Sullivan did turn his hand to more serious works, and especially to his oratorios and church music, he displayed a profound spiritual sensitivity.

Although Sullivan's background was cosmopolitan, with Italian blood on his mother's side and Irish on his father's, the dominant influence on him as a child in both religious and musical terms was firmly English and indeed Anglican. As a boy he attended both the

Church of England school and the parish church in Sandhurst where his father was a military bandsman and he fell in love with the Anglican choral tradition. His first musical composition, written at the age of eight, was an anthem *By the Waters of Babylon*. When he was 11 he became a chorister at the Chapel Royal, the ancient foundation attached to St James's Palace which, under the direction of Thomas Helmore, was at the van of the mid-nineteenth-century Anglican choral revival.

All of Sullivan's early compositions were sacred. In 1855 an anthem by the 12-year-old prodigy, 'Sing unto the Lord and bless his name', was sung at the Chapel Royal and in the same year he achieved his first published work with another anthem, *O Israel*. Like many young musicians and composers making their way in Victorian Britain, he took a salaried position as a church organist. Having declined the offer of a post in a Lutheran church because of his Anglican convictions, he became organist first at St Michael's, Chester Square, and subsequently at St Peter's, Cranleigh Gardens, two fashionable London churches. He composed more than sixty hymn tunes, several anthems and settings of the 'Te Deum' and a number of sacred oratorios, notably *The Martyr of Antioch*, *The Prodigal Son* and *The Light of the World*.

Like Gilbert, Sullivan was not a regular churchgoer and does not seem to have had particularly strong religious convictions. He became a freemason but this was probably for social reasons. His biographer Arthur Jacobs has written that

> His religion hardly went beyond a superficial conformity to the Church of England: neither on the threshold of death nor earlier in his mature years is there evidence of spiritual guidance sought or offered. A strong family piety together with a deep commitment to friendship and to his art – these purely human values were, perhaps, enough.[11]

The verdict of critics on Sullivan's sacred music has been very mixed. The distinguished hymnologist Erik Routley castigated his hymn tunes for poor craftsmanship and sloppy musicianship, reflected in his overuse of repeated notes and static marching basses, and for an insincere banality which came through the composer abandoning his theatricality and writing in a self-conscious 'churchy' style. For Routley:

Sullivan's genius was not in the least religious; it was too light for the graver themes, as the hymn tunes themselves show. We can imagine the relief with which he escaped from his early occupation with church music, in which he was not at home, into that wholly congenial field of light opera, in which, along with his twin genius, W. S. Gilbert, he was to achieve immortality.[12]

For another Sullivan scholar, David Eden, young Arthur's entry into the Chapel Royal was a disaster for his future compositional career, 'tainting him with the spiritual bankruptcy of Victorian Anglicanism. His genius only blossomed when his texts carry him away from religious themes.'[13] Yet other musicologists, like Samuel Rogal, have suggested that Sullivan did have a genuine feeling and gift for sacred music:

> Arthur Sullivan found religion not within the walls of a church or the tenets of a denomination, but from the balm provided by his own genius for composing music for hymns and sacred songs.[14]

The truth is, I believe, that Sullivan was both a deeply spiritual and also a deeply theatrical composer who displayed his genius equally in his settings of sacred texts and in his comic operas. Sullivan was at his best when dealing with real character and with real emotion. Some of his most poignant music was directly inspired by his own feelings of loss – his *In Memoriam* overture by the death of his father and both the ballad 'The Lost Chord' and the anthem 'Brother, thou art gone before us', which originally appeared in the crucifixion section of his oratorio *The Light of the World*, by the death of his brother. His genius was supremely manifested in his ability to find musical notes and harmonies which both heightened and deepened the meaning and emotional power of the words that he was setting. If this led to a danger of overegging the pudding and squeezing every ounce of sentiment out of a text, then that is a fault which he shares with many composers in the worlds of both church music and musical theatre.

Sullivan stands as the first great composer to cross over between these two worlds. He was equally happy in and equally suited to the orchestra pit and the organ loft. Indeed, he stands as the supreme and most successful exemplar of this particular 'crossover'. Subsequent composers working predominantly in the genre of musical theatre have occasionally tackled sacred texts: Leonard Bernstein with his

Mass and Andrew Lloyd Webber with his *Requiem* and setting of the Millennium prayer; but they have generally eschewed church music. The strength of Sullivan's religious music lies in its very theatricality. His eminently singable and stirring hymn tunes like 'Bishopgarth', 'St Gertrude' and 'Constance' could equally well have been written for a chorus of dragoons or policemen on the Savoy stage, just as many of his Savoy choruses have the anthemic four-part harmonies of Anglican church music. They are vulgar, incarnational even, in the best sense of the word. At times, he almost goes over the top in his striving for histrionic effect, as in the use of the military band playing 'St Gertrude' in his *Boer War Te Deum*. But, as we have already noted, there has long been a fine dividing line musically between the sanctuary, the concert hall and the opera house. That line was especially blurred in respect of that peculiarly Victorian genre in which Sullivan excelled, the sacred parlour ballad, and to which he contributed perhaps the greatest and most representative example in 'The Lost Chord'.

Sullivan was a sincere composer, and in that respect as in others he anticipates the style of the great composers of Broadway musicals like Richard Rodgers and Frederick Loewe. Genuine human dilemmas and triumphs moved him deeply. Ask him to set a text of abstract theology and he was out of his depth and left utterly cold, as his dire setting of George Matheson's profound hymn 'O Love, that wilt not let me go' exemplifies. But give him a good human scene and story, like James Drummond Burns's dramatic retelling of the Lord's call to Samuel in the hymn 'Hushed was the evening hymn' or Henry Longfellow's evocation of villagers gathering to light lamps and sing their evening hymn 'O gladsome light' in *The Golden Legend*, and he was inspired to produce marvellous lyrical melodies. He could also respond to expressions of doubt and perplexity. Perhaps his outstanding setting of a religious text is his tune 'Lux in Tenebris' for John Henry Newman's 'Lead Kindly Light'. The ambiguity of Newman's anguished spiritual searchings spoke to Sullivan who produced infinitely the most sensitive setting of that great Victorian anthem of doubt-filled faith.

Through his music Sullivan shows himself to be a spiritual seeker and wanderer. In this, as in so many respects, he seems to me to be very like Andrew Lloyd Webber – determined to avoid his musician father's life of blighted hopes and genteel poverty, driven by a love of fame, high society and the good life, passionate about musical theatre and with an underlying and unfulfilled spiritual yearning and questing. It was no coincidence that Sullivan's greatest 'hit single' should be inspired by these words by Adeline Anne Proctor, herself a leading practitioner of the 'crossover' between parlour ballad and hymn:

> I have sought but I seek it vainly
> That one lost chord divine,
> Which came from the soul of the organ
> And entered into mine.
> It may be that Death's bright angel,
> Will speak that chord again;
> It may be that only in Heaven
> I shall hear that grand Amen.

Sullivan perhaps came closest to revealing his own religious position and philosophy of life in the preface to his oratorio *The Prodigal Son*. He writes:

> The story is so natural and pathetic, and forms so complete a whole; its lesson is so thoroughly Christian; the characters, though few, are so perfectly contrasted, and the opportunity for the employment of 'local colour' is so obvious, that it is indeed astonishing to find the subject so long overlooked.[15]

The 'so thoroughly Christian' lesson that Sullivan draws from the parable is rather different from the one which is usually drawn from it. He significantly cuts out the last part of the story of the prodigal as recounted in Luke's Gospel, which deals with the reaction of the older brother, as having 'no dramatic connection with the former and principal portion'. For Sullivan the theme of this story is not about the joy that God has over the sinner who repents. Rather it is about the vagaries and restlessness of the human quest:

> The Prodigal himself has been conceived, not as of a naturally brutish and depraved disposition – a view taken by many commentators with apparently little knowledge of human nature, and no recollection of their own youthful impulses; but rather as a buoyant, restless youth, tired of the monotony of home, and anxious to see what lay beyond the narrow confines of his father's farm, going forth in the confidence of his own simplicity and ardour, and led gradually away into follies and sins which, at the outset, would have been as distasteful as they were strange to him.[16]

Here is a philosophy of life very different from Gilbert's emphasis on the arbitrariness of fate and the sorrow-filled nature of the world. The accent rather is on the natural restlessness and thirst for adventure of the human character. Follies and sins may assail the prodigal son on his way but they are alien and ultimately incidental to the 'confidence of his own simplicity and ardour'. There is a Pelagian strain here which we are going to encounter again in many classic musicals. Sullivan's prodigal son does not seem to have much need of God's grace, in marked contrast to the first person subject in that other great Victorian treatment of this parable, Henry Baker's hymn 'The King of Love my shepherd is':

Perverse and foolish oft I strayed
And yet in love he sought me.
And on his shoulder gently laid
And home rejoicing brought me.

For Sullivan, the story of the prodigal son seems rather to be about the individual human quest for adventure and derring-do. We are in the world of Don Quixote in *Man of La Mancha* dreaming the impossible dream and Maria breaking free from the convent in *The Sound of Music*. To that extent, Sullivan is perhaps closer in spirit than Gilbert to the central message of the dream theme as it was to be worked out in the golden age of Broadway musicals in songs like 'Climb Ev'ry Mountain' and 'When you walk through a storm'. He had, though, a more realistic sense than most of those writing musicals in the mid-twentieth century of the ambiguity of dreams and the ease with which they could be shattered. In this, he anticipated those writing British musicals in the late twentieth century and especially the one who was so similar to him in background, character and outlook, Andrew Lloyd Webber.

If there were many tensions between Gilbert and Sullivan and profound differences in their approaches to life, the works which they created together contain songs which show a complete fusion of outlook and attitude. One such is Mabel's aria 'Poor wandering one' in *The Pirates of Penzance*, a song which in its injunction to the one who 'hast surely strayed' to 'take heart of grace' and 'thy steps retrace' would not be out of place in a revivalist meeting. Here, Gilbert's words perfectly chime in with Sullivan's sympathy for the restless and wandering soul. Another number from the same opera in which librettist and composer speak as one individual is the unaccompanied anthem 'Hail, poetry' – perhaps the nearest that the Savoy operas have to a hymn in both its words and musical construction. It is no coincidence that it is the goddess Poetry who is both addressed and praised here. Both Gilbert and Sullivan fully subscribed to the philosophical statement which precedes this song: 'What, we ask, is life without a touch of poetry in it?' For them, a touch of poetry was what made life more explicable, more ordered and perhaps above all more palatable and pleasant. The anthem goes on to hail both the 'flowing fount of sentiment' and the quality of 'divine emollient', two terms which could stand as a description of the point and purpose of much musical theatre in the hundred years after Gilbert and Sullivan first collaborated. Until they radically changed gear in the 1970s, most musicals had an essentially sentimental and emollient quality, sweetening and soothing the vicissitudes of life and leaving their audiences feeling happier and uplifted.

This was certainly true of most of the shows written and performed during the early decades of the twentieth century when the musical stage in both the United States and the United Kingdom followed the conventions and tradition of operetta rather than of the Savoy operas. Its key protagonists, Sigmund Romberg, Lionel Monckton and Ivor Novello, gave priority to music rather than words and to star voices rather than chorus. Their musicals tended to be set in remote, romantic Ruritanian never-never lands and be equally remote from contemporary social concerns in their plot lines and subject matter. Occasionally contemporary issues were treated – there were American musicals in the 1920s dealing with the subject of prohibition – but only in a very superficial way. There were practitioners who followed Gilbert and Sullivan's emphasis on words, notably Cole Porter and Noel Coward, but their work was characterized by a very secular sophistication and subtlety. Confusion reigned more than order, and when God was mentioned, it was with some measure of uncertainty about his existence and sincerity, as in Coward's 1931 show *Cavalcade*:

Why if there's a God in the sky
Why doesn't he grin,
Up high above this dreary
Twentieth-century din?

2

'Til you find your dream –

the golden age of Broadway

There have been three defining partnerships of lyricist and composer in the history of musical theatre: Gilbert and Sullivan, whose collaboration lasted from 1875 to 1898, Rodgers and Hammerstein, who worked together between 1942 and 1960, and Rice and Lloyd Webber, who teamed up from 1968 to 1973. Each fundamentally changed the landscape of musical theatre and brought an entirely new element to the genre. In the case of Rodgers and Hammerstein it was an emphasis on character and plot, a strong moral content and message and an undergirding atmosphere of uplifting idealistic optimism.

In many ways Rodgers and Hammerstein took American musical theatre back to its roots in the Savoy operas from which it had been diverted by the counter-influence of the operetta tradition. Like Gilbert and Sullivan, they gave priority to the words. This was unusual among those writing American musicals at this time. With his first lyricist, Lorenz Hart, Richard Rodgers followed the practice of writing the tunes first. Oscar Hammerstein was also used to this way of working, which he had experienced in his early collaborations with Jerome Kern, Sigmund Romberg, Rudolf Friml and George Gershwin. But when Rodgers and Hammerstein worked together the words came first and the melodies had to be fitted to them. Hammerstein was also unusual in providing both the lyrics and libretto, or book, for his musicals. Usually, the two activities were split.

The fact that Hammerstein provided plot and dialogue as well as lyrics underlines his key role as the first real dramatist in the history of the American musical. Before Rodgers and Hammerstein, most musicals were little more than a collection of songs linked by a rather flimsy and simple storyline. Their achievement was to integrate music and story so that the songs were no longer a diversion and distraction but

a key element in the narrative, carrying forward the plot and expressing and developing the character of the key participants. What
they did, in short, was to produce musical plays rather than musical
comedies.

Ethan Morrden, the leading historian of mid-twentieth-century
American musical theatre, has written that 'musical plays are stuffed
with content; that's, really, how they differ from musical comedy'.[1]
The content with which Rodgers and Hammerstein's shows were
stuffed was not just the predictable formula of boy meeting girl, boy
losing girl and boy getting girl back in the end. They tackled serious
subjects like the nature of community, race and class, and big themes
like remorse and redemption. This kind of heavy and moralistic
approach to writing musicals, characterized as 'school-room senten-
tiousness' by the *Guardian* theatre critic, Michael Billington, would
have been anathema to Lorenz Hart who was a decidedly amoral
urban sophisticate full of clever wit and cutting cynicism. Oscar
Hammerstein, by contrast, was an idealist, a moralist and a gentleman, as evidenced by Mae West's famous piece of advice to him when
young: 'Get out of the theatre, kid, and go back to law. You've got too
much class to hang around the stage.' He was also an incurable
romantic.

While Hammerstein cut his teeth working in the 1920s as co-
librettist and lyricist on Romberg's gloriously romantic operettas, *The
Desert Song* and *The New Moon*, he showed his more serious side in
his 1927 collaboration with Jerome Kern, *Show Boat*, for which he
provided both book and lyrics. *Show Boat* is often hailed as the first
musical to have real characters facing real problems. As Peter Stone
has observed, it also portrayed 'real unhappiness, not just "My date
went home with somebody else," which was the basic unhappiness of
the musical up to that time'.[2] Tracing the lives of three generations of
families, black and white, working on the Mississippi theatre show
boat, *Cotton Blossom*, it deals with racial prejudice, alcoholism,
gambling and family breakdown. Hammerstein himself noted how it
stood out from other shows of the twenties, 'mostly feather-brained
musical comedies with wide-eyed *ingénues* and earnest young men'.
Hal Prince, who directed the 1990s Broadway and West End revival,
points to its crucial place in the history of musical theatre:

> It was a beginning. Before *Show Boat* there were operas and there
> were musical comedies. After it came *Carousel*, *West Side Story*,

Fiddler on the Roof, Cabaret, all of Sondheim. *Show Boat* made it possible to put subjects into musicals that were exclusively non-musicals' property. Now you can deal with serious subjects and people will come.[3]

In some ways, indeed, *Show Boat* seems to belong more to the angst-ridden 1990s than to the roaring twenties. Perhaps that is why it was revived so successfully in the closing decade of the twentieth century. Significantly for the revival Hal Prince restored a song, 'Mis'ry's Comin' Round' which Kern and Hammerstein had cut because they felt it was too bleak and downbeat but which was wholly in keeping with the 'gloomy doomy' mood of the 1990s. Although *Show Boat* points up the ambiguity of the human condition and does not suggest that life is simply about following your dream and thus finding happiness and fulfilment, the dream theme which was to feature so prominently in the Rodgers and Hammerstein collaborations is certainly there. The main love song, 'Only make believe' contains the reflection that 'our dreams are more romantic than the world we see'. Hammerstein's characteristic emphasis on the durability and hope-filled striving of the human spirit in adversity is most movingly expressed in the spiritual-like show-stopper, 'Ol' Man River', in which the central black character, Joe, reflects on his unremitting and back-breaking work as a stevedore. It is not, as one might expect, a protest song but rather a work song with a distinct and almost stoic philo-sophical edge in which the steady flow of the mighty river on whose banks Joe ceaselessly labours symbolizes the rhythm of all human life and hints at the hope of something beyond its pain and futility:

Ah gits weary an' sick of tryin',
Ah'm tired of livin' an' skeered of dyin',
But ol' man river, he just keeps rollin' along.

There is also something of the spiritual in 'Ol' Man River' with Joe's prayer-like plea: 'Show me that stream called the River Jordan / That's the old stream that I'd like to cross'. It is, indeed, significant that the most reflective and profound song in *Show Boat* is put on to the lips of a black man. It is striking the extent to which white American lyricists and composers have written some of their most spiritually charged words and music for black characters. The supreme example is *Porgy and Bess* (1935) in which George Gershwin made prolific use of the distinctive black musical genre of spiritual and gospel song. There has been much debate as to how far this work represents an outsider's exploitation of black culture and faith and how far Gershwin's own deep spiritual roots and experience of isolation as a Jew enabled him to empathize with the religious outlook of the American negro. His first biographer, Isaac Goldberg, pointed out how he became 'increasingly conscious of the similarity between the folk song of the Negro and of the Polish (Jewish) pietists'.[4] In other hands, *Porgy and Bess* would almost certainly have involved a much more romanticized treatment of black America. There was at one stage a move by Jerome Kern and Oscar Hammerstein to turn DuBose Heyward's novel, *Porgy*, into a musical starring Al Jolson.

Gershwin's *Porgy and Bess* is generally regarded as more of an opera than a musical, as attested by the fact that it is usually attributed simply to the composer with the lyricists Ira Gershwin and DuBose Heyward receiving little or no credit. In its final three-hour-plus version, however, it perhaps most resembles a modern through-sung musical like *Les Misérables*, although it differs from this genre and from most opera in having dialogue. The dialogue in Porgy and Bess indeed has a key role, being reserved for the largely non-singing white characters like Mr Archdale and the policemen, who are thus given a monochrome character in contrast to the musically much more colourful blacks.

Porgy and Bess also resembles *Les Misérables* in having so many songs directed to God and Jesus which are effectively prayers. Two scenes are almost entirely made up of such songs. Act 1, scene 2, which focuses on the mourning following the death of Robbins, has Porgy praying to 'Suffering Jesus' and calling on God to 'raise dis poor sinner up out of his grave'. The mourning chorus takes up this theme, crying 'send down your angels' and affirming 'Everybody helpin' now – sendin' our brother to heaven'. This scene ends with Bess's hope-filled Gospel train song:

> Oh the train is at the station,
> An' you better get on board,
> 'Cause it's leavin' today,
> 'An it's headin' for the Promise' Lan'

Act 2, scene 4 begins and ends with an extraordinary sextet in which the inhabitants of Catfish Row try to drown out the hurricane raging around them by intoning simple prayers directed respectively to Doctor Jesus, Captain Jesus, Professor Jesus, 'the Lawd above', Heavenly Father and 'the Father what die on Calbery'. Gershwin based this sequence on singing that he had heard while standing outside the Holly Rollers Church in Hendersonville. The influence of negro spirituals and gospel songs is evident through the rest of this scene. The opening sextet is followed by Clara singing 'One of dese mornings you goin' to rise up singin'.

At one level, *Porgy and Bess* constitutes a huge affirmation of simple faith and the power of prayer. Serena's prayer-like aria, 'Doctor Jesus, who done trouble water in de Sea of Galilee' cures Bess of the fever which she develops after her encounter with Crown at the picnic on Kittiwah Island. Yet there is, too, an ambivalence about religious faith, and especially the simple faith of the American south. Sporting Life, the dope peddler who eventually spirits Bess away to New York, is, like the Devil, given one of the best tunes for his 'It ain't necessarily so. De tings dat yo' li'ble to read in de Bible, it ain't necessarily so.' The God in whom the Christian characters believe is very clearly a God of judgement. The general enjoyment that follows Sporting Life's catchy put-down of Bible stories is interrupted by Serena breaking in to warn:

> When the Christians turn their backs
> You start behavin' like Sodom an' Gomoorah.
> It's a Gawd's wonder de Lord don't sen' His
> Livin' fire to burn you offen de face of the earth.

There is also a good deal of cruelty in *Porgy and Bess*. It engages with the nasty side of humanity and has a strong sense of the arbitrary power of fate. It sticks to raw reality and does not deal in dreams as it might well have done had it been written by Kern and Hammerstein. Indeed, perhaps it is this absence of the dream theme that makes *Porgy and Bess* an opera rather than a musical. Porgy's God is one who decrees individual suffering rather than one who makes dreams come true:

> When Gawd make cripple
> He mean him to be lonely.
> Night time, day time,
> He got to trabble dat lonesome road.

What relieves this somewhat bleak and fatalistic world-view is the strong belief in a better world to come. God's rule and judgement may be harsh and arbitrary-seeming in this life but he has promised his people another land. The familiar negro spiritual theme of journeying to the promised land provides the one element of real hope in *Porgy and Bess*. It is there in Serena's weary observation after Robbins's death: 'Work and me is travellers, journeyin' together to the promised land' and in Porgy's final solo as he is helped into the goat cart to set off to New York to find Bess, a song which has attained the status of a hymn (see page 7):

I'm on my way to a Heav'nly Lan'
Oh Lawd, it's a long, long way,
But You'll be there to take my han'

If *Porgy and Bess* stands in many ways as the defining American opera, then a film which appeared just four years later could be seen as the defining American musical. *The Wizard of Oz* has been described by US journalist Mark Hertsgaard as 'the closest thing we have to a national fairytale'. It introduces a theme that was to dominate American musical theatre for the middle decades of the twentieth century – the quest for right and moral purpose. In *The Wizard of Oz* this theme is expressed in the journey of a child and her companions to rescue the broomstick of the Wicked Witch of the West. It has the qualities of an epic – we are in the realm of *The Lord of the Rings* and *Harry Potter* – and it also has a political and social dimension – both lyricist Yip Harburg and composer Harold Arlen were active Democrats who passionately supported Franklin Roosevelt's New Deal. The great sense of yearning expressed in Dorothy's song 'Somewhere over the rainbow', however, is primarily focused on individual self-fulfilment even if it has an implied communal dimension. In Hertsgaard's words: 'The message of *The Wizard of Oz* is clear: Believe in yourself, stick by your friends, fight for what's right, and things will get better', or, as Dorothy sings, 'the dreams that you dare to dream really do come true'.[5]

In that last affirmation we are introduced to the key message of the dream theme as it is expounded in American musicals in the golden age of Broadway. It is in the songs of Rodgers and Hammerstein that it finds its fullest expression, perhaps supremely in the number from *South Pacific* which gives this book its title and in which Bloody Mary tells Lieutenant Cable 'You've gotta have a dream. If you don't have a dream, how you gonna have a dream come true?' The incitement to dream your own personal dream, coupled with the firm conviction that such dreams, if pursued doggedly and single-mindedly enough, really do come true, is the dominant theme of the great Rodgers and Hammerstein musicals of the 1940s and 1950s. It is a very different, much more optimistic and in many ways more secular message than the emphasis on prayer, submission to God's hard judgements and the long journey to the promised land in *Porgy and Bess*. It is significant that these latter themes continued to feature for a few years in black musicals where the gospel song and spiritual remained a powerful influence. There is a classic example of the genre in the song 'The Lord Done Fixed up my Soul' in the 1940 show *Louisiana Purchase* which, as Ethan Mordden says, 'turns up in the action only because . . . well, why not?'

> With almost all the principals facing exposure and prosecution, a minor character offers a non-solution. It's the south, and he's black, and while neither fact inexorably points to a soul rave-up, his logic seems persuasive to everyone on stage:

> BLACK MAN. I know what my mammy would do if she was in the trouble you all's in. She'd do some mighty deep praying.[6]

In another 1940 show, the all-black *Cabin in the Sky*, opposing armies from heaven and hell, led by the Lawd's General and Lucifer Junior, fight for the soul of Little Joe, the ever-sliding but well-intentioned husband of Petunia. The score includes a spiritual, 'Wade in de Water' which provides the opening number, a revivalist rave-up, 'Dem bones', and a gospel hymn, 'The Man Upstairs'.

There is room for a thesis on the influence of the spiritual on American musicals. If it reaches its sublime height in *Porgy and Bess*, it could be said to have reached its nadir in *Anything Goes* (1934) when Reno Sweeney, evangelist turned nightclub singer, attempts to lift the spirits of her fellow passengers on the SS *American* with 'Blow, Gabriel, blow'. In fact, the song had been written long before the musical, and Sweeney was made an ex-evangelist simply to make it plausible that she would suddenly launch into such a number. The result is spiritual as entertainment, the antithesis of its use in *Porgy and Bess* and the precursor of those syncopated, up-tempo treatments of 'Dem Bones' and 'Jacob's Ladder' by the Black and White Minstrels which captivated me as a child but which I now realize were travesties of the originals. Subsequent treatments of spiritual-type songs in musicals – such as 'Cold' in *Whistle Down the Wind* – have tended to play up the entertainment rather than the religious element.

Anything Goes is also worthy of mention as being the first musical of which I am aware that portrays a clergyman in a less than appealing light. He is the Reverend Dr Moon whom J. Edgar Hoover has branded as 'Public Enemy No. 13'. A slightly later show, *The Cradle Will Rock* (1937), provides another example of a thoroughly uninspiring clergyman in the person of the Reverend Salvation who obligingly changes his sermon from being pro-peace to pro-war at the behest of the strident Mrs Mister to support her husband's military machine. *Pins and Needles*, another 1937 musical brimming with social comment, features the Nazi-sympathizing radio priest, Father Coughlin. *Sing Out, Sweet Land!*, a 1940 salute to American folk and popular music, provides an equally unappealing clerical portrait, this time of the puritanical Parson Killjoy gloating over the fate of the hero, Barnaby Goodchild, whom he has put into the stocks and condemned to 'wander the desolate roads with thy singing and dancing forever'. The parson's curse, indeed, provides the musical's plot as Goodchild wanders through American history from Puritan New England to an aircraft carrier in the Pacific, always stalked by the miserable Killjoy.

The most unattractive clerical character that I can think of from the American musical stage appears in *Susannah*, the 1955 opera by Carlisle Floyd, who was himself the son of a Methodist minister. The Reverend Olin Blitch has 'come to New Hope Valley to cast out devils and conquer sin and bring sinners to repentance' but ends up seducing the innocent and sad heroine, Susannah. In the end, he is shot by her brother Sam. Its bleakness perhaps as much as its musical structure puts this work firmly into the category of opera rather than musical. Like *Porgy and Bess*, it has some moving evocations and echoes of deep gospel music and has a haunting wistful spirituality as well as a deep pessimism. Floyd himself wrote a preface to *Susannah* 'addressing the difficulty of instilling the sacred communion in a culture perhaps too amply endowed with a predilection for the profane'. Describing opera as 'a necklace of arias, duets, and ensembles strung together with brief jarring recitatives', he suggested that 'to expect absorption and belief in what is going on on the stage under these circumstances seems to me to be blindly and absurdly optimistic'.[7] This seems to me undeservedly self-deprecating and to underestimate the ability of both opera and musicals to tackle and penetrate the sacred and spiritual realm, but it does valuably point to the naturally profane leanings of both art forms with their predilection for sumptuous spectacle, illusion and over-the-top emotionalism.

Not all clergy in 1940s' musicals were models of judgementalism and hypocrisy. Mr Forsyth, the parish minister in Lerner and Loewe's 1947 hit *Brigadoon*, even though he never appears on stage, is a saintly figure who through his own prayer and self-sacrifice has protected his parishioners from harm by making a pact with God that the village should disappear, emerging for just 24 hours every century. *Brigadoon* is, indeed, a musical with significant spiritual resonances. The opening scene, in which two American tourists lose their way in a Highland forest, involves a dialogue between faith and unbelief to the background accompaniment of angelic voices singing from the misty lost village. Tommy Albright, the believer and romantic, compares the forest through which they are walking to a cathedral. His cynical companion, Jeff Douglas, expresses the wish that it was a cathedral because in that case he would be able to find the way out. The contrasting perspectives of these two men, one the dreamer who is ever searching and the other the cynic who has given up, play a significant role in the subsequent unfolding of the plot. Jeff talks Tommy out of his infatuation with Brigadoon and his love of Fiona MacKeith and persuades him to leave Brigadoon, but in the end his cynicism proves less powerful than Tommy's love which calls him back to the Highlands and conjures Brigadoon out of the mists once again.

Like its misty setting, *Brigadoon* hovers on the boundary between sentimentalism and spirituality, illusion and reality. At one level, it is pure escapist fantasy, a fairy story set in a highly romanticized and highly Americanized re-creation of the Scottish Highlands. Yet for all the feel of a never-never-land idyll, there is also a clear moral dimension and message. This surfaces in several songs – notably 'I'll go home to Bonny Jean' which, with its opening line 'I used to be a roving lad', I have heard likened by a former Salvation Army officer to a testimony of conversion – and in the overall theme that the way to ultimate fulfilment is through surrender and self-abandonment. A stranger can only stay in Brigadoon if he loves someone there strongly enough to give up everything else. This leads Mr Murdoch, the village dominie, to reflect that 'it's the hardest thing in the world to give up everything, even though it is often the only way to get everything'. It is not quite on a par with Jesus' teaching that whoever would save his life must lose it but there is an undeniable note of sacrifice in Tommy's abandonment of the bright lights of New York to return to the Highlands as well as a strong reiteration of the theme familiar in so many musicals that love conquers all.

Does *Brigadoon* have deeper spiritual resonances? There are several allusions to the power of miracles in the dialogue. Explaining the extraordinary story of the village's fate, Mr Murdoch finds himself telling the American visitors that 'what happened was a miracle. Miracles require faith and faith seems to be dead.' The reappearance of Brigadoon in front of Tommy's eyes when he returns to Scotland does, on the face of it, seem miraculous and to have been brought about through his own love and faith. Alan Jay Lerner acknowledged the presence of apparent miracles in both *Brigadoon* and *Camelot* but felt compelled to add 'I do not believe in miracles. I have seen too many.'[8] The way in which the dream theme is handled in *Brigadoon* might also suggest spiritual resonances. Visiting the enchanted village which sits 'between the mist and the stars', Tommy feels that he is in a dream and yet at the same time that this is the strongest and most real experience that he has ever had. Is Brigadoon, this strange otherworldly place protected from evil forces by a minister's prayers and self-sacrifice and where love conquers all, in fact a symbol for paradise? There is certainly a sense that it is a place of special blessing, as expressed in Fiona's statement 'we're a most blessed folk', and maybe there is an element of religious allegory in its depiction as the enchanted land of dreams and yearning which is yet very real and which is reached through sacrifice and love.

This is not a wholly wild suggestion, given Alan Lerner's own philosophy and credo. He wrote: 'I believe deeply there is a Divine Order and that life is without end, but at times Fate deals with it so frivolously that it seems without meaning.'[9] Like Hammerstein an unrepentant romantic, he also noted that he was incapable of writing satire and that 'I like to write stories that will move me, with the implicit hope that they will move others, too. This does not necessarily mean love stories, but it usually does. As a rule, it is not sadness that brings tears to my eyes, but a longing fulfilled.'[10] Lerner and his partner Frederick Loewe shared the strong Jewish roots of the founding fathers of the American musical. They also firmly belonged in the European operetta tradition – Loewe's father had created the role of

Danilo in the original Berlin production of *The Merry Widow*. Their most successful joint work, *My Fair Lady*, first performed in 1956, has often been described as the last operetta. It is certainly a robustly secular work although, as we shall see (pages 91–2), the pair's final collaboration, *Camelot*, represented a return to both the dreamlike quality and spiritual yearning of *Brigadoon*.

Richard Rodgers and Oscar Hammerstein had the same upper-class background as Alan Lerner – Frederick Loewe, by contrast, was a first-generation immigrant who had an impoverished childhood. All four shared a largely agnostic upbringing. Lerner's father was a committed atheist. Maybe his son's romantic idealism and spiritual yearning was a reaction against this – there is more than a hint in his autobiography that it might have been. Rodgers' autobiography begins with the death of his great-grandmother, an event which he takes as marking the end of the observance of orthodox Jewish customs in his family. Although taken as a boy to the imposing Temple Israel in New York, he became an atheist and as a parent strongly resisted religious instruction for his children. Yet for all his lack of belief, his music, like Hammerstein's lyrics, has a distinctly 'preachy' quality. 'I can always tell a Rodgers tune.' Cole Porter once observed, 'There's a certain holiness about it.'[11]

The most significant religious and cultural influence on Oscar Hammerstein was almost certainly the Presbyterianism of his Scottish mother, Alice Nimmo. His father was a non-practising Jew and he was not raised with any Jewish culture, traditions or education. Although his first wife was Jewish, Hammerstein did not raise his children as Jewish. In both his genetic make-up and his output, he perhaps comes closer than anyone else from the golden age of Broadway to embodying the Protestant strain which I have identified as defining the character and especially the moral world order of the twentieth-century musical. Stephen Sondheim described him as a man of infinite character but limited talent. Rodgers, by contrast, was 'a man of infinite talent – but limited soul'.[12] Even more than Lerner, Hammerstein was an idealist and, in total contrast to Rodgers' earlier collaborator, Lorenz Hart, a happy family man, most at home on his farm. There was a basic simplicity and sincerity in his character and a total absence of cynicism. There was also an essential wholesomeness about him. He would never have come up with a line like Hart's 'Thank God I can be oversexed again' from *Bewitched, Bothered and Bewildered*. Joseph Fields, who worked with him on the book for *Flower Drum*

Song, said, 'Oscar really believed that love conquers all, that virtue triumphs, that dreams do come true.'[13] Maria von Trapp, whose life story provided the inspiration for *The Sound of Music*, described him as 'a living saint. That means that a person is as close to perfection as one can get and still be alive. It just emanated from him and I'm sure he didn't know it himself.'[14] He freely confessed to being sentimental, writing 'I don't deny the ugly and tragic – but somebody has to keep saying that life's pretty wonderful, too. Because it's true. I guess I can't write anything without hope in it.'[15] In many ways, indeed, he summed up his creed in the song 'A cock-eyed optimist' in *South Pacific* with its admission: 'But I'm stuck, like a dope, with a thing called hope, and I can't get it out of my head.'

Hammerstein came to believe in the power of musicals to preach his creed of hope, love, tolerance and the eradication of racial, ethnic and class prejudices. He had initially conceived of making money out of musicals and then turning to straight plays

> in which I could say and state my reactions to the world I live in. Later on, however, I became convinced that whatever I wanted to say could be said in songs, that I was not confined to trite or light subjects . . . The longer I write the more interested I become in expressing my own true convictions and feelings in the songs I write.[16]

In Richard Rodgers, with his soaring tunes full of yearning and longing, he found the perfect partner for creating musicals which carried a significant message as well as gaining huge success at the box office.

Mark Steyn has written that 'Rodgers and Hammerstein's America, with its sense of building community through commitment and justice, is art as aspiration: this is what we'd like it to be.'[17] This is certainly true of their first collaboration, *Oklahoma!* (1943), a celebration of democracy and community at a time when the United States was engaged in a war against fascism. Its promotion of the values of brotherhood, learning to live with your traditional enemies ('the farmer and the cowman should be friends') and settling differences peacefully earned Rodgers and Hammerstein a special citation from the National Conference of Christians and Jews. In Stephen Citron's words, 'It was the first of the Rodgers and Hammerstein musicals to leave audiences glowing with feeling (and message) while giving them a good time.'[18]

Their next joint work for the stage, *Carousel* (1945), also celebrated community with the chorus especially expressing community values so that, in Steyn's words, ' "This was a real nice clambake" is about ritual and sacrament and a secular Yankee communion.'[19] But it is an altogether darker and more profound piece than its predecessor. As Stephen Sondheim observed, '*Oklahoma!* is about a picnic; *Carousel* is about life and death.'[20] It gives an unusual twist to the dream theme as it is usually expressed in Broadway musicals by making the dreamer not the romantic lead but the utterly prosaic and shallow Enoch Snow, the precise, would-be father who sings to his wife Carrie:

When the children are asleep,
We'll sit and dream
The things that ev'ry other dad and mother dream.

Snow's dreams, 'dreams that won't be interrupted', are not about climbing every mountain and walking through storms with his chin held high but rather about building ever-larger fish canning factories and having ever more children. John Bush Jones describes Snow as 'a walking exemplar of the Down East American Calvinist-Presbyterian capitalist archetype so brilliantly delineated in R. H. Tawney's classic *Religion and the Rise of Capitalism*'.[21] Billy Bigelow, the central character in *Carousel*, is not really a dreamer, although in his moving soliloquy he does allow himself to dream about what he will do with his future child. He is rather an impulsive charmer and chancer who lives for the moment and is easily led into the robbery which costs him his life.

Carousel is unique among blockbuster musicals in incorporating both a scene set in heaven (or, at least, in its ante-room) and extensive speculation about the nature of God. The film version actually begins in heaven with the Star-Keeper fixing his stars and Billy looking back on his life. In the original stage version, the topic of heaven and the nature of God is introduced in the exchange between Billy and Jigger, his partner in crime, in Act 2, scene 2.

BILLY. Suppose some day when we die we'll have to come up before . . . before
JIGGER. Before who?
BILLY. Well – before God.
JIGGER. You and me? Not a chance!

BILLY. Why not?

JIGGER. What's the highest court they ever dragged you into?

BILLY. Just perlice magistrates, I guess.

JIGGER. Sure. Never been before a Supreme Court Judge, have you?

BILLY. No.

JIGGER. Same thing in the next world. For rich folks, the Heavenly Court and the high judge. For you and me – perlice magistrates . . . For the rich, fine music and chubby little angels –

BILLY. Won't we get any music?

JIGGER. *NOT A NOTE*. All we get is justice! There'll be plenty of that for you and me. Yes, sir! Nothin' but justice.

What is striking about this exchange is not so much its use of the classic imagery of angels and music to portray heaven as the emphasis on judgement. This is where the two-tier nature of the afterlife is expressed: the rich will be judged by the highest judge of all while the poor must make do with police magistrates. For everyone, there will be plenty of justice, by which seems to be meant judgement. This emphasis may well reflect the outlook of Hammerstein, who was, in Stephen Sondheim's words, 'judgmental and a true moralist', and, indeed, of Rodgers, who, according to his wife, Dorothy, felt that religion was based on fear and contributed to 'feelings of guilt'.[22]

This theme comes up again later in the scene after Billy has been killed in the fracas following the robbery, and finds himself in what appears to be purgatory. Here he is greeted by the Heavenly Friend who announces that he has come down to fetch him and take him up to the judge.

BILLY. Judge! Am I goin' before the Lord God himself?

HEAVENLY FRIEND. What hev you ever done that you should come before Him?

BILLY. So that's it. Just like Jigger said: 'No Supreme Court for little people – just perlice magistrates!'

HEAVENLY FRIEND. Who said anythin' about . . .

BILLY. I tell you if they kick me around up there like they did on earth, I'm goin' to do somethin' about it! I'm dead now and I got nothin' to lose. I'm goin' to stand up for my rights! I tell you I'm goin' before the Lord God Himself – straight to the top!

This leads in to one of the very few songs from a musical that I know of that describes heaven as it is understood by religious believers rather than as a place where dreams come true or a state of general ecstacy and wish-fulfilment. It is worth quoting 'The Highest Judge of All' in full, not least because it is sadly often cut in modern amateur performances.

Take me beyond the pearly gates,
Through a beautiful marble hall.
Take me before the highest throne
And let me judged by the highest judge of all!

Let the Lord shout and yell,
Let His eyes flash flame,
I promise not to quiver when He calls my name.
Let him send me to hell,
But before I go,
I feel I'm entitled to a hell of a show!
Want pink-faced angels on a purple cloud,
Twangin' on their harps till their fingers get red.
Want organ music, let it roll out loud,
Rollin' like a wave, washin' over my head!
Want ev'ry star in heaven
Hangin' in the room,
Shinin' in my eyes when I hear my doom!

Reckon my sins are good, big sins,
And the punishment won't be small.
So take me before the highest throne
And let me be judged by the Highest Judge of all!

Here again, alongside the traditional Sunday School images of pearly gates, angels on clouds, organ music and stars, all of which Billy desperately wants as part of his 'heaven experience', is the emphasis on judgement. What he wants more than anything else is to be judged by the Highest Judge of all. That is how he sees God.

In the original version of *Carousel* Billy went to heaven and did get to meet God there. However, this aspect of the story was radically changed during the show's pre-Broadway try-out in Boston, as Elliot Norton describes:

The original heaven of *Carousel* was a New England parlor, bare and plain. In it sat a stern Yankee, listed on the program as He. At a harmonium, playing softly, sat his quiet consort, identified as She. Later some observers (including Rodgers) referred to this celestial couple as Mr. and Mrs. God . . .

Richard Rodgers, walking back to the hotel with his collaborator afterwards put it to Oscar Hammerstein bluntly:

'We've got to get God out of that parlor!'

Mild Oscar Hammerstein agreed.

'I know you're right', he said, 'But where shall I put Him?'

'I don't care where you put Him,' said Richard Rodgers. 'Put Him up on a ladder, for all I care, only get Him out of that parlor.'

So Oscar Hammerstein put Him up on a ladder. He discarded the sitting room too, and put his deity into a brand new sequence. On a ladder in the backyard of heaven, He became the Star-Keeper, polishing stars which hung on lines strung across the floor of infinity, while a sullen Billy Bigelow looked and listened to his quiet admonitions.[23]

Quite how the Star-Keeper who greets Billy at the back gates to heaven – the mother-of-pearly ones, as opposed to the pearly ones – fits into the celestial hierarchy is not quite clear. Billy tries to establish who he is but is told to mind his own business. The Star-Keeper does not seem to be God himself since he says at one point 'I got my orders'. He does, however, seem to control entry into heaven and engages in a long conversation with Billy as to how he can gain entrance in the course of which Billy is asked if he is sorry that he hit his pregnant wife, Julie:

BILLY. Ain't sorry for anythin' –
STAR-KEEPER. You ken be as stubborn and perniketty as you want. Up here patience is as endless as time. We ken wait. Now look here, son, it's only fair to tell you – you're in a pretty tight corner. Fact is you haven't done enough good in yer life to get in there – not even through the back door.
BILLY. All right. If I can't get in – I can't.
STAR-KEEPER. I didn't say you can't. Said you ain't done enough so *FAR*. You might still make it – if you tried hard enough.

Here the emphasis has swung away from judgement and towards grace. There is plenty of time for Billy to repent of his sins. 'Up here patience is as endless as time.' The Star-Keeper seems to be preaching a gospel of forgiveness and of salvation through works. Billy has not done enough good in his life to get to heaven but he can still get there if he tries hard enough. Here is the familiar Pelagian strain that runs through so many musicals coupled with a portrayal of God which is much more centred on the attributes of forgiveness and grace than on judgement.

Billy takes up the Star-Keeper's offer that he can go down to earth for a day and 'do somethin' real fine for someone'. He tries to give his 15-year-old daughter, Louise, a star but she refuses to take it and in despair he impulsively and involuntarily hits her. Ferenc Molnar's play, *Liliom*, on which *Carousel* was based, ended at this point, leaving Billy Bigelow in despair, a loser in death as in life. But this was altogether too pessimistic an ending for Hammerstein and he added an extra scene where Billy is given one last chance and goes on to Louise's high school graduation. The oration is given by the local country doctor, Dr Seldon, a man of transparent goodness who reminds Billy of the Star-Keeper up on his ladder – an observation which provokes the Heavenly Friend to reflect: 'Yes, a lot of these country doctors and ministers remind you of him.' In productions of *Carousel* the Star-Keeper and Dr Seldon are usually played by the same actor, reinforcing the God-like character of the saintly doctor whose speech to the graduating students provides a perfect exposition of the gospel according to Rodgers and Hammerstein:

DOCTOR. I can't tell you any sure way to happiness. All I know is you got to go out and find it fer yourselves. You can't lean on the success of your parents. That's their success. And don't be held back by their failures! Makes no difference what they did or didn't do. You jest stand on yer own two feet.
BILLY (To LOUISE). Listen to him. Believe him.
DOCTOR. The world belongs to you as much as to the next feller. Don't give it up! And try not to be skeered o' people not liking you – jest you try likin' *THEM* – Jest keep yer faith and courage – and you'll come out right. It's like what we used to sing every mornin' when I went to school. Maybe you still sing it – I dunno.

As the doctor starts reciting the song, which is taken up by the whole company, Billy tells Julie that he loves her and is then led away back to heaven by the Heavenly Friend. The stage direction at this point reads:

'The Doctor watches and smiles wisely.' Is this, in fact, a divine blessing and an acknowledgement that Billy has taken his chance of redemption and not blown it, as happened in *Liliom*? Ethan Mordden is surely justified in pointing to 'the ascetically religious nature of the finale, whose sense of sorrow and ecstacy has the air of a church service', and asserting that '*Carousel* takes on the format of a parable'.[24]

The religious feeling of the final scene of *Carousel* is, of course, enormously heightened by the anthem-like quality of the song which is sung as the curtain goes down. 'You'll never walk alone' gives the show not so much a happy ending as a morally uplifting one. In the words of one of my students, 'it turns the show into a salvation narrative'. More than any other song from a musical it has crossed over from the theatre to the sanctuary and is found in several hymn books and regularly heard on the BBC's *Songs of Praise*. It is among the top ten most requested songs for funerals in the United Kingdom and has attained the status of a communal anthem sung across the western world at times both of great tragedy and of great celebration. To give just three recent examples, it was chosen as the most appropriate number with which to close the 2001 Emmy Awards ceremony which took place just two months after the terrorist attack on the World Trade Center in New York, and it was sung spontaneously by crowds in the street in Rotterdam following the funeral of the Dutch politician, Pim Fortuyn, in May 2002, and in London's Mall during Queen Elizabeth II's jubilee celebrations a month later. A recent BBC radio series, *Soul Music*, ranked it alongside 'Silent Night' and 'Abide With Me' in terms of its impact and iconic status and focused particularly on its role as the anthem of Liverpool Football Club and its enormous pastoral influence in the aftermath of the Hillsborough disaster in 1989 when 95 Liverpool fans were crushed to death and over 200 injured when police mistakenly opened a gate to ease pressure outside the ground on the eve of an FA Cup semi-final.

There is no doubting the hymnodic quality of both the words and music of 'You'll never walk alone'. Irving Berlin reckoned it was Rodgers and Hammerstein's greatest song because when he heard it at a funeral he realized that it had as much impact on him as the 23rd Psalm. Its initial injunction to 'keep your chin up high and don't be afraid of the dark' is the very stuff of muscular Christianity, or strenuous humanism, and could come straight out of a hymn by Lowell Mason or Norman Macleod's 'Courage, brother, do not stumble'. The incitement to 'walk on through the wind, walk on through the rain, though your dreams be tossed and blown', prefaced with the assurance that 'at the end of the storm is a golden sky and the sweet, silver song of the lark' supplies the inevitable dream reference which, while acknowledging that dreams do get buffeted, presents the message of gritty determination and ultimate optimism found in a thousand popular songs of the 'Keep right on to the end of the road' variety. It is the last phrase which gives it its real originality and its particular spiritual resonance:

Walk on, walk on with hope in your heart,
And you'll never walk alone!

It is, of course, possible to take several different meanings from these words, sung to Rodgers' deliberate pulsating minims. Do they simply imply that there are other humans treading the road of suffering and offering some kind of companionship and solidarity, even if it is unseen? Or do they suggest the companionship of some divine being and convey a similar message to the much loved and quoted poem 'Footprints' that when you are least conscious of his presence, God is carrying you? This is certainly how they have been interpreted by many people and it is certainly an interpretation that both the words and tune bear very easily. Kurt Ganzl in his authoritative history of the musical has no hesitation in describing the song as 'a rousingly religious piece in which a round-voiced mezzo soprano soared forth the maxim that "You'll never walk alone" while you walk with God'.[25] In this respect, 'You'll never walk alone' has a wholly different message from the song 'No One is Alone' from Sondheim's *Into the Woods* to which it is often compared by writers on musicals.[26] The key message of Sondheim's song is a reminder that every action has consequences for others, that no man is an island. There is no suggestion in it of a spiritual or supernatural dimension as there is in 'You'll never walk alone'. Perhaps a better comparison is with Sydney Carter's 'One more step along the world I go' with its refrain 'Keep me travelling along with you' addressed to an implied but never explicitly stated divine companion.

Carousel abounds in moral lessons and messages. It points to the transforming effect of parenthood, as when Billy sings 'You can have fun with a son but you've got to be a father to a girl'. It points up the virtue of fidelity and standing by your man. In her song 'What's the use of wond'rin' Julie reflects that there is no point in worrying whether your man is good or bad. You have to accept him for what he is, which is in some sense the result of the actions of a designer or creator – 'something made him the way he is'. Even though 'common sense may tell you that the ending may be sad', you are called to unquestioning love and faithfulness. There is also a strong emphasis on getting on with life, whatever difficulties it throws up. This is well expressed in the exhortation which Carrie Pepperidge delivers to Julie just after Billy's death and just before she sings 'When you walk through a storm' to her: 'Keep on living. Keep on going'. In many ways, we are back to Gilbert and Sullivan's philosophy of taking life as it comes.

The success of *Carousel* confirmed the triumph of musical theatre over musical comedy. Rodgers and Hammerstein's next three big hits, *South Pacific* (1949), *The King and I* (1951) and *Flower Drum Song* were lighter than *Carousel* but were similarly plot-led. All three had oriental settings and were concerned with race relations, purveying the message that cultural differences are only skin-deep and that, fundamentally, human beings are the same everywhere. This was a message that Hammerstein himself sincerely believed in and put into practice in his own life. A prominent member of the Hollywood Anti-Nazi League, he supported the emerging black civil rights movement in the United States. His championing of the value of diversity is well expressed in the opening number of the somewhat neglected Rodgers and Hammerstein musical, *Pipe Dream* (1955), 'It takes all kinds of people to make up the world'.

South Pacific contains one of Hammerstein's most biting pieces of social commentary and criticism in the song 'You've got to be carefully taught' with its message that racial and class prejudice is acquired and instilled rather than natural and inborn. It also contains perhaps the ultimate dream song which sums up the philosophy of the mid-twentieth-century Broadway musical. 'You gotta have a dream', Bloody Mary tells Cable in the song 'Happy Talk', because 'if you don't have a dream, how you gonna have a dream come true?' Here having your own dream is as important as walking on through the storm and climbing every mountain. Indeed, it is the essential prerequisite for the dedicated and fulfilled life which has a purpose. The point is reinforced in 'Bali Ha'i' when Mary tells Cable of the importance of having 'our own special dream'. Bali Ha'i is presented as the paradise island where dreams come true but only for those who have them:

Your own special hopes,
Your own special dreams
Bloom on the hillside
And shine in the streams.

The injunction to follow, or in this case find, your dream is, of course, a prominent theme in Rodgers and Hammerstein's last collaboration, *The Sound of Music* (1959). In many ways it is more of an operetta than a musical, showing Rodgers at his most Romberg-like and the ailing Hammerstein, who was dying of cancer as he wrote the lyrics, at his most sentimental. Critics castigated its saccharine sweetness. Noel Coward complained that 'there were too many nuns careening about and crossing themselves and singing jaunty little songs, and there was, I must admit, a heavy pall of Jewish–Catholic schmaltz enveloping the whole thing' and Kenneth Tynan described the show as 'Rodgers's and Hammerstein's Great Leap Backward'.[27] Yet the creators of *The Sound of Music* could put their hands on their hearts and say that nothing in it was contrived. The whole work was utterly sincere. Hammerstein felt compelled to point out that '*The Sound of Music* was based on the autobiography of Maria von Trapp. No incidents were dragged in or invented to play on the sentimental susceptibilities of the audience as some critics seem to feel.'[28] Rodgers for his part wrote:

Most of us feel that Nature can have attractive manifestations, that children aren't necessarily monsters and that deep affection between two people is nothing to be ashamed of. I feel that rather strongly, or obviously it would not be possible for me to write the music that goes with Oscar's words.[29]

Responding to criticisms of the particularly sentimental feel of the 1965 film version, he wrote:

What I enjoy particularly is what it has done for the un-selfconscious people of the world – the selfconscious ones sneer a little at it. It is sentimental, but I don't see anything particularly wrong with that. I think people have been given a great deal of hope by that picture.[30]

Like all Rodgers and Hammerstein shows *The Sound of Music* is full of moral messages – the celebration of Austrian patriotism, the strong anti-Nazi strain, the transparent goodness of Maria, the wisdom of the Mother Abbess. Unlike any of their other works, it has an explicitly religious setting and context, the original stage version consider-ably more so than the film. It begins and ends in a convent and contains substantial passages of liturgical music, notably the opening 'Preludium' and the complex 'Gaudeamus', 'Gloria' and 'Alleluia' sequence that makes up the Processional in Act 2. Rodgers took enormous trouble to get these right. He was apprehensive about setting Christian liturgical texts but felt that they were essential to establishing the authentic atmosphere of the convent setting. For the first time in his life he engaged in musical research, attending Catholic services and consulting the nun in charge of the music department at Manhattanville College in Purchase, New York, who staged a special concert for him at which the nuns ran through their liturgical reper-toire from Gregorian chant to Fauré. Another nun, Sister Gregory, head of drama at Rosary College, River Forest, Illinois, was brought in to instruct Mary Martin, who created the role of Maria, and other members of the cast in the nature and manner of the religious life.

The Sound of Music gives a very positive impression of Christianity and particularly of the dedicated religious life. Indeed, among musi-cals only *Fiddler on the Roof* seems to me to provide a more sympa-thetic and positive portrayal of a religious community. Perhaps both lyricist and composer were simply moved by the child-like enthusiasm and simplicity in the Catholic faith of Maria von Trapp and the nuns whom they brought in as advisers. On stage the nuns are given great character. They are evidently fulfilled in their vocation, they display ingenuity and guts in their efforts to shield the fleeing von Trapps from the Nazis and above all they are full of warmth and humour, as exemplified in that marvellous line 'Maria makes me laugh'.

The character of the Mother Abbess is drawn and developed with particular sensitivity and sympathy. In the film version her role is con-siderably diminished, partly through the general downgrading of the convent setting in favour of more scenic mountain locations but also because of the overall dominance of Julie Andrews's Maria and more specific slights like losing the song 'My Favorite Things'. In the original stage version the Abbess is a much more dominant figure. Indeed, it is hardly too much to say that she really steers the whole plot, guiding Maria to realize that the love of a man and a woman is a holy thing and that being the husband of Captain von Trapp and the mother of his children is just as much a God-given vocation for her as pursuing the religious life. She comes over as full of humanity, understanding and wisdom as well as being a significant exponent of incarnational theology. As she originally sings it to Maria, 'My Favorite Things' carries the message that joy and comfort can be derived from the simplest ordinary things in life. Although there is no specific religious allusion in the song, the fact that it is sung by the Abbess, who is certainly not afraid to talk about God and invoke his presence, almost gives it something of the message of George Herbert's 'Teach me, my God and King, in all things thee to see'.

The Mother Abbess is at her most sermonic in her great anthem, 'Climb Ev'ry Mountain'. In many respects, of course, this song reasserts the Rodgers and Hammerstein gospel of single-mindedly pursuing your dream, with its strongly Pelagian suggestion that all you need to do is go for it and you will ultimately find it, albeit that in this case the quest will be particularly strenuous and demanding – 'A dream that will need all the love you can give / Every day of your life for as long as you live'. However, there is a distinctiveness about the way the dream theme is framed here. For the Mother Abbess, the destiny that Maria must seek out and pursue is very much a God-given one. Her first rendition of 'Climb Ev'ry Mountain' is preceded by the dialogue in which she tells Maria that her love for Captain von Trapp does not mean that she loves God any less and that 'You must find the life you were born for'. It is significant that 'Climb Ev'ry Mountain' is about finding rather than having your dream. The dream is already there in God's providential purposes – the human task is to identify and find it, not to construct it. The song is very emphatically not saying what appeared as the English translation of the last line on the supertext screen during a recent performance in Hungarian which I attended at the Budapest operetta theatre: 'Your life's calling you. So go, dream away'.

As originally conceived by Hammerstein, the Mother Abbess's song was, in fact, about anything but dreaming away. Initially entitling it 'Face Life', he outlined its theme in a note scribbled on the manuscript of an early draft:

You can't hide here. Don't think these walls shut out problems. You have to face life wherever you are. You have to look for life, for the life you were meant to lead. Until you find it you are not living.[31]

Early versions of the song contained lines about climbing a hill and getting to the top 'which doesn't bring you much closer to the moon, but closer to the next hill, which you must also climb'. They also contained the lines beginning 'A song is no song till you sing it' which were later transferred to open the reprise of the duet 'You are sixteen'. Had they been kept in the Mother Superior's song, following her dialogue about God being found in human relationships as much as in the cloistered life of the convent, they would have made it even more theological as an apologia for kenotic, self-giving love (see page 16).

In its final form, 'Climb Ev'ry Mountain' was purged of its verses and left with just two simple, spare stanzas. This structure, together with Rodgers' slow, soaring tune with its straightforward open harmonies, reinforces its anthem-like feel. The composer himself marked the music 'with deep feeling, like a prayer'.[32] Although shorn of some of the deeper and more theological resonances that were present in Hammerstein's earlier drafts, it still packs a significant spiritual punch. This was certainly how it struck Sister Gregory when she received a manuscript copy of the final version of the song, as she told Mary Martin and other members of the original cast:

> It drove me to the Chapel (Relax, chums. I'm sure it will not affect your audiences in the same way). It made me acutely aware of how tremendously fortunate are those who find a dream that will absorb all their love and, finding it, embrace it to the end . . . It was the lyrics that drove me to the Chapel. Mr Hammerstein's lyrics seem perfectly yet effortlessly to combine what we ordinary souls feel but cannot communicate.[33]

The Sound of Music went on, of course, to become one of the most successful musicals of all time. The stage version established itself as the longest-running American musical in London until overtaken by *Chicago* in 2003. The film version grossed $66,000,000 within two years and was easily the most successful film of the 1960s, outperforming both *Gone With the Wind* and *Dr Zhivago*. The soundtrack album became the all-time best-selling long-playing record, standing at the top of the UK charts for 70 weeks and selling more copies than the entire recorded output of Frank Sinatra, and the film has been seen by an estimated one billion people across the world. Its global reach and iconic status is well illustrated in the central role which a family trip to see it for the third time in the Indian city of

Kerala plays in Arundhati Roy's novel, *The God of Small Things*, which won the 1997 Booker Prize. Forty years after its release, the film still draws huge audiences for its regular airings on Christmas Day and Bank Holiday television and the video version continues to sell. It also continues to provoke strong reactions, not least among Christians – a single recent issue of the *Church Times* contained separate references to members of the Church of England who both loathed and loved it. An obituary of a traditionalist clergyman concluded 'He had no time for 100 *Hymns for Today*, the film version of *The Sound of Music*, or the ASB lectionary', while a book review of the diary of a Yorkshire vicar noted that a highlight of his church social calendar 'is the Mothers' Union outing to a Leeds cinema to see *The Sound of Music*'.[34] One Leeds cinema in fact screened nothing but this film for three years.

For the devoted fans who went to see the film again and again, or who repeatedly watch the video version, *The Sound of Music* has fulfilled a pastoral role and provided the companionship, hope, consolation and uplifting message often associated with a church service. Indeed, it has probably come closer than any other work to establishing the musical almost as a para-church or new religious movement. During the cold war, the BBC prepared a 100-day schedule of films to play to boost the morale of those trapped in bunkers in the event of a nuclear attack. *The Sound of Music* topped the bill. It has recently become the subject of a whole new ritual and cult following. A singalong screening at the Gay and Lesbian Film Festival in London's National Film Theatre in April 1999 sold out within 24 hours. Since then singalong performances have played to packed houses up and down the country with members of the audience enthusiastically dressing up as nuns, Nazis, lonely goatherds or even brown paper packages tied up with string, hissing the Baroness and joining in all the songs. Although originally taken up by the gay community, *The Singalong Sound of Music* is now hugely popular with families and across the entire social and cultural spectrum, providing a rare uninhibited communal-bonding experience in our increasingly atomized and self-conscious society.

While we are on the subject of musicals about religious communities, it is worth giving at least passing mention to the extraordinary success of *Nunsense*, the 'habit-forming' musical featuring the Little Sisters of Hoboken in New Jersey, first performed in 1986 and beaten only by *The Fantasticks* as the longest-running off-Broadway show in history. *Nunsense* has been translated into ten different languages and is currently playing in over 300 theatres around the world. Enormously popular for high school and college productions, the original show has spawned several successors, including *Nunsense II – The Second Coming* and *Nunsense A-Men*. As can be guessed from song titles like 'The Padre Polka', 'Just a Coupl'a Sisters' and 'Tackle that Temptation with a Time-Step', the *Nunsense* shows make no serious theological message and lack the explicit moral uplift and 'preachy' quality of Rodgers and Hammerstein. They do demonstrate, however, that *The Sound of Music* far from exhausted the dramatic possibilities presented by putting nuns in a musical and they share its hugely positive picture of the dedicated religious life. Explaining the show's origins, Dan Goggin, who combined the roles of writer, lyricist, composer and director, has written: 'I spent a great deal of my life around nuns. And most of my experiences left wonderful memories. I wrote *Nunsense* because I wanted to share what I knew to be the humour of the nun.'[35]

There is, too, another show from the golden age of Broadway which portrays a Christian community in a generally sympathetic and favourable light. Frank Loesser's *Guys and Dolls* (1950) has, like *The Sound of Music*, maintained its popularity over five decades and is now a favourite choice for school productions. Rather than an Austrian convent full of nuns, the location is the down-town New York mission hall from which the uniformed officers of the Save-A-Soul Mission sally forth urging the gamblers and drunkards of Broadway to:

Follow the fold, and stray no more,
Stray no more, stray no more,
Put down the bottle and we'll say no more,
Follow, follow the fold!

At the heart of the story of *Guys and Dolls* is the relationship between Sergeant Sarah Brown, the beautiful and upright new officer from the mission, who introduces herself with the sermonic utterance, 'Brothers, sisters, resist the Devil and he will flee from you. That's what the Bible tells us', and Sky Masterson, the ace gambler and wide boy who makes a bet with his friend Nathan Detroit that he will whisk Sarah off to Havana. He initially impresses her by pointing out that the text above the mission hall door, 'No peace unto the wicked', has been misattributed to Proverbs when it in fact comes from Isaiah. Sarah is both amazed and infuriated to find that he is so well up on the Bible and somewhat nonplussed when he tells her why this is: 'There are two things been in every hotel room in the country: Sky Masterson and the Gideon Bible. I must have read the Good Book ten or twelve times.' He promises to fill the mission hall with sinners for the Thursday night meeting if she will have dinner with him in Havana. She refuses, saying that he is not the sort of man she would ever go out with.

It looks as though Sky is going to lose his bet with Nathan. However, the situation changes when General Cartwright from the Save-A-Soul Mission headquarters appears and announces that he is going to have to close the Broadway mission because of its failure to win any converts to Christ. Sky's guarantee that he can bring in a dozen sinners now looks irresistible and Sarah agrees to the Havana date on which she gets drunk. She and Sky come back late to New York to find a crap game going on in the mission hall. Sarah is furious but Sky is more than ever determined to fulfil his part of the deal. His pals, however, are reluctant to come to the sinners' meeting. Harry the Horse accuses Sky of reading the Bible too much. 'So what?' comes the retort, 'Maybe the Bible don't read as lively as the Scratch Sheet, but it is at least twice as accurate.'

Inevitably, Sky has to bet his pals for their souls. He wins and so they duly turn up at the mission hall and give their testimony. In Nicely Nicely Johnson's case this takes the form of a dream about heaven:

> I dreamed last night I got a boat to heaven,
> And by some chance I had brought my dice along and there I stood,
> And I hollered 'Someone fade me',
> But the passengers, they knew right from wrong,
> For the people all said, 'Sit down,
> Sit down, you're rocking the boat.'

The fact that the obligatory dream song in *Guys and Dolls* is about heaven or at least going to heaven inevitably invites comparisons with 'The highest judge of all' in *Carousel* and there is a similar emphasis on the theme of judgement and punishment. In the second verse, for example, a wave crashes over Nicely Nicely as he gets his bottle of whisky out. As Ethan Mordden has observed, 'Sit down you're rocking the boat' is a song which 'manages to spoof revivalist hymns while serving as a perfectly legitimate revivalist hymn'.[36]

Sarah offers a different kind of Christianity to the black-and-white judgementalism that the gamblers take it to involve. She lies to a police officer about the crap game in the mission hall to save the players from arrest. Sky is won over and marries Sarah. As Brother Masterson he becomes a leading figure in the Save-A-Soul Mission, preaching his own earthy brand of revivalism: 'Brothers and sisters! Life is one big crap game, and the Devil is using loaded dice!' At least that is what happens in the stage version of *Guys and Dolls*. In the 1955 film version Sky does not join the Save-A-Soul Mission. The director, Joseph Manckiewicz, felt that this was stretching his conversion too far: 'We know Sky is going to be a good husband and father, but he won't be a brass-buttoned, uniformed Save-A-Soul-er. He's not the type. It just wouldn't happen.'[37]

Guys and Dolls may have an altogether grittier and rougher feel than Rodgers and Hammerstein's shows but it is every bit as much a religious parable as *Carousel* or *The Sound of Music* and even more a story of redemption and conversion. Sky is not the only one to change his ways. Nathan Detroit finally stops dangling his long-suffering and ever-faithful fiancée Adelaide and agrees to marry her in the mission hall. It may be the case that the primary agent of redemption in both cases is the love of a good woman and that 'the guy's only doing it for some doll'. Yet the religious element is there, in the mission hall setting and Sarah's transparent and upfront Christianity, and there is no denying the spiritual dimension to the show's main message, which is the power of forgiveness.

3

To dream the impossible dream –

the rhythm of life and the brotherhood of man

The influence of Rodgers and Hammerstein on American musical theatre lingered for a long time. Throughout the 1960s and for much of the 1970s most Broadway shows were both optimistic and moralistic, extolling the values of community and brotherhood, celebrating the variety and vitality of life and continuing to centre on idealized and idealistic dreams.

It could have been very different. The year 1957, which brought *My Fair Lady*, the last great operetta, also saw the arrival of a very different style of musical, full of in-your-face realism and shattered dreams and focusing unrelentingly on the seamy side of life. *West Side Story* is about conflict rather than community. In so far as it is set in one of the seedier parts of New York, it resembles *Guys and Dolls* but in this case there is no Save-A-Soul Mission or happy ending. It is, in Scott Miller's words, 'a musical about hatred and prejudice, a musical that says that love cannot triumph over all'.[1] Leonard Bernstein and Jerome Robbins originally thought of basing their updated version of *Romeo and Juliet* on the gang warfare between New York's Catholics and Jews during the period of Easter and Passover. However, they decided to re-enact the feuding between the Montagues and the Capulets in racial rather than religious terms and to focus on rival gangs of Puerto Ricans and whites. It is not entirely clear why they made this change – possibly they felt that race provided a more potent and obvious source of conflict at a time when the hold of religion was waning, or maybe it was simply that the Puerto Rican element provided more exciting possibilities in terms of music and choreography.

In many ways the relentless realism, brash rhythms and tragic overtones of *West Side Story* anticipate the frenetic British rock musicals of the early 1970s like *Tommy* and *Jesus Christ Superstar*. Throughout the 1960s, however, in the United Kingdom just as much as in the

To dream the impossible dream

United States musical theatre remained true to the gentle, romantic and idealistic traditions of Rodgers and Hammerstein. The three most successful British shows of the decade, Lionel Bart's *Oliver* (1960), Leslie Bricusse and Cyril Ornadel's *Pickwick* (1963) and Nevill Coghill and Martin Starkie's *The Canterbury Tales* (1968) share a nostalgic historical setting, a strong affirmation of the values of community and the vitality of human character and an idealized utopianism supremely expressed in the great dream anthem from *Pickwick* 'If I ruled the world'.

These elements are also conspicuous in the first major American success of the 1960s, Lerner and Loewe's *Camelot* (1960). Set in the far-off days of medieval chivalry and Arthurian romance, it is full of incitements to dream dreams of a better world and 'to live as if' such dreams came true. At its heart is the conviction that for one brief moment in history there was a place where the knightly virtues of courage, liberty, humility, honesty, diligence, charity and fidelity did reign and that this world could be recreated again. Although it was written and opened before his inauguration, *Camelot* became a metaphor and a blueprint for the thousand-day presidency of John F. Kennedy, who had been a Harvard classmate of both Alan Lerner and Theodore White, the author of *The Sword in the Stone*, on which the musical was based. Kennedy's assassination in November 1963 reinforced the 'if only' feel about re-creating Camelot and added enormously to the poignancy of the show's message. In an interview a week after Kennedy's death, his widow told White how much both the original Arthurian legend and its reworking in the musical had meant to her late husband:

> History made Jack what he was. You must think of him as a little boy, sick so much of the time reading in bed, reading history, reading the Knights of the Round Table. For Jack, history was full of heroes . . . Jack had this hero idea of history, the idealistic view. When Jack quoted something it was usually classical; but all I kept thinking about is this line from a musical comedy. At night, before we'd go to sleep, Jack liked to play some records and the song he loved most came at the very end of this record. The lines he loved to hear were:
>
> > Don't let it be forgot
> > That once there was a spot,

For one, brief, shining moment
That was known as Camelot![2]

Lerner recalled that after Kennedy's assassination 'Camelot became the symbol of those thousand days when people the world over saw a bright new light of hope shining from the White House'.[3] The final song from the musical, as quoted above, was sung at Kennedy's funeral in what was perhaps the first instance of a show song being used liturgically. Both the music and lyrics of this song are printed on the final page of Samuel Morison's monumental *Oxford History of the American People*, which was published in 1965 and ends with Kennedy's death.

In his autobiography Lerner has described what really fired him to write *Camelot* and what he sees as its essential message:

> I believe it is the idealism expressed in the concept of the Round Table that accounts for the indestructibility of the Arthurian legend. Stripped of its tales of derring-do, its magic, its love potions and medieval trimmings and trappings, there lies buried in its heart the aspirations of mankind, and if Arthur lived at all, he was a light in the Dark Ages. If the Arthurian legend is pure fantasy, it is even more significant. To me, the greatest contribution of Jesus Christ is contained in three words, the 'Brotherhood of Man'. Arthur is more related to that dream than to the monarchical pageantry of English history.[4]

Here is a fascinating apologia for the centrality of the dream theme in the Broadway musical in its heyday. For Lerner, the agnostic Jew, the great contribution of Jesus Christ to the world is the message of human brotherhood. This message is seen very significantly as a dream – a dream which has been expressed in history by such legends as the story of Arthur and the knights of the round table. There is a wistfulness about this dream which almost makes one feel it is better to go on dreaming it, or perhaps even more to go on singing about it, than to actualize it and make it a reality.

A darker and more profound spiritual note was struck in Tom Jones' and Harvey Schmidt's *The Fantasticks* which opened in New York's Sullivan Street Playhouse two months after *Camelot* and continued in a record-breaking run there until finally closing in January 2002. Since first coming across the character of John Barleycorn in the preface to George Bernard Shaw's *Androcles and the Lion* and subsequently reading James Frazer's *The Golden Bough*, Jones had become fascinated by the cycle of birth, death and regeneration/resurrection found in the primal mythology of the 'dying and rising' gods of nature and expounded in Jesus' words in John 12.24–5 about the necessity of the corn of wheat falling into the ground and dying if it is to produce fruit. The show is woven together by images of seasonal rituals and the changing cycle of vegetation, and the theme of sacrifice looms large with the two central characters, Matt and Luisa, realizing that they must sacrifice something of themselves if they are to grow. As the omniscient narrator figure El Gallo observes at the end:

There is a curious paradox
That no one can explain.
Who understands the secret
Of the reaping of the grain?
Who understands why Spring is born
Out of Winter's labouring pain?
Or why we all must die a bit
Before we grow again.
I do not know the answer.
I merely know it's true.
I hurt them for that reason.
And myself a little bit too.

The theme of human brotherhood which looms so large in *Camelot* is given equally prominent if slightly less wistful treatment in Frank Loesser's *How to Succeed in Business without Really Trying* which appeared just a year after *Camelot*. In the final scene of the show Wally Womper, one-time window washer who has risen to become chairman of the board of World Wide Wickets, announces to his staff 'I'd like to say a few words about humanity'. He then launches into a Gospel-style song which celebrates the 'one great club that all of us are in' and proclaims that there is something more important than loyalty to the company and climbing over everyone else to get up the corporate ladder:

There is a brotherhood of man,
A benevolent brotherhood of man,
A noble tie that binds
Our human hearts and minds
Into one brotherhood of man.

Here is the message of 'The cowman and the farmer should be friends' transplanted from the plains of Oklahoma to the world of metropolitan big business. It is at one level a purely secular message – the essence of the humanist creed, indeed – although there are phrases in the song which teeter on the brink of theological language, such as: 'Keep forgiving each brother all you can' and 'mediocrity is not a mortal sin'. The melody and orchestration put 'The brotherhood of man' squarely in the mock Gospel-song category alongside 'Blow, Gabriel, blow' and 'Sit down you're rocking the boat' and, in Scott Miller's words, present 'the moment of confession and ethical rebirth for these crooked businessmen, as a musical revival meeting complete with hand-clapping and tambourines'.[5]

Loesser is undoubtedly in part creating a send-up of the quasi-religious atmosphere and revivalist spirit that underlies corporate team building and business life. Miller is right to suggest that by making 'The Brotherhood of Man' a hand-clapping, foot-stomping revival spiritual, he is 'underlining not just the charade of the sleazy executives pretending to confess their sins and to be born again but also the devoutly practiced religion of business'.[6] There are other touches in the musical which point up this theme, like the solemn funereal organ music played before the board meeting and the prayer-like quality of J. Pierrepont Finch's song of self-congratulation, 'I believe in you'. Geoffrey Block has argued that such 'secular religiosity' is a recurrent feature of Loesser's music, evident in his first hit, 'Praise the Lord and Pass the Ammunition' and the song 'Make a miracle' from *Where's Charley?* where he inserts a cadence marked 'religioso' at several points to underline the miracle theme.[7]

Yet it is impossible to listen to 'The brotherhood of man' without feeling that it is not just a send-up and that it has a basic integrity and sincerity. It does proclaim that there are other and more important bonds between human beings than the cash nexus and the principles of market economics. Loesser's song is a great deal less cynical than Tom Lehrer's 'National Brotherhood Week', written in 1964, with its acid reminder that basically we all hate each other and that while we can just about manage to bury our tribal, racial and religious differences for an artificially contrived week of national brotherhood, we are profoundly grateful that such enforced fraternity and good neighbourliness 'doesn't last all year'. This kind of cynical realism might fit the mood of the sophisticated Harvard-trained mathematician but it was not what the dreamers of Broadway wanted to believe, nor what their audiences wanted to hear.

The message of human brotherhood and community is even more emphatically emphasized in what was the most successful and from the theological point of view the most important and fascinating of all the 1960s' musicals, *Fiddler on the Roof* (1964). What makes it particularly fascinating is the fact that in this case it is not universal brotherhood which is being celebrated but rather the ties of religious faith and tradition and specifically, of course, that particularly potent mixture of the ethnic and spiritual which is Jewishness. No musical gives a more sympathetic or idealized portrait of religious faith and its impact and hold on a community. I always ask the students in my theology of the musical class whether they could conceive of a musical being based around a Christian community and treating it with the same measure of idealized affection and gentle humour and reverence. The answer is invariably no – somehow one cannot imagine it. The portrayal of the nuns in *The Sound of Music* perhaps comes closest but even in the stage version they do not play the dominant role that Jewish tradition and observance does in *Fiddler*. Nor does any other musical feature as much religious ritual and theological musing in its plot and songs. Perhaps Judaism with its particular combination of folk tradition, sentiment and zany self-deprecating humour lends itself more than any other faith to being portrayed on the musical stage.

Fiddler on the Roof could have been written by Frank Loesser, Lerner and Loewe, Rodgers and Hammerstein or any of the other American lyricists and composers of the first half of the twentieth century who came from Jewish backgrounds and could relate directly to the persecution and pogroms which had brought their parents or grandparents to the USA from Europe. It was, indeed, a show waiting to be written and it is in many ways surprising that it was not until the 1960s that anyone hit on the obvious suitability for the musical stage of so much in the Jewish experience – its poignancy, traditions, humour and distinctive and haunting music. The early years of that decade in fact saw five Jewish-themed musicals open on Broadway – the others being *Milk and Honey* (1961), *A Family Affair* (1962), *I Can Get It for You Wholesale* (1962) and *Funny Girl* (1964) – but it was *Fiddler* that was both the most Jewish-focused and the most successful. The lyricist, Sheldon Harnick, had fallen in love with musical theatre as a schoolboy violinist accompanying amateur Gilbert and Sullivan productions at the Goodman Theatre, Chicago, in the late

1930s. He resolved to make writing musicals his career after listening to a college friend's record of *Finian's Rainbow*. 'If ever there was an actual turning point in my life, I think that was it,' he later wrote. 'I was dazzled. To be able to say such pertinent things; and to say them in such entertaining ways – that was a career worth pursuing.'[8]

Harnick's early lyrics were sophisticated and satirical. He particularly delighted in pricking the bubble of schmaltzy religiosity and piety that surrounded so many American popular songs of the 1940s and 1950s:

> I kissed you under the nave
> At the Basilica of St Anne . . .
> There in a scene celestial
> You acted clean and I acted bestial.
>
> My father's so meek that it's criminal,
> Incredibly gentle and mild.
> To hear him sing hymns from a hyminal
> You'd never believe I'm his child.[9]

Joseph Stein's book for *Fiddler on the Roof*, based on stories by Sholom Aleichem about life in the Jewish shtetls, or settlements, in Tsarist Russia, brought out a much less flippant side in Harnick. Like *Oklahoma!* and *How to Succeed in Business without Really Trying*, *Fiddler on the Roof* is a great celebration of the values of community and humanity. It is about a people brought closer together through adversity. It is also about the power of the human spirit. The song 'To life' with its line 'Let's live another day' echoes the philosophy of *carpe diem* expressed in the works of Gilbert and Sullivan but gives it a more theological twist by introducing God into the picture as the author of human joy:

> Life has a way of confusing us,
> Blessing and bruising us.
> Drink, l'chaim, to life.
> God would like us to be joyful,
> Even when our hearts lie panting on the floor.
> How much more can we be joyful
> When there's really something to be joyful for?

This mention of God is not incidental. It is the power and hold of religious faith which both binds and defines the community of

Anatevka. This is centred on the family unit, widens out to encompass the whole shtetl with all its characters, most important of them all 'our beloved Rabbi', and acknowledges those others who make 'a bigger circle', 'his honour the constable, his honour the priest, and his honour . . . many others. We don't bother them and so far they don't bother us.' In so describing life in his village, Tevye is expressing the central importance of his Jewish faith which, for all its stubborn conservatism, is the precious lifeblood that keeps Anatevka going.

The centrality of religious faith in *Fiddler* is beautifully expressed in the song 'Tradition' which Jerome Robbins, the director, suggested as an opening number to replace the song 'We've Never Missed a Sabbath Yet' with which Harnick and composer Jerry Bock had originally intended opening the show. Its message is powerfully reinforced in the film version where symbols of Judaism like the star of David, the menorah and the Torah are flashed up on screen while 'Tradition' is sung. On both stage and screen the song is introduced by Tevye in a speech which spells out the intimate connection between religious faith and tradition, moral order and a sense of community.

Because of our traditions, we've kept our balance for many, many years. Here in Anatevka we have traditions for everything . . . how to eat, how to sleep, how to work, how to wear clothes. For instance, we always keep our heads covered and always wear a little prayer shawl. This shows our constant devotion to God. You may ask how did this tradition get started. I'll tell you – I don't know. But it's a tradition. Because of our traditions, everyone here knows who he is and what God expects him to do.

Religious ritual is treated particularly sympathetically in *Fiddler on the Roof*. The staging of the 'Sabbath Prayer' must surely count as the straightest and fullest depiction of an act of worship in any musical. The song could have come straight out of a Jewish hymnbook and is sung with absolute sincerity and fidelity. Significantly, the dream scene in this musical has an explicitly religious dimension when Grandmother Tzeitel appears to Tevye to tell him that the match between his daughter Tzeitel and Motel the tailor was 'made in heaven'. The song 'Miracle of Miracles', sung by Motel when he gets Tevye's blessing to marry Tzeitel, provides another example of Harnick's sympathetic treatment of Jewish faith and theocentric emphasis. Comparing what has happened to him with the triumph of Daniel in the lion's den, the walls of Jericho tumbling down, Moses softening Pharaoh's heart, the parting of the Red Sea, David's slaughter of Goliath and the manna falling from heaven, Motel reflects

> But of all God's miracles, large and small,
> The most miraculous one of all
> Is that out of a worthless lump of clay
> God has made a man today.

In putting his own happiness at having won the girl of his heart alongside the epic triumphs of the people of Israel as described in the Hebrew Bible, Motel could easily have slipped into blasphemy or at least extreme bathos. Yet when he concludes the song by affirming

> But of all God's miracles, large and small,
> The most miraculous one of all
> Is the one I thought could never be:
> God has given you to me!

he is expressing his own profound faith. God is seen as the one who is the author of all these miracles, large and small. It is God who is being thanked for giving Tzeitel to Motel. By comparing his own position with the outcome of the great biblical miracle stories, Motel is not trivializing them in any way. Rather he is affirming his faith in miracles and his utter thankfulness to God for effecting one for him.

No character in *Fiddler*, nor perhaps in any musical, quotes as freely from the Scriptures nor speaks as often and as familiarly to God as Tevye. Part of his charm is, of course, that his quotations from the Good Book are so often inaccurate. He has to be put right as to whether it was Abraham or Moses who said 'I am a stranger in a strange land' and reminded that it was Moses rather than David who was 'slow of speech and slow of tongue'. Tevye has a wonderful sense of familiarity with God and a great appreciation of both the sense of humour and the real compassion at the heart of the divine. This is perhaps most evident in the song which was cut from Fiddler during its pre-Broadway run in Philadelphia, in which he speculates about the long-awaited Messiah's eventual arrival on earth:

> When Messiah comes
> He will say to us,
> 'I apologize that I took so long,
> But I had a little trouble finding you.

Over here a few and over there a few.
You were hard to reunite
But ev'rything is going to be all right!
Up in heaven there
How I wrung my hands
When they exiled you from the Promised Land.
Into Babylon you went like castaways
On the first of many, many moving days.
What a day and what a blow!
How terrible I felt you'll never know!'

The Messiah envisaged here is equally far from the angst-ridden figure of *Jesus Christ Superstar* and the stern unmovable judge of *Carousel*. The God with whom Tevye regularly engages in banter and conversation in *Fiddler on the Roof* is an approachable figure. Indeed, he is an old friend, exasperating at times, to be chided and bargained with but one whose existence is very real and never to be doubted. 'Sometimes I think when things are too quiet up there, you say to yourself: Let's see, what kind of mischief can I play on my friend, Tevye?' That mild complaint, expressed in the form of light-hearted banter and addressed to 'my friend', sums up how Tevye sees God, as someone to talk to and moan at. It introduces the scene which contains the great dream song in *Fiddler*, 'If I were a rich man', in which Tevye tries to persuade God to give him worldly wealth by describing all the good things he would do if he had it.

At one level this song clearly asserts the doctrine of predestination in its acknowledgement of God's sovereignity:

Lord, who made the lion and the lamb,
You decreed I should be what I am.
Would it spoil some vast, eternal plan
If I were a wealthy man?

What is particularly striking, however, is not its theology but the fact that at the heart and climax of Tevye's dream of what riches would bring is not the sybaritic life, nor even the happiness of his beloved wife, but rather the effect it would have on his spiritual life:

If I were rich I'd have the time that I lack
To sit in the synagogue and pray
And maybe have a seat by the eastern wall.

And I'd discuss the holy books with the learned men
Seven hours ev'ry day.
That would be the sweetest thing of all.

For me those are the most moving lines in the entire musical. Admittedly it is all very idealized and Americanized. This is Judaism as the second and third generation descendants of those who had escaped the pogroms of central and eastern Europe like to think of it. Some Jews that I know are profoundly uneasy about *Fiddler on the Roof*. They regard it as corny and cloying, producing a stereotyped and wholly unrealistic picture of Judaism which one described to me as 'post-Holocaust idealism'. Yet it has an aura of sincerity and it treats religious faith seriously and sympathetically. For many non-Jews this musical provides the defining images of Judaism – and they are very positive ones. When Homer Simpson, a fictional character who is not unlike Tevye in holding frequent and familiar conversations with God, needs $50,000 for a heart bypass, he goes to the local rabbi, pretending to be Jewish in the only way that he knows how: 'Now, I know that I haven't been the best Jew, but I have rented *Fiddler on the Roof* and I will watch it.'[10]

If *Fiddler on the Roof* stands as the supreme musical tribute to the community-binding power of religious faith, a show which opened a year later in many ways represents the culmination of the idealistic dream theme pioneered by Rodgers and Hammerstein. Dale Wasserman was inspired to write *Man of La Mancha*, based on the life of Miguel de Cervantes and his famous creation Don Quixote, by a quotation he came across in the works of Miguel de Unamuno: 'Only he who attempts the absurd is capable of achieving the impossible.' In a very different way from *Fiddler*, the 'musical play' which he wrote with its emphasis on the thin dividing line between illusion and reality and between sanity and absurdity and its central character's quest 'to dream the impossible dream' is a profoundly religious work. Indeed, it is perhaps the first musical to have inspired a reaction from its audience that could best be described as a religious experience – much as *Les Misérables* did twenty years later. Albert Marre, the director, noted of the response of audiences 'They're not just watching a play, they're having a religious experience.'[11] Wasserman himself wrote of his creation:

To me the most interesting aspect of the success of *Man of La Mancha* is the fact that it plows squarely upstream against the prevailing current of philosophy in the theater. That current is best described by its catch-labels – Theater of the Absurd, Black Comedy, the Theater of Cruelty – which is to say the theater of alienation, of moral anarchy and despair. To the practitioners of those philosophies *Man of la Mancha* must seem hopelessly naive in its espousal of illusion as man's strongest spiritual need, the most meaningful function of his imagination. But I've no unhappiness about that. 'Facts are the enemy of truth,' says Cervantes-Don Quixote. And that is precisely what I felt and meant.[12]

The depiction of illusion, and specifically of dreaming, as an essentially spiritual quality in *Man of La Mancha* is greatly helped by the sensitive and inspiring lyrics written by Joe Darion. Like the original story on which it is based, the musical takes the form of a play within a play. It opens with Miguel de Cervantes languishing in a Spanish gaol awaiting trial by the Inquisition. As is customary he is 'tried' by his fellow prisoners and pleads guilty to their charge that he is an idealist, a bad poet and an honest man. He continues his defence by entertaining the other prisoners and the Governor with the story of Don Quixote, himself playing the title role. Quixote is presented as the mad rash knight bent on adventures in the cause of virtue and against his wicked enemy the Enchanter. He is, in the words of his faithful servant, Sancho Panza, 'the defender of the right and pursuer of lofty undertakings'. Above all Quixote is a dreamer who blurs reality and illusion by seeing what he wants to see rather than what is actually in front of him. A simple inn is for him a castle and a shaving basin the golden helmet of Mambrino which will protect its wearer from all wounds. Aldonza, a serving wench and village whore, becomes in his eyes the fair lady Dulcinea.

Don Quixote's dreams consistently lead him to see the best in everyone and spur him on in his quest to accomplish selfless deeds of derring-do in the best tradition of medieval chivalry. When he first encounters Aldonza serving in the inn and being harried by muleteers, he immediately sees her as the one whom he has long been called to protect:

I have dreamed thee too long,
Never seen thee or touched thee, but known thee with all of my
  heart,
Half a prayer, half a song,
Thou hast always been with me, though we have been always apart.

He goes on to sing that he sees Heaven when he sees her and that her name – which he insists is Dulcinea rather than Aldonza – 'is like a prayer an angel whispers'. Later Quixote expounds his aim in life to her as being 'to add some measure of grace to the world'. She cynically retorts that 'the world's a dungheap and we are maggots that crawl on it' but he tells her that she knows better than that in her heart and goes on to say that 'Whether I win or lose does not matter'. In response to her question as to what does matter, he replies 'only that I follow the quest' and launches into his show-stopping anthem:

To dream the impossible dream,
To fight the unbeatable foe,
To bear with unbearable sorrow,
To run where the brave dare not go.

To right the unrightable wrong,
To love, pure and chaste, from afar,
To try, when your arms are too weary,
To reach the unreachable star!

This is my Quest, to follow that star,
No matter how hopeless, no matter how far,
To fight for the right without question or pause,
To be willing to march into hell for a heavenly cause!

This dream song from *Man of La Mancha* has a similar uplifting hymn-like quality to 'When you walk through a storm' from *Carousel* and 'Climb Ev'ry Mountain' from *The Sound of Music*. In its call to reach the unreachable star and fight for the right it is more strenuous and demanding than either of the Rodgers and Hammerstein numbers and it also differs from them in being a personal mission statement rather than a piece of advice and encouragement. Indeed, it is altogether more heroic and sacrificial than any other Broadway anthem, conjuring up visions not just of knightly chivalry but of an almost Christ-like quality of self-abandonment and bearing unbearable sorrow. The reference later in the song to 'one man, scorned and covered in scars' echoes the suffering servant passage in Isaiah and the Gospels' description of the crucified Jesus, and there is a direct use of Christian imagery in the line about marching into hell for a heavenly cause. Taken together with Don Quixote's earlier references to prayer, angels and grace and his use of the archaic and biblically resonant term 'thee', the overall feel here is distinctly Christian.

In the context of the musical as a whole, 'To dream the impossible dream' is above all an affirmation of the importance of dreaming dreams which become goals and aspirations in one's life. In the middle of the play which he is putting on for his fellow prisoners Cervantes reflects on the despair in so many lives and suggests that while 'to surrender to dreams – this may be madness', maddest of all is perhaps 'to see life as it is and not as it should be.' Don Quixote is someone who surrenders totally to his dreams. Indeed, he is in an almost permanent dream state, seeing objects, people and situations as they should be and as he would like to see them rather than as they are. His dreams inspire his own reckless selflessness. They also have a trans-formative, redemptive power which actually changes those whom he encounters into the idealized image which he has of them. This is most strikingly achieved in the case of Aldonza. Everyone tries to tell Don Quixote that she is far from being the fair and chaste Lady Dulcinea whom he makes her through his dream, not least Aldonza herself who beseeches him to look at her and see her for what she is, 'the kitchen slut reeking of sweat, born on a dungheap to die on a dungheap, a strumpet men use and forget!' Yet when Don Quixote is on his deathbed at the end of the play, Aldonza comes to tell him that he has changed her whole life not just by the way he insisted of thinking of her as a lady rather than a whore but more radically by his idealism and pursuit of the impossible dream. 'You spoke to me and everything was different . . . You spoke of a dream and about the Quest.'

Man of La Mancha can be read as a testament to the philosophy of idealism or as another assertion of the essentially Pelagian 'follow your star and pursue your quest' message of so many mid-twentieth-century Broadway shows. But it also has a deeper spiritual resonance. Quixote's world is built on the unseen rather than the seen, on belief rather than reality. Like St Paul, he walks by faith rather than by sight. His dreams literally keep him going – it is when he loses them that he dies. Yet his death does not mean the end of his dreams. They live on in the changed and transformed lives of those he has touched, notably Sancho and Aldonza. Their redemptive quality makes them somehow more than dreams – they perhaps point to the ultimate and deeper reality, the presence of the divine which is in everyone and everything but which is so often obscured from our limited earthly sight. Perhaps the last word should be with the Padre, who feels that Don Quixote is 'either the wisest madman or the maddest wise man in the world'. While the dreamer is holding vigil in the chapel of his imaginary castle in preparation for becoming a proper knight, the man of God reflects on both the absurdity and the nobility of his fantasy over Dulcinea:

There is no Dulcinea,
She's made of flame and air,
And yet how lovely life would seem
If every man could weave a dream
To keep him from despair.

There is considerably less theological or spiritual nuance in the next big Broadway hit after *Man of La Mancha*, Dorothy Fields and Cy Coleman's *Sweet Charity* (1966). It is of interest, however, for its electrifying and compulsive song 'Rhythm of Life', which has crossed over from the musical stage to the church choir repertoire (see page 7). The plot is not without ecclesiastical resonances. Charity Hope Valentine, a dance hall hostess looking for real love, meets Oscar Lindquist, an accountant, when they get stuck in the lift at the YMCA. After they have been freed, he asks her if she would like to go to church with him. He belongs to a mailing list, the church of the month club, and the featured place this month is the Rhythm of Life Church which started off as a jazz group and turned into a religious cult. Charity and Oscar go along to the basement garage where the church meets to be greeted by the leader, Johan Sebastian Brubeck, otherwise known as 'Daddy' who preaches a sermon entitled 'We have beaten our swords into ploughshares and the beat goes on'. Having announced that 'time is running out on the great LP of life and the greatest disc jockey is going to lead us to the flip side of life called eternity', he proclaims his sixties gospel: 'Thou shalt dig thy neighbour as thou wouldst have him dig thee.' Daddy then incites his followers to spread the religion of the rhythm of life.

In the original version of the song, memorably rendered by Sammy Davis Junior in the 1969 film of *Sweet Charity*, the members of the Rhythm of Life Church are incited to 'clip your wings and fly to Daddy'. This and other phrases have been changed in the version of the song by Richard Barnes which has become a standard with male voice and church choirs but the key message remains the same, that 'the rhythm of life has a powerful beat', as does the familiar Pelagian refrain: 'Clip your wings and fly up high. You can do it if you try.'

The nod to the new religious movements and cults of the swinging sixties represented by the Rhythm of Life Church in *Sweet Charity* became a full-scale tribute with *Hair* the following year. Generally seen as the ultimate musical tribute to flower-power and hippydom, *Hair* is in fact almost as remarkable for its explicit Christian references as for its mentions of drugs, draft dodging and global pollution. The second song, a hymn to drugs, suddenly switches from a catalogue of hallucinogenic substances to the lines 'This is the body and blood of Christ' and 'Here are your rosary beads, baby'. The syncretistic sense that the sacramental and liturgical expressions of Christianity take their place in the panoply of religious experiences that mark the dawning new age of Aquarius is reinforced by the fact that John the Baptist is listed among the hippies' heroes. Overall, the atmosphere is of irreverence, as in the lines 'I am the Son of God. Beware, I shall vanish and be forgotten' and 'As Mary Magdalene once said, "Jesus, I'm getting stoned"', but in this postmodern spiritual pot pourri there is still room for straight lifts from the Bible, as in the song 'What a piece of work is man? In action how like an angel', and for ethical reflection, as in the number about how much easier it is to be charitable to strangers than to those nearer home.

In some ways *Hair* is one long dream sequence from beginning to end – the dream in this case being more a drug-induced hallucination and fantasy than a vision of a better world. What really separates it from most of the other major musicals of the 1960s is its uncompromisingly contemporary setting. *Camelot* is set in Arthurian Britain, *Fiddler on the Roof* in Russia at the dawning of the twentieth century, *Man of La Mancha* in sixteenth-century Spain. The dreams which they project point backwards to a lost age of medieval chivalry or community life in the Tsarist shtetls. There is a nostalgic yearning in all of them for the recovery of a lost golden age. *Hair*, by contrast, proclaims that a new golden age is about to dawn. The *New York Times* critic hailed it as 'the first Broadway musical in some time to have the authentic voice of today rather than that of the day before yesterday'.

Hair does belong to the 1960s in one key respect. It is essentially optimistic. The 1970s were to be characterized by a darker, more cynical and anguished style of musical theatre. A little-noticed 1970 show provides a fitting epitaph to the decade in its nostalgic setting, its celebration of the rhythm of life and its optimism about the human condition. *Purlie* tells the story of a self-ordained black preacher, Purlie Victorious Judson, who returns to his home town in the

American South to save Big Bethel, the chapel which Ol' Cap'n Cotchipee, the white bigot who owns the local cotton plantation, wants to destroy. Set in the early twentieth century, it has something of the feel and message of *Show Boat*. The score is full of optimistic Gospel-style numbers in which Purlie sings the praise of life here and now rather than the uncertainties of life in the hereafter, asking 'How 'bout some glory days before we are dead' and proclaiming that 'The World is Comin' To A Start'.

If *Purlie* marks the last of the 1960s-style musicals, a show which opened just a few months earlier anticipates the angst-filled musicals of the 1970s. In *Celebration* Tom Jones returned to the theme of the cycle of birth, death and regeneration that he had first explored in *The Fantasticks*. He was inspired to write it after reading about an ancient Sumerian ritual battle between summer, symbolizing youth, growth and fertility, and winter, representing age, decay and death. Despite its title, *Celebration* has an altogether bleaker feel than *The Fantasticks*, as represented by the musings of Potemkin, a de-frocked priest and drugged-out drop-out:

God is dead
That's what they said.
Done in by Darwin, Marx and Freud.
Free are we
From Deity.
Of course, it sort of leaves a little void.

A later 1970 show confirmed the new more cynical direction in which musical theatre was moving. Stephen Sondheim's *Company*, often described as the first concept musical, broke not just with the whole romantic, idealistic mould that Rodgers and Hammerstein had created but also with their legacy of strong unfolding narrative and overarching moral purpose. It harks back in some ways to the older tradition of revue, providing a series of almost disconnected snapshots or improvisations on a theme, in this case marriage. Sophisticated, witty, amoral and utterly secular, the lyrics are much closer to those of Cole Porter and Lorenz Hart than to Hammerstein, and Sondheim's music is curiously truncated and unfulfilled – the very antithesis of Rodgers' soaring cadences and broad flowing melodies. As Scott Miller observes, '*Company* is about the chic, intellectual, spiritually empty people living in the Big Apple.'[13] This is a community without dreams. The *Village Voice* critic noted percipiently 'in *Company* no one dreams, only survives'.[14] John Bush Jones describes it as the ultimate 'fragmented musical', marking a reaction against the integrated musical with its themes of community and wholeness and ushering in a new style of show mirroring the much more fragmented society of the 1970s.

As it had been shaped by Broadway, with more than a little help from Hollywood, the dream motif disappeared from musicals after 1970. However, a new kind of dream, more ambiguous, tentative and angst-ridden, was being fashioned by a young British librettist and composer who together were to transform musical theatre in the 1970s, and who found their initial inspiration to do so in the unlikely source of Bible stories.

4

Any dream will do –

the biblical superstars of the 1970s

It may not be their main claim to fame but Tim Rice and Andrew Lloyd Webber, who dominated the musical theatre scene in the 1970s and relocated its centre of gravity from New York to London, have arguably done more than most priests and preachers in the last thirty-five years to promote biblical knowledge and theological awareness. *Joseph and the Amazing Technicolor Dreamcoat*, their first successful collaboration, which began life as a 20-minute prep school cantata and was later reworked into a two-hour extravaganza built around the teenybopper appeal of Jason Donovan and Donny Osmond, has become the staple fare of junior school concerts. It has been estimated that it has been performed in more than 15,000 schools. Bill Kenwright's touring version, which has been on a virtually perpetual progress throughout the United Kingdom for over twenty years, holds the record for the longest-running touring musical and has been seen by over 15 million people. *Jesus Christ Superstar*, their most original and daring work, which provides a highly unusual slant on the last weeks of Jesus' life by looking primarily through the eyes of Judas, overtook *Oliver* in 1978 as the longest-running musical in West End history, has been filmed twice, translated into 11 languages, performed in 22 countries and grossed over £100 million. Lloyd Webber achieved a third spectacular piece of Christian product placement in 1985 when the 'Pie Jesu' from his *Requiem* reached the top ten of British pop singles, the only liturgical item ever to have made it into the hit parade.

Religion bulked large in both men's childhoods. Rice spent a formative year aged 11 at a school run by 'a bunch of rather aggressive Canadian monks, whose order, the Brothers of Christian Instruction, clearly regarded corporal punishment as an essential stop en route to heaven'.[1] Although his main memory from this brush with Catholicism is of the beatings, he records that it also produced a lifelong interest in Bible stories and the language of Christianity. In Lloyd Webber's case the religious influence was more direct, coming from his strongly Methodist mother, Jean, and his church musician father, William, who was successively organist of the Anglo-Catholic All Saints Church in Margaret Street, London and the Methodist Central Hall, Westminster. William Lloyd Webber was a moderately successful composer whose output included a number of sacred works, among them *The Saviour* and *The Samaritan*, two dramatic cantatas very much in the style of Sullivan and Stainer, and two Latin masses. His son inherited a passionate love of English church music.

Perhaps the dominant characteristic shared by Rice and Lloyd Webber is their quintessential Englishness. Both had a Home Counties preparatory and public school education. A photograph of Lancing College Chapel is juxtaposed with family snaps and grainy images of early girlfriends in Rice's autobiography. Although Lloyd Webber's upbringing was more bohemian, his great passions are essentially those of an English country gentlemen – country churches, bell-ringing, horses and Pre-Raphaelite paintings. He got into Oxford on the strength of an idiosyncratic paper on the merits of Victorian architecture and for being able to tell K. B. Macfarlane, the medieval history don at Magdalen College, the date of the nave of Westminster Abbey. In fact, the dreaming spires held him only briefly in their thrall – he left university after one term having realized that of his two great childhood ambitions it was the dream of being the next Richard Rodgers that fired him more than the prospect of ending up as Chief Inspector of Ancient Monuments.

Significantly, the first joint project on which the 17-year-old composer and the 20-year-old lyricist collaborated was a musical about Dr Barnardo. Undoubtedly influenced by Jean Lloyd Webber's Methodist passion for social reform and helping underprivileged East End children, *The Likes of Us*, which never reached the stage, had an uplifting moral feel and cast the Victorian philanthropist as a Christ-like figure. Although they have been largely responsible for creating the contemporary genre of rock opera, both men are highly traditional, indeed nostalgic in their own tastes. Lloyd Webber was teased for his teenage enthusiasm for Rodgers and Hammerstein by contemporaries who were being drawn to the emerging pop music scene. Rice was a more enthusiastic devotee of rock and roll but found his greatest source of inspiration in the Savoy operas whose patter songs he regarded as the supreme example of the lyricist's art.

Comparisons with Gilbert and Sullivan are inevitably often made in respect of Rice and Lloyd Webber. There are some striking similarities between the personalities of the dominant British lyricist and composer in late twentieth-century British musical theatre and their Victorian predecessors. Rice, like Gilbert, embarked briefly on a legal career before finding his true metier as an urbane, witty wordsmith. His passion for cricket and his knighthood epitomize his outlook and lifestyle as a relatively uncomplicated establishment figure and English gentleman. Lloyd Webber is an altogether more complex, mercurial and tortured figure, well described by his biographer, Michael Coveney, as 'a mixed up, misplaced Victorian'.[1] Stephen Citron finds considerable similarities between Lloyd Webber's beloved Victorian churches and his musicals: 'They are romantic. They are emotionally direct. They are visual extravangazas' – attributes which equally apply to Sullivan's operettas.[2] Like Sullivan, Lloyd Webber's work displays an undoubted if unconventional spirituality. Coveney suggests that the central theme running through all of his music is a quest for the spiritual dimension of life. In the extraordinary edition of *Songs of Praise* celebrating his fiftieth birthday he admitted to praying, though unsure to whom, and expressed his belief that 'there is something we don't understand'.

At first sight it may seem ironic that Rice and Lloyd Webber broke both the mould and the hold of the Rodgers and Hammerstein-style Broadway musical in favour of a more irreverent and contemporary approach on the basis of two big hits based on stories from the Bible. The fact is, however, that they were not alone among lyricists and composers at the tail-end of the 1960s in turning to the Scriptures as a source for new musicals. Why this should be is not entirely clear – perhaps the influence of John Robinson's best-selling *Honest to God* and more generally of what became known as South Bank theology combined with the tenets of hippydom to break down taboos at the same time as creating an interest in some of the more radical aspects of Christianity. Maybe it was just chance. It is certainly striking that the great enduring trinity of Bible-based musicals, *Joseph, Jesus Christ Superstar* and Stephen Schwartz's *Godspell* all date from this period.

Even Richard Rodgers wrote a biblical musical in 1970. *Two by Two*, the veteran composer's last full-scale work on which he collaborated with lyricist Martin Charnin, was based on the story of Noah's ark, updated so that the flood became a metaphor for the atomic bomb and the whole story an allegory about humankind's response to the threat of ultimate and mass destruction. As in earlier Rodgers and Hammerstein shows, the overwhelming impression is of a God of vengeance and judgement. The plot has a despairing Japheth leaving the ark, feeling that he must stand up to an avenging God who must surely love 'something, somewhere'. At the end Noah makes a bargain with the Almighty. If he will not devastate the world, his creatures will not forget his name. Then if humankind destroys itself, it won't be God's fault. Noah sings:

> Now it is in man's hands to make or destroy the world.
> You will be definitely off the hook.

Two by Two ran for just under a year, hampered by uncertainty as to how Jewish the show should be and by increasingly erratic and unpredictable performances by Danny Kaye in the role of Noah.

In Britain there had through the 1960s been a string of successful pop cantatas for schools based on biblical stories, which perhaps provided a more direct inspiration for *Joseph*. The earliest was Herbert Chappell's *Daniel Jazz* in 1963. Its witty libretto and catchy syncopated tunes were very popular and inspired other similar works like Michael Hurd's *Jonah-man Jazz* (1966) and *Captain Noah and His Floating Zoo* by Michael Flanders and Joseph Horowitz (1970). In many ways *Joseph and the Amazing Technicolor Dreamcoat* was a natural follow-on to these end-of-term school shows. Where it differed from them was in its expansion from a 20-minute cantata for Colet Court prep school to a two-hour West End spectacular.

The original brief to Lloyd Webber and Rice from Alan Doggett, head of music at Colet Court and a friend of William Lloyd Webber, was for a short piece which would appeal equally to the 8- to 13-year-old boys who would perform it and the parents and grandparents who would form the audience. The 19-year-old composer and his 24-year-old collaborator initially toyed with the idea of a mini-musical about a James Bond-like figure but Doggett steered them towards a biblical subject, playing them a tape of *Daniel Jazz* which the school choir had just performed with considerable success. Rice, whose favourite Bible story from school was that of Joseph and his coat of many colours, dug out his copy of *The Wonder Book of Bible Stories*, which became his principal source text.

Joseph was first performed in its original 20-minute form at Colet Court School in March 1968. It was slightly expanded for a second performance two months later, as part of a concert at Central Hall, Westminster, where it received a mixed reception from the critics present. Merion Bowen from the *Times Educational Supplement* dismissed it as 'a series of pop tunes of the crusading type featured by Cliff Richard'. Derek Jewell, the *Sunday Times* critic, who was there because his son was in the chorus, by contrast, enthused about its 'infectious overall character and wonderfully singable tunes' and described it as 'a considerable piece of barrier-breaking'.[3] The show's third performance, with further expansion, took place in November 1968 in the nave of St Paul's Cathedral as part of a festival called 'Pop into St Paul's' organized by the Cathedral's progressive Australian dean, Martin Sullivan, who himself parachuted down from the dome as part of the fun. This version was released as a record by Decca in January 1969 and performed by the Young Vic Company at the Edinburgh Festival in 1972 where it was paired with an adaptation from the Wakefield Mystery Plays of the story of Genesis from the creation to Jacob to make a two-handed show entitled *Bible One – Two Looks at the Book of Genesis*. Expanded to 40 minutes, this production transferred to the Round House in London, where it had a six-week run. It made its West End debut in a yet further enlarged form in February 1973 at the Albery Theatre as part of another biblical double-bill, its companion-piece this time being *Jacob's Journey* which was intended as a prologue telling the story of Jacob from the time of his row with Esau. Despite having lyrics by Rice, music by Lloyd Webber and book by television scriptwriters Alan Simpson and Ray Galton, who turned Isaac's family into porridge-eating Scots and made God an absent-minded Lancastrian who always arrived with a heavenly host in tow 'because otherwise nobody ever believes it's really me', the new piece was a flop and hastily withdrawn.

Joseph, by contrast, went from strength to strength, undergoing yet further expansion so that it could stand on its own as a full evening's show. It was first performed in this form at the Haymarket Theatre, Leicester, ran for seven months in Washington, DC in 1980 and received its first Broadway performance in 1982. In June 1991 a new and much more spectacular two-hour production opened at the London Palladium, with teenage idol Jason Donovan in the title role. It ran for two and a half years, was seen by over two million people and took over £47 million at the box office. This production subsequently went to the United States where it starred Donny Osmond who also played Joseph in the video version released in 2000.

Joseph has retained something of its original naivety and freshness throughout its many metamorphoses. Every performance of the current professional touring version features a locally recruited children's choir on stage. The exhaustive list of colours for Joseph's coat – 24 in all – made up by the Colet Court boys for the original performance has been retained, as have simple and stylized props like the model sheep and camels which reinforce the sense of a Sunday school performance. The video version cleverly sets the show in the context of a school concert with the cast coming into a school hall as teachers, led by headmaster Richard Attenborough who goes on to play Jacob. At several points there are reaction shots from the audience of children watching the story unfold and more than once they invade the stage and involve themselves in the action, which is played out in a highly stylized cartoon-like set. There is a raunchier, more tacky and vulgar side to the video, epitomized by Joan Collins's performance as Potiphar's wife and Robert Torti's hip-grinding Pharaoh, as there is in all the professional productions of *Joseph*. Overall, however, it justifies its description on the box as a 'classic family musical'. *Joseph* works its magic whether it is being given a highly lavish and glitzy production with a star-studded cast or performed in a school or church hall with piano accompaniment. Apart from the works of Gilbert and Sullivan, I can think of no other musical which works as well in both professional and amateur performance. Perhaps that is why it has to a large extent supplanted G & S as the staple fare of school and church concerts. Steven Pimlott, who directed both the Palladium production and the video, is surely right to describe *Joseph* as Rice and Lloyd Webber's *HMS Pinafore* in its brightness and freshness and its joyous sense of discovery of what two new collaborators could achieve.

Joseph's genesis and its early pairing with other biblically-inspired works might suggest that it could be classified as a 'Christian musical', a category into which its progenitors *Daniel Jazz* and *Jonah-man Jazz* can fairly clearly be placed. It sticks close to the biblical narrative recounted in Genesis 37–46. Indeed, the audience is reminded of this fact and almost invited to check up on the show's biblical accuracy when Potiphar notes of his wife's lusting after Joseph 'it's all there in Chapter 39 of Genesis'. In the video version the Bible itself appears as a prominent prop, being leafed through by the narrator at several points and consulted by Joseph in the middle of Pharaoh's exposition of his dream. There are moments when the musical appears to be conveying a theological message, perhaps most obviously in the ballad 'Close every door' which goes considerably deeper than the Genesis account of Joseph and gets to the very heart of the central Exodus theme with its lines: 'Children of Israel are never alone' and 'We have been promised a land of our own'. Remarks by Rice in his autobiography suggest that part at least of his objective in writing *Joseph* was to point up the religious meaning and dimension of the biblical story. He notes that it was written for 'children learning about music and language – and maybe God too' and comments more broadly on its overall theme:

> This great tale has everything – plausible, sympathetic characters, a flawed hero and redeemed villains. The figures of power can be portrayed comically yet they retain their potency and even their dignity. The storyline is both original (perhaps not surprisingly as it is one of the first ever told) and unpredictable, yet moves with unerring force towards a happy conclusion. It is a symbolic, spiritual, religious and human story – even in our light-hearted retelling of it the presence of God is inescapable. The props, coat and goat, and locations, bleak (Canaan) and extravagant (Egypt), are magnificent. It is a story of triumph against the odds, of love and hate, of forgiveness and optimism.[4]

Yet the fact is that, far from being inescapable, the presence of God is completely missing from *Joseph and the Amazing Technicolor Dreamcoat*. In marked contrast to the Genesis narrative on which it is otherwise so closely based, there is not one single reference to God in the entire libretto of the musical. He is effectively airbrushed out of the story.

This radical process of secularization is particularly evident in the way that Joseph's dreams are dealt with in the musical. In the Genesis story, these are clearly portrayed as prophetic messages from God and Joseph is unequivocal in his insistence that it is not he but God who interprets dreams (see, for example, Genesis 40.8 and 41.16). As the Old Testament scholar, Walter Moberly, has pointed out, the emphasis is very much on Joseph as the agent of God rather than on his own remarkable abilities as a dream interpreter:

The text portrays Joseph as locating himself in relation to God in such a way that his words will be responsive to God. Integrity and accountability, rather than charisma as such, is the concern. Or, to put it differently, the concern of the text is not to separate divine action from human action, but rather to locate divine action within human action of a particular kind.[5]

In the musical, Joseph is portrayed not as God's agent in the interpretation of divine prophecy but rather as a charismatic seer who himself has the power to interpret dreams. He is portrayed even more as the quintessential dreamer who lives out more than most the message of all those Rodgers and Hammerstein anthems about having and following your own dream. This is especially evident in the prologue which was written at a relatively late stage of *Joseph*'s long process of evolution and locates the whole message of the subsequent story firmly in the 'dream theme' that we have already identified at the heart of the mid-twentieth-century musical:

Some folk dream of the wonders they'll do
Before their time on this planet is through.
Some just don't have anything planned,
They hide their hopes and their heads in the sand.
Now I don't say who is wrong, who is right
But if by chance you are here for the night,
Then all I need is an hour or two
To tell the tale of a dreamer like you.

We all dream a lot – some are lucky, some are not,
But if you think it, want it, dream it, then it's real.
You are what you feel!

But all that I say can be told another way
In the story of a boy whose dream came true
And he could be you!

Here is a complete departure from the biblical story of Joseph which is not in any way about a man who dreams of what he might do during his time on earth, nor an invitation to its readers to follow their own particular dreams. Rice and Lloyd Webber's Joseph is not the mouthpiece of God but one who himself dreams of what he might do and whose own dreams come true. He is someone with whom we can all identify – 'a dreamer like you'. It is true that the biblical account does at one point portray Joseph as a dreamer, or at least suggest that this is how his brothers regard him when they see him coming and say to one another 'Here comes the dreamer' (Genesis 37.19). The word used here, which has been translated in one concordance as 'master of dreams' is, in fact, applied to no other figure in the Bible. But to sum up the Genesis story of Joseph as that 'of a boy whose dream came true – and he could be you!' is something of a distortion. This is the message of 'Climb Ev'ry Mountain', 'You've got to have a dream' and 'When you walk through a storm' rather than of Genesis 37–45. The prologue's message that 'if you think it, want it, dream it, then it's real' goes even beyond Rodgers and Hammerstein, let alone anything suggested in the biblical story of Joseph, in its emphasis on the immanence of the dream experience and the ability of the individual to actualize it effortlessly and instantaneously.

Another significant way in which the musical distorts the emphasis of the biblical story on which it is based is by portraying Joseph very much as a star. This is clearly articulated in the narrator's lines near the beginning of Act 2:

> Strange as it seems
> There's been a
> Run of crazy dreams
> And a man who can interpret
> Could go far
> Could become a star

This sentiment is echoed by the chorus with the words 'could be famous, could be a big success'. This treatment of Joseph provides a much more one-dimensional and much less human figure than the Joseph of Genesis. In the biblical account, Joseph is referred to at least three times as weeping (Genesis 42.24; 43.30; and 4.14). In the musical, he shows very little emotion except for a certain introspective moodiness when he is thrown into prison. There is also virtually no development in his character as there is in the Old Testament story where the experience of being in prison changes him. Rice and Lloyd Webber's Joseph struts his stuff as a biblical superstar from the beginning of the show when he proudly boasts 'I look handsome, I look smart' to the end where he appears in his shimmering chariot of gold.

Physically, he is made a cross between an Arian god and a Chippendale, with bare rippling chest and dazzling blond hair. In several recent productions he makes an entry in the second act riding on a motorbike to the strains of the 'Superstar' theme from *Jesus Christ Superstar*, a gimmick introduced by Lloyd Webber when he was conducting a recording for Granada Television in the 1970s, much to the director's annoyance. It is, in fact, wholly appropriate – as presented in the musical Joseph is given a cult-superstar status which almost suggests divinity. Donny Osmond in the video version, with his long hair, white robes and entrance wafting through clouds of dry ice followed by adoring children carrying candles, resembles nothing more than a Pre-Raphaelite, Sunday School Jesus.

There are, indeed, intriguing messianic and Christological references and overtones in *Joseph and the Amazing Technicolor Dreamcoat* for those disposed to find them. There is the reference to Joseph laying down his life for others in the brothers' line in 'One more angel in heaven': 'If he had not laid down his life, we would not all be here'. In 'Close every door to me' Joseph presents himself as an innocent victim and exhibits something of the combination of confusion and resignation found in Jesus' anguished words to God in the garden of Gethsemane. There are close parallels between this song and 'Gethsemane' in *Jesus Christ Superstar*, particularly when Joseph sings 'If my life were important, I would ask should I live or die, but I know the answers lie far from this world'. He seems both to acknowledge and to address God in 'Hate me and laugh at me, do what you want with me'.

My students have also found both Christological and messianic references in the soft rock showstopper ballad 'Any dream will do', notably in the phrases 'and in the east, the dawn was breaking' and 'the world and I, we are still waiting'. This is a song which can bear many interpretations. Could it be about the cries of prophets which so often go unheard and missed as is perhaps suggested by the lines 'Far far away, someone was weeping/But the world was sleeping'? This is surely to read too much into a quintessential example of undemanding easy listening. Yet, as described by Rice himself, 'Any dream' is not without complexity and meaning:

Its message, expressed in deliberately obscure terms is that most of us would rather dream about anything at all than face reality. The coat is the dream and the singer is only truly happy when he is asleep, when he can 'draw back the curtain' and see colours that are 'wonderful and new'. When he awakes he only wants to 'return to the beginning' of his dream.[6]

The audience's appreciation of this really quite subtle message, which seems directly to contradict the narrator's opening observation that 'if you think it, want it, dream it, then it's real', is hardly helped by the easy, seductive accessibility of the tune. We are confronted here with the same kind of mismatch that we noticed with Sullivan's sublimely melodic settings for some of Gilbert's most pessimistic and discordant words (see page 51). In this case, as with nearly all of Lloyd Webber's output, the tune preceded the words and had originally been set to a song entitled 'I fancy you' written by Rice for the group Herman's Hermits after he had met one of them in the lavatories at EMI studios. Rice himself has noted that '"Any dream will do" combines a rather sad, resigned lyric with a very sweet and catchy tune – a paradoxical mix that usually proves very powerful.'[7] In this particular case the effect is certainly powerful but perhaps also deceptive. I suspect very few people even who know this song well would be aware that in it the coat symbolizes the dream or that its message is actually about our unwillingness to face reality. This observation on the human condition, which although still far from the theme of the biblical story of Joseph does at least inject a philosophical note into the musical, is lost not just because of the tune but because it is wholly swamped by the message of the song's much-repeated punch line 'Any dream will do'. The relativisim of this statement goes beyond the Rodgers and Hammerstein dream theme in suggesting that it does not matter what kind of dream you have.

Taken together with the prologue, this song comes over as a perfect expression of a postmodern approach to dreaming – it does not matter how you approach it, or what you make of it, because any dream will do and, as the narrator says, 'you are what you feel'. The relativism of 'Any dream will do' chimes in with the studied non-judgementalism of the narrator in stating at the outset of the show: 'Now I don't say who is wrong who is right'. We are a world away from the moralistic Pelagianism of Rodgers and Hammerstein and mid-twentieth-century Broadway. There is no injunction here to follow every dream, however tossed and blown, as one would climb a mountain or ford a stream, and certainly no call to do anything as strenuous as to dream an impossible dream. There is no point in doing anything very much, in fact, as it is really all down to luck – in the words of the prologue 'some are lucky, some are not'. Perhaps the key message of *Joseph* is contained in the original title that Rice and Lloyd Webber proposed for the musical – 'How to succeed in Egypt without really trying' – and in Joseph's reflection:

Anyone from anywhere can make it
If they get a lucky break.

How serious are the implications of this considerable distortion of the themes of a Bible story, given the huge popularity of *Joseph and the Amazing Technicolor Dreamcoat* particularly within schools and among young people? Rowan Williams expressed his unease about the message of the show's most popular song in his 2002 Dimbleby Lecture delivered shortly before his enthronement as Archbishop of Canterbury:

You may have sat through – as I have, many times – school choirs performing *Joseph and the Amazing Technicolor Dreamcoat*. I have a very soft spot for it – but as I listen to 'Any dream will do' my conscience bothers me: it's as though the ideal personal goal recommended were simply activating your potential in any direction you happen to set your heart on. It is a vision that has nothing to say about shared humanity and the hard labour of creating and keeping going a shared world of values.[8]

Terence Copley, Professor of Religious Education at the University of Exeter, believes that the musical has done serious harm in the context of religious education. He points out that the traditions of the major religions present us with three Josephs: the Jewish Joseph of the Hebrew Bible, the Christian Joseph who becomes a 'type' for Mary's husband who is also credited with receiving special revelation from God via angels and dreams, and the Islamic Yusuf of the Qur'an. These three readings of Joseph agree in portraying him as a seer, sage and prophet and in making Yahweh/God/Allah the central agent in his story. The Joseph with whom most children are familiar, however, is the very different figure created by Rice and Lloyd Webber.

In this treatment Joseph is something of an opportunist, yet possessing integrity: a person who strikes lucky and makes the best of his 'breaks' without abusing others. He is the epitome of a secular westerner in the late twentieth century . . . The themes, although distantly biblical ('I have been promised a land of my own'), caught a mood of assertive individualism which was sweeping Europe and continues to dominate western society, notably that 'Any dream will do', the significant lyrics for the finale. For the Joseph/Jusuf of the Bible and the Qur'an, any dream will simply not do, since dreams and visions are one way of mediating direct messages from 'the Lord'/God/Allah. But *Technicolor Dreamcoat* translated the Joseph/Yusuf saga into a highly entertaining, memorable, religion-less pop oratorio which found itself in tune with an increasingly secular society. The Prologue includes a terse statement of western relativist values:

> But if you think it, want it, dream it, then it's real!
> You are what you feel.[9]

Copley makes these remarks in the context of a broader complaint about the creeping secularization within religious education in which the religious narrative is being censored. He is worried that the Joseph of the musical is the only one presented to many children and calls for a comparative study of the four Josephs of Judaism, Christianity, Islam and Lloyd Webber/Rice as part of a wider call to encourage the genuine 'theologising' of RE. Such a project would enable *Joseph and the Amazing Technicolor Dreamcoat* to play a significant role in encouraging theological thought among young people. I suspect that it is, in fact, already happening and that both primary and Sunday school teachers, having 'hooked' children with the Rice and Lloyd Webber version do go on to look at the other Josephs. If they do, I wonder if they are struck, as I am, by the extent to which Rice in some ways creates a character more reminiscent of the Islamic Yusuf than the Jewish one. I doubt very much if he had a potted version of the Qur'an to hand as a source along with his *Wonder Book of Bible Stories* but it would have given him more warrant for portraying Joseph as both a pin-up and an angel. Both attributes are found in the way that the story is treated in Sura 12 where the Egyptian's wife (she is not given a name in the Qur'an), having failed to seduce Yusuf, parades him before her women friends who are so overcome by his physical attributes and his star quality that they cut themselves with their dinner knives and proclaim him 'a gracious angel'.

In the Hebrew Bible and the Qur'an the story of Joseph is significant because he is a messenger or prophet of God and for what it says about faith and obedience. There are other themes in the story as well and some of these are tackled in the musical. Interviewed in a 'behind-the-scenes' compilation for the video, Stephen Pimlott gives his view that 'Joseph is about families and family relationships, depression, learning about ourselves and forgiveness – turning bad thoughts into gold. The story ends in forgiveness.' Forgiveness is certainly a key theme in the Genesis story and it is picked up in the musical when Joseph reveals himself to his brothers – although predictably there is no mention of God in this encounter in marked contrast to the biblical account where God is mentioned four times in six verses (Genesis 45.4–10). But it is perhaps time to remind ourselves that *Joseph and the Amazing Technicolor Dreamcoat* was not written primarily as a theological or educational aid, and certainly not as an evangelistic work, but first and foremost as an entertaining romp in the best pantomime tradition – which it has proved itself to be for 35 years.

The success of *Joseph* inspired Rice and Lloyd Webber to tackle another Old Testament theme and they decided to write a musical on the life of King David. While running along Fulham Road to buy an old Ricky Nelson album, Lloyd Webber came up with a strong opening melody to which Rice set the lines 'Samuel, Samuel, this is the first book of Samuel'. However, the project was abandoned in favour of another cantata for schools, *Come Back Richard, Your Country Needs You*, about Richard the Lionheart and the Crusades, which was performed by Alan Doggett at the City of London School. The young composer and lyricist returned to the Bible for their next collaboration, although it was to the New Testament that they now looked for inspiration, spurning the advice of their Jewish agent, David Land, who implored them to do anything but the life of Jesus. The hours that both men had spent in chapel during their public school days played a significant part in their choice of subject. 'If one had had religion sort of rammed down one's throat when one was in school', Lloyd Webber commented, 'it was inevitable, I should think, that Christ would be one of the first subjects one would choose.'[10] Long fascinated by the story of Christ's passion and crucifixion, Rice forsook his *Wonder Book of Bible Stories* and turned instead to Fulton Sheen's *Life of Christ* for its calibration and comparison of the four Gospel writers' accounts of the last week of Jesus' life.

Jesus Christ Superstar, the most original and significant work in the Rice and Lloyd Webber canon, began life as a single (that is, short-playing record), released in November 1969. On one side was the title song which used the tune of the 'Samuel' song from the aborted King David musical and on the other an orchestral piece entitled 'John 19:41' which was to become the last musical item in the subsequent stage show. Although the record had little impact in the UK, it crept into the US top hundred in the last week of the 1960s and eventually made No. 14 in the US singles chart. A double long-playing album released in October 1970 sold two million copies within twelve months.

The stage version of *Jesus Christ Superstar* opened on Broadway in October 1971. Best described as a rock opera, it introduced a radically new style into musical theatre with its through-sung score, harsh, shrieked vocal lines, intense, angst-ridden atmosphere and huge publicity build-up and hype. The Broadway production, which ran for nearly two years, also introduced a virtually unprecedented level of spectacle and over-the-top visual effects with huge angels swinging about on psychedelic wings, dancing dwarfs and lepers and a cruci-fixion scene set on a dazzling golden triangle. A simpler and starker production opened in London in August 1972, running for eight years and overtaking *Oliver!* as the longest-running musical in West End history. A film version made on location in Israel and directed by Norman Jewison with screenplay by Melvyn Bragg was released in 1973. A new, less glitzy production by Gale Edwards, more focused on the relationship between Jesus and Judas, began a two-year run at the Lyceum Theatre, London, in 1996, toured the UK from 1998 and was the basis for a video version released in 2000. A modified version of this new production opened in New York in 2000 where it received a standing ovation from the audience but a predictable panning from the critics.

From the outset, Rice and Lloyd Webber's project was bound to be controversial. Coming hard on the heels of John Lennon's remark that the Beatles were more popular than Jesus, the title of their hit song and of the show which followed it seemed to be equating the founder of Christianity with the idols of pop music and show business. Rice had got the idea for the title from a description of Tom Jones in *Melody Maker* as 'the World's Number One Superstar'. *Joseph*, as we have seen, had invested one Old Testament character with several of the attributes of a star from the world of entertainment. Now the central figure in the New Testament was being portrayed as a superstar. He was also being made the object of some very direct questions that some might consider blasphemous. The chorus which Rice wrote for the initial hit single, originally called 'Judas' song' and reflecting the lyricist's long-standing fascination with the character of the apostle who betrayed Christ, began:

Jesus Christ, Jesus Christ
Who are you? What have you sacrificed?

To which he later added a further question:

Jesus Christ, Superstar,
Do you think you're what they say you are?

For enthusiasts of 'Honest to God' South Bank theology, these kinds of question, expressed through the medium of contemporary rock music, were exciting and welcome. Martin Sullivan gave his blessing to the whole *Superstar* project and offered to stage the rock opera in his cathedral, giving rise to newspaper stories that St Paul's Cathedral would be playing host to John Lennon as Christ and Yoko Ono as Mary Magdalene in the first performance of the new work. The St Paul's performance never came off – nor did a plan to unveil the new rock opera to the press at Oberammergau with a one-off performance on the stage used for the village's famous passion play – but the long-playing album of the show's songs was launched in a Lutheran Church in New York and the sleeve notes for the single version of the 'Superstar' song carried Sullivan's enthusiastic endorsement:

There are people who may be shocked by this record. I ask them to listen to it and think again. It is a desperate cry. 'Who are you, Jesus Christ?' is the urgent enquiry, and a very proper one at that. The record probes some answers and makes some comparisons. The onus is on the listener to come up with his replies. If he is a Christian let him answer for Christ. The singer says, 'Don't get me wrong, I only want to know.' He is entitled to some response.[11]

When *Jesus Christ Superstar* opened on Broadway, the reaction from religious groups was predictably mixed. The show was attacked in equal measure by Christian fundamentalists and atheists. On opening night the theatre was picketed by the National Secular Society with leaflets headed 'Jesus Christ Supersham' and by an irate nun carrying a banner declaring 'I am a Bride of Christ, not Mrs Superstar'. A Roman Catholic priest in New Jersey used the lyrics of the title song as the basis for a sermon and said 'this is exactly what the youth are asking for today'. Billy Graham denounced the musical as bordering on 'blasphemy and sacrilege' because of its failure to acknowledge or celebrate the divine aspects of Christ: 'I object to the fact that it leaves out the Resurrection. If there is no Resurrection, there is no Christianity.' However, he went on to acknowledge that 'the opera asks questions millions of young people are asking, such as "Jesus Christ, are You who they say You are?" If the rock opera causes religious discussion and causes young people to search their bibles, to that extent it may be beneficial.' In Britain, David Sheppard, the Bishop of Woolwich, hailed 'an utterly genuine attempt of two young men to enter into the story of the Cross'.[12]

The 1973 film provoked similarly diverse reactions. The critic for the liberal Protestant weekly, *The Christian Century*, applauded it as the first biblical film to portray Jesus 'in a first-century setting with twentieth-century sensitivity' and described it as 'superb cinema and stimulating theology'. For the conservative *Christianity Today* reviewer, by contrast, it was 'a theological disaster but an ecumenical triumph', the former because 'Jesus looks and acts incompetent, insecure and petulant', the latter because it had managed to unite Protestants, Catholics and Jews in condemnation. The secular press was equally divided in its verdict on the film. *Time* magazine concluded that 'it has reverence, taste, good vibes and it really rocks out', while for *Newsweek* it was 'one of the true fiascoes of modern cinema'.[13]

British theatre critics were similarly polarized in their views of *Jesus Christ Superstar*. For Sheridan Morley

> in terms of taste, it was as unimpeachable as vanilla ice cream and every bit as bland, but judged on its own level as a pop opera designed to reassure the middle-aged without actively alienating the young, it had to be reckoned a rousing success.[14]

Derek Jewell, by contrast, described it in the *Sunday Times* 'as every bit as valid as (and, to me, often more moving than) Handel's *Messiah*'.[15] Reviewing the first night in the *Daily Mail*, Peter Lewis found it 'a pageant-concert of simplified beat numbers' while for Milton Shulman, writing in the *Evening Standard*, the musical's Christ-figure, constantly bathed in a silvery glow and wearing a robe so spotlessly white it could be a testimonial for a biblical detergent called Jeez, is a symbol in the tradition of the palatable knick-knacks sold in the bazaars of Lourdes to commemorate the agony of Christ. The measure of its religious appeal can be judged by the fact that King Herod's song, an irrelevant camp pastiche of a 1920s jazz number, received the most ecstatic reception.[16]

One thing was certain from the reception and coverage that *Jesus Christ Superstar* received from the outset – and it has been confirmed by its huge continuing success since: whether you liked or loathed it, you could not ignore it. The night after the opening, Kevin Sanders, reporter for New York's ABC affiliate TV station (WABC-TV) noted that the musical was 'drawing bigger houses than any church in town, and they're supposed to be telling the same story'. He then turned the programme back to the anchorman, Roger Grimsby, who commented 'I just can't get over their last supper!'[17] Their remarks raise the whole question of how far Rice and Lloyd Webber were trying seriously to retell the Gospel story of the last days of Jesus Christ in a contemporary idiom and how far they were primarily out to entertain and create a blockbuster musical. The work has had a very different feel in its various incarnations. The original Broadway production certainly had a blockbuster feel and anticipates many of the lavish glitzy features which came to be one of the hallmarks of Lloyd Webber musicals. The 1973 film, by contrast, with its setting in the Holy Land, its spare, angular sets and its quieter and more intimate atmosphere had a greater sense of faithfulness to the Gospel story. The 1996 production and 2000 video have a relentless intensity and harshness which hardly qualifies as entertaining but undoubtedly provides an extremely powerful aural and visual experience.

Both composer and librettist have always been very clear that they were not in any way trying to write a 'Christian' musical and that they approached the story of Jesus' last week on earth as a wholly human story. As with *Joseph*, although more obviously and self-consciously, the divine dimension is largely left out although God cannot be wholly airbrushed out of the Jesus story and is a key if unseen presence in the Gethsemane scene. A trio of American academics have recently written that 'the Webber/Rice Superstar Jesus seems to exist as a postmodern Christological phenomenon: He is there, not to show us the way to the Father, but to his own identity'.[18] In an early radio interview Rice stated:

> We approached the opera from the point of view of Christ the man, rather than Christ the God. We had been well-coached in the mechanics of Christianity and its legends and beliefs. That was drummed into us at school. They treated the legends so we decided to treat the bloke as a man. We read the gospels very carefully and that was it. What we did not read was eighty-three other people's interpretations of Christ because we didn't want to be affected by their views.
>
> We tried to humanize Christ, because, for me, I find Jesus as portrayed in the gospels as a God as a very unrealistic figure. He doesn't really get through to me. The same is true, on the other hand, for Judas who is portrayed just as a sort of cardboard cut-out figure of evil. It seems to me there must be much more to these central characters of the story. We tried to make them both human beings. As a result of that, for me, Christ becomes a much more exciting and inspiring man.[19]

Whether Rice and Lloyd Webber succeed in emphasizing the humanity of Jesus is another matter. He is certainly portrayed as a loner, seeming aloof from the other characters on stage and almost permanently anguished and angst-ridden. He is certainly given several human vices, notably a distinct petulance and irritability, clearly displayed in his dealings with his disciples and with the halt and the lame who crowd round him begging to be healed, only to be shooed off with the unbiblical rebuff:

> There's too many of you – don't push me.
> There's too little of me – don't crowd me.
> Heal yourselves!

There is also the repeated reference to Jesus' humanity in Mary Magdalene's line 'He's a man, he's just a man'. I have to confess that I do not myself find the Jesus of *Superstar* a particularly human figure but I have met one woman who came back to church and to faith as a direct result of seeing the show and who told me:

> I was struck for the first time by the human-ness of Jesus – the fact

that he was anguished and angry. It was so different from the anaemic Jesus portrayed in Sunday School and it got me wanting to know him and know more about him.

What *Jesus Christ Superstar* undoubtedly does, and does very well, is to raise a series of significant questions about the person of Jesus – essentially the questions asked in the title song about who he is and what he has sacrificed. The way that these are framed, and left unanswered, leaves open the key question as to whether he is the Son of God. It is, of course, highly significant that these questions are first asked by Judas, who is in many ways portrayed throughout as a much stronger character than Jesus. Rice has said that the key inspiration for both the initial 'Superstar' song and the subsequent rock opera came from a line in a Bob Dylan song: 'I can't think for you, you'll have to decide, Did Judas Iscariot have God on his side?' From the age of ten Rice had been fascinated by the figure of Judas and had harboured an ambition to write a play centring on him with Jesus as a purely incidental character.

Jesus Christ Superstar really looks at Jesus through the eyes of Judas, the intellectual and the analyst among the disciples, one who in the beginning had been his greatest follower but has come to be worried that Jesus is being taken in by the adulation and the star treatment heaped upon him. In Rice's words:

We made him a type of Everyman. Judas did not think of himself as a traitor. He did what he did, not because he was basically evil, but because he was intelligent. He could see Christ becoming something he considered harmful to the Jews. Judas felt they had been persecuted enough . . .

As far as what Christ was saying, general principles of how human beings should live together – Judas approved of this. What Judas was worried about was that as Christ got bigger and bigger and more popular, people began switching their attentions from what Christ was saying to Christ himself. They were saying that Jesus is God, here is the new Messiah, and Judas was terrified because a) he didn't agree with it – he thought Christ was getting out of control and it was affecting Him and b) Judas reckoned that if the movement got too big and people began worshipping Christ as a god, the Romans who were occupying Israel would come down and clobber them.[20]

It is these thoughts which Judas expresses in the opening song in the show – and it is, of course, significant that it is he rather than Jesus who has the opening number. Here he signals his concern about the mythologizing of Jesus: 'if you strip away the myth from the man, you will see where we all soon will be'. Things have got out of hand: 'I remember when this whole thing began/No talk of God then – we called you a man'. The trouble is that Jesus has started to believe the things people say about him: 'You really do believe this talk of God is true'. The genuine value and significance of the human Jesus, a prophet with important and true things to say, has been destroyed by being spiritualized by disciples who have 'too much heaven on their minds'.

This cool analysis contrasts with the excitable, malleable temperament of the other disciples, exemplified by their introductory song, 'What's the buzz? tell me what's happening' which wonderfully expresses their restless urge for gossip and action. Jesus makes his first appearance with the piercing falsetto scream 'Why should you want to know?' which immediately establishes his cantankerous character and gives him the air of a rather sullen, angst-ridden adolescent. His subsequent remarks about not minding about the future and saving tomorrow for tomorrow have a similarly petulant and despairing ring, wholly different from the way that they are treated, for example, in the epic 1965 film *The Greatest Story Ever Told* where the same words are delivered by Jesus in a way which suggests wisdom, calm, reassuring authority and a confidence about the future. In *Jesus Christ Superstar*, by contrast, they are spat out in a way which, in the words of a recent study, depicts Jesus as 'a frustrated "loose cannon" with little sense of direction and little hope for the future and little sense of his role in that future, whatever it might be'.[21]

An altogether gentler note is introduced by Mary Magdalene, whose first song 'Try not to get worried' provides one of the few peaceful and calming numbers in the opera. The extent to which *Jesus Christ Superstar* suggests a sexual relationship between Mary and Jesus has been much discussed by critics and commentators. The most recent production seems to hint at a triangular relationship between Judas, Mary and Jesus. Mary is evidently deeply moved and affected by Jesus but her feelings for him are complex and ambiguous. Her key song, 'I don't know how to love him' works at one level as the show's standard love ballad, tailored for the hit parade and engineered for maximum emotional impact. Yet it also contains some very penetrating observations about the disconcerting effect that Jesus must have had on those close to him. For all her repeated reassurance to herself that 'he's just a man', it is clear that for Mary Magdalene Jesus does have a strange and unfathomable quality unlike any other man she has met, which is both frightening – 'He scares me so' – and transformative – 'I've been changed, yes really changed' – maybe even redemptive?

The most clearly drawn figures in *Superstar* are Caiaphas, Annas and the other Jewish priests, sinister, calculating, portrayed in both stage and film versions in grotesque costumes, unqualified baddies with no redeeming features. It is largely their caricatured and totally unsympathetic portrayal that has led to accusations of anti-Semitism being periodically made against Rice and Lloyd Webber. It is, in fact, difficult to see that their treatment of the Jewish authorities is any more anti-Semitic than that of the Gospels. Here, as elsewhere, the rock opera follows both the biblical narrative and the nuances of the Gospel writers fairly closely. This faithfulness to the scriptural account is also evident in the handling of the entrance into Jerusalem where the crowd are willing a reluctant Jesus to be king. The 'Hosanna, Heysanna' chorus seems to me to contain considerable food for theological thought and I have taken it as a text for a Palm Sunday sermon. The line 'Hey JC, JC, won't you smile at me?' perfectly encapsulates the crowd's desire for a friendly, benevolent monarch, just as the subsequent request 'Will you fight for me?' expresses their hope for a military leader who will take up the Zealot cause and defend the Jews from Roman oppression. Here the crowd are very much treating Jesus like a superstar and celebrity pop idol, wanting his acknowledgement of their adulation – 'Christ you know I love you, did you see I waved?' – and his assurance of their salvation – 'So tell me that I'm saved'. What they get is neither smile, military action, nor assurance but rather a typically grumpy and seemingly ungrateful put-down in which they are told that none of them understand 'what power is, what glory is' and that 'to conquer death you only have to die'.

Jesus Christ Superstar is so starkly realistic and uncompromisingly 'in your face' as to represent in many ways the complete antithesis of the whole 'dream theme' that I have characterized as being central to the ethos of the musicals of the mid-twentieth century (and which is certainly present in several of both Rice's and Lloyd Webber's other works). There is, however, one significant song about a dream, Pilate's 'I dreamed I met a Galilean, a most amazing man'. It is unlike almost anything else in the show in its gentle, understated wistfulness. Set in the soulful key of B flat minor, it gives another dimension to Jesus' humanity – 'He had that look you very rarely find – the haunting hunted kind' – and also provides the opera's only real acknowledgement of the huge impact that he was to have after his death – 'I saw thousands of millions crying for this man'.

There is another scene which evokes a dream-like atmosphere. The Last Supper is accompanied by a relaxing and rather surreal ballad, 'Look at all my trials and tribulations sinking in a gentle pool of wine', in which the slightly drunken disciples congratulate themselves on making it as apostles and look forward to writing the gospels in their retirement 'so they'll still talk about us when we've died'. Their self-indulgent fantasizing is brought very sharply to an end by Jesus' angry words:

> For all you care about this wine could be my blood
> For all you care this bread could be my body.

This remarkable couplet, which turns the conventional Christian understanding of the Eucharist on its head, is surely the most original and radical theological statement in the entire opera. Far from instituting a sacrament and a perpetual remembrance of his passion, Jesus' words about bread and wine here simply serve to point up the fickleness and lack of understanding of his followers. He goes on to reflect despairingly: 'I must be mad thinking I'll be remembered'. Here more than anywhere else in *Superstar* is conveyed a real sense of Jesus as the man of sorrows, despised and rejected, the one who, in the familiar words of John's Gospel, 'came to his own and his own received him not'.

This sense of Jesus as one who is lonely, isolated and misunderstood is reinforced in his anguished soliloquy 'Gethsemane'. Here God is a very real presence – but one to be railed against and bombarded with angry questions. In this song Jesus betrays a clear feeling of failure and disillusion – 'Then I was inspired/Now I'm sad and tired' – yet he also acknowledges God's sovereignty, albeit in a slightly unconventional manner – 'God thy will is hard/But you hold every card'. This song wrestles in a harrowing way with the whole question of patripassianism and the necessity for Jesus' suffering. Throughout it Jesus remains faithful and obedient to God even though he does not begin to understand why he is being inflicted with so much excruciating pain and suffering:

I will drink your cup of poison, nail me to the cross and break me
Bleed me, beat me, kill me, take me now – before I change my mind.

It is left to the mysteriously resurrected Judas (a significant departure from the Gospel story which has been strangely little noticed by evangelical critics) to ask the key questions about Jesus' identity and mission with the backing of a particularly vulgar line of chorus girls. He also has a host of supplementary queries for a man whom he now seems to regard in a rather different light from his dismissive verdict in the show's opening song:

Why'd you choose such a backward time and such a strange land?
If you'd come back today you'd have reached a whole nation
Israel in 4 BC had no mass communication.

Tell me what you think about your friends at the top
Who d'you think besides yourself's the pick of the crop?
Buddah was he where it's at? Is he where you are?
Could Mahomet move a mountain or was that just PR?

Jesus Christ Superstar ends with a rare moment of silence and stillness as the crucifixion is depicted in stark and simple terms. The contrast with the heavily amplified rock music of the rest of the work is palpable and highly moving. The fact that it ends with the Crucifixion and has no hint of a Resurrection has, not surprisingly, been the cause of much Christian criticism. To have included a Resurrection scene would, of course, have been to have answered the question about the nature and person of Jesus which the rock opera deliberately leaves open. It would also almost certainly have invited a vulgar, over-the-top *coup de théâtre* which would have produced a shining Superstar Jesus looking even more like a Chippendale or an Arian blond bombshell than Joseph does in his technicolor dream coat. It is extraordinarily difficult to portray the Resurrection convincingly and satisfactorily on stage – and we should acknowledge that theologians and preachers themselves have huge problems with conceptualizing and visualizing it. By ending with the Crucifixion, *Jesus Christ Superstar* not only leaves open the question as to who Jesus was. It also puts a premium on faith. Are those who want to see a definite Resurrection appearance at the end of the show rather like Thomas, wanting visual proof and certainty where we can only walk in faith and trust?

Does the Crucifixion ending possibly also compensate in some way for what is perhaps the most serious theological weakness in *Jesus Christ Superstar*, the total absence of any allusion to or suggestion of a doctrine of atonement? Does the image of Calvary at the end emphasize Jesus' sacrifice? This is certainly the view of a reviewer of the video for the *Church Times*: 'The ending is Johannine: we witness God's glory when all is accomplished through Christ's self-sacrifice.'[22] I am not convinced myself that *Jesus Christ Superstar* really conveys any sense of God's glory, either in its final moments or at any other point. That is not what Rice and Lloyd Webber were out to do. They certainly convey the agony of Jesus' death, and for all his protestations that he dies without knowing why, they also convey a sense of redemptive power at work in him, though it is demonstrated in his life rather than through his death. Jesus has changed Mary Magdalene, the man-hating prostitute, into someone who loves and cares for a particular man very much in the way that Don Quixote changes Aldonza by the way he treats here in *Man of La Mancha*. He has also transformed Judas, the one who distrusts and betrays him, into a man full of remorse who finds himself singing 'I don't know how to love him'. In so far as there is a theological theme or agenda in the rock opera, however, it is focused on the figure of Judas rather than Jesus and specifically on the question of how far he was a free and voluntary agent and how far an instrument of God in the events leading up to the Crucifixion.

It is difficult to sum up *Jesus Christ Superstar*. Its staggering success over three decades suggests that it touches a chord with many people. It can hardly be its entertainment value. Apart from King Herod's song, inserted late in the day to provide some light relief and reuse a tune originally written for *Richard the Lionheart*, the score is unremittingly tense and anguished. It is the first of the gloomy, doomy, through-sung blockbusters that were to dominate musical theatre throughout the last three decades of the twentieth century. Described by one critic as 'entertainment designed to overwhelm', it certainly leaves its audience drained and exhausted. At the same time it has presented millions of theatre- and cinema-goers with a highly original and theologically nuanced presentation of the life and death of Jesus and left them with a host of significant questions about who he was and what it meant. In raising these questions, it is in a way a much more theological work than Bach's great settings of the passion narratives which are full of drama but accept the Gospel texts at face value.

Five months before *Jesus Christ Superstar* hit Broadway with such spectacular razzmatazz and hype, another musical based on the Gospel accounts of Jesus' life opened with very little fanfare or fuss at the Cherry Lane Theatre, New York. *Godspell*, which clocked up 2,651 performances in its opening run, has proved every bit as durable as *Superstar*, if somewhat less lucrative for its creators. In the year following its off-Broadway opening, seven professional companies were touring the US with the show and by the mid-1970s there were 25 companies performing it around the world. *Godspell* had a three-year opening run in London from 1971 and finally made it to Broadway in 1976. A film version was released in 1973. Easier to stage and much more accessible to amateur performance than *Jesus Christ Superstar,* and having something of the exuberance and freshness of *Joseph,* it has become a favourite with schools, churches and colleges. In 1999 it was the most performed show at the Edinburgh Festival fringe. It has been staged at the White House and the Vatican. In 2002 a new British touring production opened under the direction of Scott Schwartz, son of the composer.

Godspell was the work of two young men who were almost exact contemporaries of Rice and Lloyd Webber. John-Michael Tebelak and Stephen Schwartz first met as fellow students at Carnegie Mellon University. For his master's course in drama the 21-year-old Tebelak was required to direct a production of a classic or modern work. He asked if he could write a play of his own and turned to St Matthew's Gospel for his story line. He left the university without finishing his coursework but was given a degree on the strength of *Godspell* which he first performed in 1970 with a cast made up of friends and acquaintances who sang his simple settings of hymn texts from the Episcopal Church hymnal. A professional producer who saw the piece recognized its commercial potential and its need for a stronger score and brought in Stephen Schwartz, who had recently graduated from Carnegie Mellon and had just finished his own musical *Pippin*, about the son of King Charlemagne, to compose new settings for the songs.

In contrast to the Englishness of the cricket-mad Rice and the Victorian church enthusiast Lloyd Webber, Tebalek and Schwartz were quintessentially American college boys. Yet ironically, it is *Godspell* which is the more 'British' musical in terms of being under-stated, gently humorous and not taking itself too seriously, while *Superstar* has the brash vulgarity that, rightly or wrongly, tends to be associated with American musicals. *Godspell* has an altogether more amateur and low-key feel to it and displays another British trait in closely resembling the form and style of the medieval mystery play in its dramatization of Gospel stories through such devices as dressing up, song and mime, its concern to universalize the message and bring in contemporary references and its direct involvement of the audience. Robert Ellis pointed to this aspect in one of the earliest academic assessments of the work: 'When a modern theatre-goer takes in *Godspell*, he is seeing the closest approximation our times have made to the medieval religious drama.'[23]

How does the portrayal of Jesus compare in these two virtually contemporaneous musicals? Both bear the hallmarks of the period in which they were conceived and written and both are about a human rather than a divine figure. While the Jesus of *Superstar* is the outsider of Camus' novels and the angry young man of John Osborne's plays, the Jesus of *Godspell* is the relaxed, laid-back, child-like hippy of Haight Ashbury. In this respect, *Godspell* is the more American show. If *Superstar*'s most obvious antecedent is Pete Townshend's pioneering 1969 rock opera, *Tommy*, *Godspell*'s is *Hair*. It has, indeed, been well described as '*Hair* with a haircut'. The *Godspell* Jesus is a man slightly apart from others but not in the petulant, moody way of the *Superstar* Jesus. He is a clown with a painted face, a joker, a teacher, a story teller, a person whom it is fun to be with and yet who has a clear and charismatic authority and is very much the leader of the gang – altogether a much more relaxed and confident figure than Rice and Lloyd Webber's Jesus. In his script notes Schwartz wrote: 'he must be the most charismatic individual in the cast. High energy, charming, funny, gentle but with strength. He is the sort of person others instinctively follow.'[24] This last point is particularly important. There is a much greater sense than in *Superstar* of people giving up their homes and careers to follow Jesus and much more obvious reason why they should be motivated to do so – not just by the temptation to drop out and lead a counter-cultural flower power lifestyle but through the irresistible call of a strong and prophetic leader.

Godspell's focus in terms of plot is at once both broader and narrower than that of *Superstar*. While covering the whole of Jesus' ministry from his baptism by John to the crucifixion rather than just the last week of his life, it concentrates exclusively on his preaching and teaching and his relationship with his small coterie of disciples. There are no crowd scenes in *Godspell*, no cleansing of the temple or trial and no appearance by Herod, Pilate or the Jewish high priests.

Indeed, the only named biblical characters who appear are Jesus, John the Baptist and Judas, the latter two in early productions being played by the same person as a composite figure who, according to the script notes, 'has attributes of both biblical figures: he is both Jesus' lieutenant and most ardent disciple and the doubter who begins to question and rebel. He is the most serious and intellectual of the group.'[25] The rest of the cast simply assume their own names and play the disciples as contemporary modern figures.

Godspell is a much more conventional musical than the through-sung *Superstar* in its structure with substantial dialogue scenes interspersed with songs. Virtually all the dialogue is made up of direct quotation from Jesus' aphorisms and parables as recorded in the Gospels. To this extent, it has more of the feel of a 'Christian' musical with an evangelistic purpose of putting across Jesus' teaching in a relevant contemporary form. Tebelak, who had seriously considered entering the Episcopal priesthood, was moved to write *Godspell* after attending an Easter morning service at St Paul's Episcopal Cathedral in Pittsburgh in 1970. He found it uninspired and lacking in joy with the clergy rushing mechanically through the liturgy: 'I left with the feeling that rather than rolling the rock away from the tomb, they were piling more on.' He sensed a hostility on the part of several of the congregation to his own appearance as a long-haired student. After the service, he was stopped by a policeman and frisked for drugs outside the cathedral. *Godspell*, he later noted, was written

> as a statement against the organized Church – as an indictment of it for keeping religion so serious and removed from the people . . . it was designed to be part of the Jesus awareness, but neither the cast nor I could be styled as Jesus freaks, nor would we want to be.[26]

Critics have been divided about the extent to which *Godspell* is in fact about 'Jesus awareness'. For the *New York Times* critic, the film version is 'less a celebration of the life and teachings of Jesus than a celebration of theater, music, youthful high spirits, New York City locations and the zoom lens'. The *New Republic* critic concurred: 'In anything remotely resembling something that could begin to be called a religious sense, *Godspell* is a zero; it is Age-of-Aquarius love fed through a quasi-gospel funnel, with a few light-hearted supernatural touches.' The Jesuit periodical *America* suggested that 'what is proclaimed in this musical is not Christ, but a nostalgic escape into a lost childhood, when, according to most adults, the grass was always green and every day was Sunday'. However the *Saturday Review* concluded that 'with no religious trappings whatsoever [it] provides a religious experience of extraordinary intensity' and *Christianity Today* praised its portrayal of 'the free frolicking joy of following Christ'.[27]

Conservative evangelical critics are predictably uneasy about *Godspell*'s portrayal of Jesus as a clown and the absence of a Resurrection scene and any expression of atonement theory. A website entitled 'Godspell the ultimate blasphemy' states 'The Lord Jesus Christ was beaten, smitten, mocked and crucified as a "curse" for your sins. He didn't come bouncing along as a clown!' and asks 'how in the name of sanity does an afro-haired, Superman-shirted, clown-face-painted, harlequin-Jesus possibly remind anyone with a brain that Jesus was an historical figure, the son of God?' It goes on to ask 'where is the blood?', making the point that 'if there is no blood, there is no Gospel' and complains 'Godspell ends with a DEAD Jesus – no resurrection! And no Resurrection = No Gospel.'[28] The question as to whether the show is fundamentally Christian or not is one of the liveliest and most frequently surfacing debates on the *Godspell* chat page in the Musicals.NetForum website, another being how best to stage a Resurrection scene at the end of the musical. While it continues to offend Christian fundamentalists, *Godspell* also falls foul of the politically correct lobby for being too Christian. In 1999 a school board in Allegheny County, Pennsylvania, upheld the complaint of a Jewish parent that 'If you're not a Christian, this is not your history' and voted 7:1 against a production of a musical which it felt was 'trying to convert people from one religion to another'.

Godspell has been noticeably more popular for performance by church groups than *Jesus Christ Superstar*, although this may have as much to do with its greater accessibility and simplicity as with the nature of its message. Its creators have also been happy to mark significant milestones in its history with religious services and church-based events. Shooting of the 1973 film version began with a prayer service in front of the Empire diner in New York. A special performance in the Cathedral of St John the Divine in New York in 1977 celebrated its success and the tenth anniversary of the show's opening in Los Angeles was celebrated by a benefit show at the First Christian Church of North Hollywood.

Godspell's great strength is that it can function both as a piece of Christian musical theatre pointing up the radical kingdom message of

Jesus' teaching and as an exuberant exploration of the theme of community. I suspect that this may reflect different emphases on the part of its two creators. Tebelak undoubtedly wrote the work originally with a clear message in mind for a Church which, in his view, 'has become so dour and pessimistic: it has to reclaim its joy and hope. I see *Godspell* as a celebration of life'. He also sought to put across the broader universal message of Jesus' teaching as is clear from his remark that 'I chose the parables very carefully. The Prodigal Son, for instance, is extremely important to young people today because it deals with the problem of the generation gap. The woman take in adultery stresses compassion and understanding'.[29] For Schwartz the emphasis in *Godspell* is rather on the importance and dynamics of community. He has written:

> The first act of *Godspell* must be about the formation of a community. Eight separate individuals, led and guided by Jesus (who is helped by his assistant, John the Baptist/Judas), gradually come to form a communal unit. This happens through the playing of games and the telling and absorption of lessons, and each of the eight individuals has his or her own moment of committing to Jesus and to the community. When Jesus applies clown make-up to their faces after 'Save the People' he is having them take on an external physical manifestation that they are his disciples, temporarily separating themselves from the rest of society. But the internal journey of each character is separate and takes its individual course and period of time. Exactly when and why this moment of commitment occurs is one of the important choices each of the actors must make, in collaboration of course with the director.
>
> In the second act, after an opening number that continues the sense of playfulness and includes some good-natured teasing by Jesus and his followers, Jesus announces: 'This is the beginning'. By this he means that now that the community has been formed, they are ready to move through the challenging sequence of events leading to the Crucifixion. When Jesus removes their make-up, just prior to the Last Supper, he is saying that they have assimilated his teachings into themselves and no longer need the outward trappings to brand them as disciples. And when Jesus is taken from them at the end, the rest of the company remain fused as a community, ready and able to carry forth the lessons they have learned.
>
> If this basic dramatic arc is not achieved, *Godspell* does not exist;

no matter how amusing and tuneful individual moments may be, the production has failed.[30]

What is striking about the community of *Godspell* is its very self-contained nature. In the musical Jesus has no interaction with the crowd or with humanity as a whole. He is simply shown in his relationship with his disciples who are themselves cut off from the rest of the world. This isolation is reinforced by the urban playground set surrounded by a high wire netting fence on which Jesus is crucified at the end. In the film the streets and parks through which Jesus leads the disciples skipping and dancing are strangely deserted of all other life. There are intriguing theological and biblical resonances here – of the Marcan secrecy motif and the Johannine emphasis on Jesus and those who follow him standing against and in opposition to the world. But they are counterbalanced by a tendency towards universalism, particularly marked in the film version's treatment of the parable of the sheep and the goats where Jesus comes back to rescue the goats left bleating and apparently damned and tells them to join the saved sheep, and by the involvement of the audience in the community of Jesus and his disciples. This involvement takes various forms: through being encouraged to laugh and sing along with the cast, in the 2002 Scott Schwartz production, through John the Baptist 'baptizing' the audience by flicking them with a sponge dipped in a bucket after he has baptized Jesus, and most significantly of all, by the invitation to take a glass of wine or fruit juice during the interval. In some productions what Tebelak called 'this party between the acts' takes place on stage while in others those playing the disciples bring trays of glasses down into the auditorium. Either way there is a real sense here of communion and of an almost liturgical participation by the audience in the shared life of the disciples.

There are other interesting theological nuances in *Godspell*. The physical portrayal of Jesus with the painted face and clothes of a clown was directly influenced by Harvey Cox's depiction of 'Christ the Harlequin' in his book *The Feast of Fools*. There is, of course, a long tradition which Tebelak tapped into of 'the painted jester whose foolishness is wiser than wisdom' and of the clown as the one who stands outside the norm, inverting the world order and sensing another reality. In painting the faces of his disciples, Jesus establishes them as entering into this other realm. He also confirms their apartness and membership of the gang. The theme of discipleship is also treated in a theological way. There is a considerable emphasis on the notion of vocation and calling which is completely absent in *Jesus Christ Superstar*.

The emphasis on Jesus' call to discipleship is brilliantly conveyed in the 1973 film which is set in New York and begins with John the Baptist wheeling his handcart across Brooklyn Bridge, proclaiming the jubilee on his shofar or ram's horn and singing 'Prepare ye the way of the Lord'. The eight characters who will be his disciples, respectively a car park attendant, a taxi driver, a fashion model, a shop assistant, a waitress in a diner, a ballet dancer, a college student and a smart businesswoman about town, are seen leaving their places of work when they hear the horn or see him. They join John the Baptist at a fountain in Central Park where Jesus appears to be baptized and then leads his motley band of followers, pied-piper like, through the deserted streets and parks of the city until they end up in the run-down garage lot full of broken-down cars and tyres which becomes their playground.

Stage versions of *Godspell* have a rather different beginning which introduces a more intellectual and philosophical note. After an opening speech by Jesus about the majesty of God, the first scene represents the Tower of Babel (or Babble) with competing messages from Socrates, Thomas Aquinas, Galileo, Martin Luther, Leonard da Vinci, Edward Gibbon, Frederic Nietzsche, Jean Paul Sartre and Buckminster Fuller rising to a cacophonous crescendo. In Scott Schwartz's 2002 production Socrates sends an e-mail, Galileo is on line and the others text messages on mobile phones. The discordant babble of their competing philosophies is finally silenced by John the Baptist blowing his shofar and singing 'Prepare ye the way of the Lord'. There is almost a suggestion of a strong *Logos* theology here in the way that the announcement of the coming of Jesus cuts through the chaos in its simplicity and call to order.

The songs in *Godspell* are of three kinds. There are straight settings of verses from the Bible, like 'Prepare ye the way of the Lord', 'O Bless the Lord, my soul' (Psalm 103), 'You are the light of the world' (Matthew 5.13–16), 'Alas, alas, for you, lawyers and Pharisees' (Matthew 23.13–37) and 'On the willows' (Psalm 137). Then there are traditional hymns set to catchy contemporary tunes. Jesus' first song is the nineteenth-century radical Chartist hymn by Ebenezer Elliot, 'When wilt thou save the people?' which is picked up as a rallying cry by the disciples. The harvest favourite, 'We plough the fields and scatter', and Thomas Pollock's 1870 hymn 'Father, hear thy children's call' are also given an upbeat makeover. Schwartz's most dramatic transformation is achieved with 'Turn back, O man', Clifford Bax's great humanist anthem of repentance, which is turned into a seductive and suggestive vamp for a femme fatale. These four hymns represent a rather bizarre choice for a musical about Jesus with a self-consciously modern feel to it. They are noticeably archaic in their language and between them include no Christological references, being almost determinedly universalist and unitarian in character. Of similar provenance is the show's greatest hit, a setting of the thirteenth-century prayer attributed to St Richard of Chichester:

Day by day, day by day,
Oh, dear Lord, three things I pray.
To see Thee more clearly,
Love Thee more dearly,
Follow Thee more nearly,
Day by day.

The third and smaller group of songs are those in which both words and music are original and specially written for the show, mostly by Stephen Schwartz. The most effective, 'All for the Best', is a wonderful vaudeville parody which has Jesus signing against Judas. Jesus describes this life as being full of cares and reflects on the reality and depth of human depression:

Your mood and your robe are both a deep blue
You'd bet that Job had nothing on you.

His ultimate message, however, is hopeful:

Don't forget that
When you go to heaven you'll be blest
Yes, it's all for the best.

Judas, in contrast, represents and reflects on those who have everything in this world:

They get the centre of the meat
Cushions on the seat
Houses on the street where it's sunny

The implication here is that those who suffer in this world will prosper in the next. In keeping with the universalist tendency throughout the show, the song refrains from suggesting that those who have an easy time here will be damned later. It merely repeats the refrain: 'It's all for the best'. It is, perhaps, significant that a song originally in the first act which has a rather less universalist message was later dropped. 'Learn your lesson well' warns sinners:

> You'd better pay attention, build your comprehension.
> There's gonna be a quiz at your ascension
> Not to mention any threat of hell.

Although, even here, there is a strong implication that the way to heaven is open to everyone:

> Ev'ry bright description of the promised land meant
> You can reach it if you keep alert.

In general, *Godspell* has a distinctly light-hearted and playful atmosphere, its catchy folky tunes a world away from the anguished shrieks and shrill chords of *Superstar*. It is not without its own pathos and agony, however. The crucifixion is represented by Jesus being spreadeagled on the wire fence round the playground and subjected to violent convulsions, as if the fence is electrified. He sings 'Oh God, I'm bleeding', 'Oh God, I'm dying', 'Oh God, I'm dead' as the disciples wind long red ribbons around him. Robert Ellis sees a further parallel here with the medieval mystery plays:

> In *Godspell* Christ is one of us. That playground fence we have all scaled becomes His cross. We are invited, in late medieval fashion, to participate in the agony. 'We hung up our lives', the last line of the last song, is, like many of the earlier lyrics, ambiguous. If it suggests to the traditionally minded the fact of man's sinfulness, it also points to the common bond of suffering. We do not know what to do about this death or even what to make of it, but we are together in our feeling, and we do not come away overwhelmed by the futility of the death. The festal freshness of the first act has passed into an extended sobriety. *Godspell*, lacking the Resurrection which would soon follow in the medieval cycle, cannot end comically or joyously. Within its limits it is too honest.[31]

In fact, productions of *Godspell* very rarely end with Jesus left hanging on the cross. In both the original stage production and in the film the crucifixion scene is followed by the disciples taking his body off the fence, hoisting it on their shoulders and walking out singing 'Long live God' with the show ending with a final reprise of 'Prepare ye the way of the Lord' in the case of the original stage version and of 'Day by Day' in the film. Many productions, especially those in churches, have added a resurrection scene but Schwartz is adamant that this is a mistake:

> *Godspell* is not meant to have a resurrection. *Godspell* was never meant to be a musical version of the story of Jesus. It is rather a story about the formation of a community. By the end of the play we are supposed to feel this community is going to thrive after Jesus is gone based on the lessons learned from his teachings. Many productions have added a resurrection, and some have used the song 'Long Live God/Prepare Ye' for this purpose, but it isn't true to the original intent of the creators of the show.[32]

The 2002 professional production of *Godspell* dispenses with 'Long live God' and 'Prepare ye the way of the Lord', with their implication of a continuing divine presence or even, perhaps, a second coming, and ends instead with a more humanist, or certainly human-centred, anthem, 'We can build a beautiful city'. This song, originally written by Schwartz for the 1973 film to replace 'We beseech thee, hear us' and subsequently reworked, has featured in several different places in the show in recent productions. In the 2000 off-Broadway production it was placed between 'We beseech thee' and 'On the willows' and in the 2001 recording it is sung by Jesus leading the company at the opening of Act 2. In many ways, it takes us back to the optimistic Pelagian spirit of Rodgers and Hammerstein:

We can build a beautiful city,
Yes we can, yes we can.
We can build a beautiful city,
And call it the city of man.

In its earliest version the song even picked up the familiar dream theme and proclaimed 'We're not afraid of voicing all the things we're dreaming of'. Schwartz came to find the original lyrics too sentimental and in the early 1990s for a projected new production in Los Angeles, which had just experienced violent race riots, he changed them to reflect the less optimistic mood of the times:

> Out of the ruins and rubble
> Out of the smoke
> Out of our night of struggle
> Can we see a ray of hope?
> One pale thin ray reaching for the day.

In its new form, this song gives an uplifting end to *Godspell* but one which clearly envisages the future hope for the world lying with humankind rather than with God, or the angels:

> We can build a beautiful city,
> Yes we can, yes we can.
> We can build a beautiful city,
> Not a city of angels
> But we can build a city of man.[33]

The introduction of this song and its subsequent reworkings perhaps underline the extent to which *Godspell* has moved in a more consciously humanist direction over the thirty years or more since it was written by John-Michael Tebelak 'as a part of the Jesus awareness'. Stephen Schwartz has always insisted that despite its subject matter and strong reliance on the Gospels, *Godspell* is not primarily a religious work. This perspective is shared by his son, Scott, director of the most recent professional production:

> The show was ultimately meant for an audience that did not need to be religious or believe in Jesus as the Son of God, but would hopefully come to respect Jesus as a very good and wise man . . .
>
> It is the story of Jesus and deals with the coming together of the apostles and then the last days of Christ on earth. If you're not a religious person or you're not interested in religion, I think that what the show really is about is a group of people who are strangers and these strangers come together slowly under the leadership of a man who happens to be named Jesus but who could just as well be called Daniel or Jonathan. This guy has some messages that he wants to get out there and they're very good messages, all around

the theme of love thy neighbour. What happens is these strangers get to know each other and come together to form a community and learn how to communicate with each other – communication is a very important theme in the show. Once this community is formed, it's about the challenges that communities go through in the real world, specifically the challenge of losing the leader and then seeing what happens – does the community choose to rally together and go on or does it dissolve?[34]

A somewhat mixed message comes out of this statement. Is *Godspell* basically about the personality and teachings of Jesus or is it about the forming and sustaining of a community? Scott Schwartz's suggestion that it is about what happens when a community loses its leader seems hard to square with the abrupt ending after the crucifixion. The musical does not begin to explore what happens to the disciples after Jesus has gone. For all that it ends with his agonizing death, indeed, *Godspell* comes over first and foremost as an exuberant and light-hearted celebration of life and of the life-affirming if challenging messages of Jesus' teaching in the parables. In that respect, it stands in marked contrast to the unremitting angst of *Jesus Christ Superstar* and the gloomy doomy through-sung blockbusters which followed in its wake.

5

Now life has killed the dream I dreamed –

Les Misérables

Les Misérables is the most significant single work in this study. As I have already mentioned, it was the experience of attending a matinée performance attended largely by young people that awakened me to the spiritual power of musicals. I have subsequently learned of three separate 'conversions' to Christianity which came about through the experience of watching a performance of the show. No other musical has anything approaching its spiritual power and epic scope. For some it is unbearably pretentious, over-long, over-loud and hugely over-hyped. For others it represents an unparalleled theatrical experience. It has been seen by well over 50 million people in more than 35 countries.

There is a direct link between *Les Misérables* and *Jesus Christ Superstar*. Alain Boublil was bowled over by the Rice and Lloyd Webber rock opera when he attended its New York premiere in 1973 and resolved to find a suitably epic and sweeping subject which he could treat in a similar way. He and composer Claude-Michel Schönberg first attempted a musical on the French Revolution which became a best-selling record and had a respectable run at the Palais des Sports in Paris with Schönberg playing the part of Louis XVI. Their decision to write a musical based on Victor Hugo's classic novel *Les Misérables* was partly inspired by another British musical. Seeing a revival of *Oliver!* produced by Cameron Mackintosh led Boublil to reflect on the riches of characterization and plot in the great nineteenth-century picaresque novels. He was struck particularly by *Oliver!*'s graphic depiction of the underworld and by the character of the Artful Dodger which gave him the inspiration for Gavroche, the little street urchin who plays a key role in the musical.

First performed in Paris in 1980 and brought five years later to London where it has played ever since, *Les Misérables* represents a decisive break with the 'dream theme' of the classic Broadway shows and ushers in the age of the 'gloomy doomy' blockbusters which dominated both the British and the world stage through the last two decades of the twentieth century. When Cameron Mackintosh, whose gut instinct and commercial acumen transformed the French hit show into a global mega-hit, shared Boublil's words and Schönberg's music with Alan Jay Lerner in the hope that he might agree to write English lyrics, the veteran Broadway lyricist commented 'I think it's terrific but it's just not for me. I write about people's dreams, and this is about people's suffering.'[1] He had identified the crucial respect in which the new-style musical of the 1980s differed from the old. In *Les Misérables* dreams are not so much sought and followed as shattered and wasted.

Les Misérables became more overtly religious in tone as it went through its various stages of conception and gestation. The original French concept album recorded in 1980 does contain some significant religious language and Christian references but, as might be expected from a concept album made to generate interest in the future show from potential promoters, its emphasis is on love and the cause of political and social revolution rather than on the themes of forgiveness, redemption and sacrifice which loom so large in Victor Hugo's novel. As the show was gradually reworked for stage presentation by Boublil and Schönberg, more emphasis was put on the religious aspects of the novel. This aspect was further developed by the British creative team assembled by Cameron Mackintosh. As a result, the final English version by Herbert Kretzmer reads almost like a liturgical text with 31 references to God, many of which are in the context of prayers (the original French concept album had just 12 and no prayers), 6 references to Jesus (there are none in the French album), 8 mentions of Heaven and of prayer and 4 of the soul and explicit allusions to Calvary, the passion and the blood of Christ, the blood of the martyrs, the way of the Lord, sacrifice, salvation and sainthood. One of the show-stopping numbers is essentially a prayer set to music ('Bring him home') and the musical ends with the recitation of part of the Lord's Prayer and a theological statement of some profundity: 'To love another person is to see the face of God.'

The extent to which the musical was given a more explicitly religious dimension is evident even in a number as simple and incidental as the chorus sung at the wedding of Marius and Cossette. In the original French concept album, this is a straightforward celebration of human happiness and love:

> Soyez hereux, chérissez-vous toujours
> Et faites-vous des enfants de l'amour.

Kretzmer's translation, however, invokes the heavenly powers and introduces a more metaphysical note into the celebrations:

> Ring out the bells
> Upon this day of days
> May all the angels
> Of the Lord above
> In jubilation
> Sing their songs of praise.

Trevor Nunn, responsible for realizing the English version on stage, and his co-director, John Caird, felt, quite rightly, that the original French version had underplayed the religious element in Hugo's novel. Nunn has said that for him *Les Misérables* is primarily a show about God, and more specifically about the very different ways in which he is perceived by the three central male characters:

> Javert is someone who believes in a vengeful, Old Testament God who will bring down plague and pestilence on all those who disobey the law; Valjean, in the light of his own experience, has come to believe in redemption and that justice can exist in our world; Thenardier not only believes that God is dead but that he died a long time ago and that we are all fair game for him.[2]

In fact, these are not the only perspectives on God represented by characters in the show. There is also the Bishop of Digne's saintly embodiment of and witness to a divine being of infinite mercy, compassion and forgiveness and Fantine's loss of faith in the whole concept of a loving and forgiving God as her dreams are shattered by the reality of life. God is certainly a dominant and ubiquitous if unseen presence throughout the musical. He is first mentioned very near the beginning when the Bishop blesses Valjean and tells him that he has bought his soul for God. He is invoked in the closing lines of Act 1 ('Tomorrow we'll discover/What our God in Heaven has in store') and in the Act 2 showstopper, 'God on high, hear my prayer' and is the last word in the last song of the show before the final reprise of the student anthem: 'To love another person is to see the face of God'.

Some critics and commentators have attributed the wide appeal of *Les Misérables* across cultural and linguistic boundaries to the centrality and universality of its theme of the struggle against oppression and social iniquity. But Edward Behr is surely right to suggest that this is neither its dominant motif nor the grounds of its huge global appeal:

> The universal aspect of *Les Misérables* has less to do with political upheavals and revolution than with the eternal truths about human nature – and belief in God. In essence, the story of Jean Valjean is that of a sudden, Pauline conversion, and a determination to retain the almost impossible ethical standards he has set himself. The quest for saintliness is the one thing that all religions have in common.[3]

For Scott Miller, 'It is a show about the nobility of the human spirit, faith, redemption, and other spiritual concepts. Religion and spirituality – as well as the distortion of it and the lack of it – informs most of the action of the show.'[4] This is perhaps putting it a little too strongly but what is surely incontestable is that *Les Misérables* the musical is essentially expounding two deeply spiritual (and deeply Christian) themes – the power of forgiveness to beget forgiveness and the redemptive quality of sacrificial love.

These two themes are primarily worked out through the treatment and development of the central character, Jean Valjean. In Hugo's novel there is an ambiguity about Valjean. As Peter Washington points out in his introduction to the Everyman's Library English language edition, it 'allows us to view Valjean, should we wish, either as a Christ figure, carrying the sins of a whole society on his shoulders, or as an existential hero, a precursor of Camus' Outsider'.[5] In the musical, following Valjean's 'redemption' by the Bishop of Digne, it is his Christ-like attributes which are very clearly to the fore. This is underlined in his line 'This never ending road to Calvary' in the song 'One day more' which closes Act 1. There is a reference to Calvary in the original 1980 French version of the song but it has a rather different emphasis, asking 'Comment faire verrai-je un jour le fin de ce calvaire?' The English version, by contrast, has much more suggestion of Valjean himself treading the road to Calvary.

In both Hugo's novel and the English version of the musical the trigger for Valjean's transformation from desperate criminal filled with hatred of humanity to sacrificial hero fired by altruism is the forgiveness he receives from the Bishop of Digne after stealing his silverware. In a sermon preached in Canterbury Cathedral on Easter Sunday 1999 George Carey described the encounter between Valjean and the bishop as offering 'the finest description of grace outside the New Testament' and setting Valjean on his way to redemption and wholeness. This encounter is missing from the original French concept album and production. Indeed, the bishop did not figure at all in the musical as it was initially conceived by Boublil and Schönberg. This is in marked contrast to his prominent role in Hugo's novel which begins with a 65-page portrait which sets the bishop up as an utter saint, exchanging his palace for the local hospital because it is so crowded and giving away his carriage allowance to the poor. Hugo gives him a debate about sacrifice with an unbelieving senator who scoffs, 'My head is not turned with your Jesus, who preaches in every corn-field renunciation and self-sacrifice.'[6] The novel's opening chapter ends with a marvellous picture of a man who does not delve into the mystery of suffering but simply throws himself wholeheartedly into the business of relieving it:

> There are men who labour for the extraction of gold; he worked for the extraction of pity. The misery of the universe was his mine. Grief everywhere was only an occasion for good always. Love one another – he declared that to be complete; he desired nothing more, and it was his whole doctrine.[7]

Hugo even uses the scene where the bishop's silver is stolen to highlight his sanctity. As Valjean pauses before the bishop's bed on his way to force the lock of the safe, he sees a reflection of unseen light on the churchman's forehead. His whole face shone as if surrounded by a halo – 'it was a luminous transparency, for this heaven was within him'. Clearly visible in the moonlight was the crucifix above his bed 'apparently extending its arms towards both men, with a benediction for one and a pardon for the other'.[8]

None of this is included in the musical but it does reflect with great faithfulness the bishop's pardon when the gendarmes bring the arrested Valjean before him and his overflowing grace in offering the thief his candlesticks as well on condition that he uses them to become an honest man. This scene, indeed, provides the first example of how the musical, at least in its English-language version, uses more explicitly Christian language than Hugo did. In the novel, the bishop's words are: 'Jean Valjean, my brother: you belong no longer to evil, but to good. It is your soul that I am buying for you. I withdraw it from dark thoughts and from the spirit of perdition, and I give it to God.'[9] In the musical, they become:

> And remember this, my brother
> See in this some higher plan.
> You must use this precious sliver
> To become an honest man.
> By the witness of the martyrs
> By the Passion and the Blood
> God has raised you out of darkness
> I have bought your soul for God!

In the novel, the transformation wrought in Valjean by the bishop's act of gracious forgiveness is not instantaneous. He commits another crime, stealing 40 sous from a little gipsy boy, before feeling utter remorse and seeing a light which he first takes to be a torch but which then assumes human form in the shape of the bishop. Valjean sees his own life in the light of that light – 'it seemed to him that he was look-ing upon Satan by the light of Paradise' – and this leads to his radical change of heart and abandonment of his old life of brooding intro-spection and hatred. In the musical Valjean's 'conversion' is instanta-neous and happens immediately after his experience of forgiveness at the hands of the bishop. It is expressed in his powerful soliloquy, 'What have I done, Sweet Jesus', which reflects on the transforming effect of this single encounter:

> Yet why did I allow that man
> To touch my soul and teach me love?
> He treated me like any other.
> He gave me his trust.
> He called me Brother.
> My life he claims for God above.
> Can such things be?
> For I had come to hate the world
> This world that always hated me!

This song identifies the key existential crisis in Valjean's life and the moment when he decisively changes his character and resolves 'Another story must begin'. It is portrayed as an act of pure *metanoia* when, confronted with the miracle of grace, he accepts it and becomes an agent of grace himself. The sense of Valjean as a new man who has given himself (or been given?) to God, almost in a reverse Faustian compact, is further reinforced in his soliloquy 'Who am I?':

> My soul belongs to God, I know,
> I made that bargain long ago.
> He gave me hope when hope was gone
> He gave me strength to journey on.

This song in which Valjean agonizes over his true identity and wrestles with his conscience as to whether he should reveal who he is in order to save a man who has been mistaken for him from prison has interesting parallels with a poem written by Dietrich Bonhoeffer in his prison cell:

> Who am I? This or the Other?
> Am I one person today and tomorrow another? . . .
> Who am I? They mock me, these lonely questions of mine.
> Whoever I am, Thou knowest, O God, I am thine.[10]

From this point on Valjean is very much portrayed in the musical as going 'in the strength of the Lord', as the Salvation Army song puts it. He is certainly conscious of being upheld by God, affirming at the beginning of 'Bring him home':

> God on high, hear my prayer.
> In my need you have always been there.

His path down the never-ending road to Calvary, treading the road of sacrificial suffering and carrying so many others on his shoulders, literally in the case of Marius, is not easy but it is one from which he does not flinch and in which he is sustained by God. There is no sense in the musical as there is in Hugo's novel of Valjean continuing to wrestle with his conscience. Hugo indeed explicitly compares him to Wrestling Jacob and has him agonize particularly over whether he should surrender Cosette to Marius when she is the only companion he has in older age. Nor, surprisingly perhaps, does the musical pick up the strongly spiritual resonances in Hugo's portrayal of the

interaction between Valjean and the ailing Fantine. In Book 6 of the
novel, Fantine, in her ravings, sees Valjean, in his guise as Monsieur
Madeleine, gazing at the crucifix on the wall above her head and he
appears to her to be transfigured and clothed with light. She asks him
what he is doing and he says, 'I was praying to the martyr who is on
high.' He goes on to tell her that her suffering will make her an angel
– 'this hell from which you have come out is the first step towards
Heaven'.[11] There is no mention of this Christ-like appearance of
Valjean in the musical, nor any such explicit endorsement by him of
the salvific purpose of suffering, although the dying Fantine does
declare from her hospital bed, 'Good M'sieur, you come from God in
heaven.'

There are other allusions to Valjean's saintliness and Christ-like
salvific quality in the novel which are not picked up in the musical,
doubtless for reasons of compression. Hugo has Valjean's old retainer,
Touissant, recognize his master as a saint and he also has Combeferre
respond to Bossuet's query 'Who is this man?' when Valjean makes
his appearance on the revolutionaries' barricade and strips off his
National Guard coat: 'He is a man who saves others.' But there is no
doubting the superhuman sacrificial qualities of the Valjean of the
musical, nor the spiritual aura that attends him. This is particularly
evident in the final scene where he kneels before an altar-like table
which is set with two candlesticks and a Cross. The departed spirits of
Fantine and Eponine return to lead him to heaven as he prays to God
to forgive him his trespasses and take him to glory. Hugo's novel ends
with Valjean dying in his bed, with Cosette and Marius beside him.
There are no appearances by the departed spirits of Fantine or
Eponine, although there is an allusion to the Bishop of Digne being 'a
witness of this death agony' and of Valjean seeing him above his head.
In his lengthy last speech Valjean tells Cosette and Marius that they
must forgive the wicked Thenadiers and reflects on the immense
suffering and unhappiness of Fantine:

Such are the distributions of God. He is on high, he sees us all, and
he knows what he does in the midst of his great stars. So I am going
away, my children. Love each other dearly always. There is scarcely
anything else in the world but that: to love one another.[12]

The English-language version of the musical conflates this into the line
sung by Valjean, Fantine and Eponine together that 'to love another

person is to see the face of God'. The original French version of the show, like the novel, has no appearances by Fantine and Eponine and has Valjean alone with Marius and Cosette. In its closing lines, Valjean enjoins the couple to love one another, reminding them that 'Qui aime sa femme sans le savoir, aime Dieu.' This concluding observation, which accords a significantly higher value to the marriage relationship than the more generalized and universal exaltation of human love in the English text, is prefaced by a fascinating theological meditation on the possibility of God returning to earth:

La lumière, au matin de justice
Puisse enfin décapiter nos vices
Dans un monde où Dieu pourrait se plaire
S'il décidait un jour de rescendre sur la terre

Inevitably, there is much more subtlety and much more philosophy in Hugo's 1,450-page novel than in *Les Misérables* the musical, long and complex though it is by the standards of most shows. Hugo suggests at several points that one of his main themes is the interconnectedness of all things. This is most explicitly stated in the description of the garden of Valjean's house in the Rue Plumet:

Nothing is really small; whoever is open to the deep penetration of nature knows this. Although indeed no absolute satisfaction may be vouchsafed to philosophy, no more in circumscribing the cause than in limiting the effect, the contemplator falls into unfathomable ecstacies in view of all these decompositions of forces resulting in unity. All works for all . . .
  Who then can calculate the path of the molecule? how do we know that the creations of worlds are not determined by the fall of grains of sand? Who then understands the reciprocal flux and reflux of the infinitely great and the infinitely small, the echoing of causes in the abysses of being, and the avalanches of creation? A flesh worm is of account; the small is great, the great is small; all is in equilibrium in necessity; fearful vision for the mind. There are marvellous relations between beings and things; in this inexhaustible whole, from sun to grub, there is no scorn; all need each other.[13]

This is fascinating stuff and strikingly reminiscent of the 'grand law of the universe' built on the principles of sacrifice and inter-dependence promulgated by the Anglican clergyman F. W. Robertson and other mid-nineteenth-century English and Scottish divines wrestling with the theological implications of the theory of evolution and the witness of the natural world to the necessity of decay for growth and death for life.[14] None of this is reflected in the musical. The official website states that '*Les Misérables* reminds us that we are each part of the same human family, and that whatever our outward differences may be, our longings for individual liberty and peace are the same.'[15] However, this is not really the message that comes across in the musical which is much more focused on the theme of human self-sacrifice and its redemptive power.

Towards the end of *Les Misérables* Victor Hugo provides his clearest statement of the novel's central theme:

> The book which the reader has now before his eyes is, from one end to the other, in its whole and in its details, whatever may be the intermissions, the exceptions, or the defaults, the march from evil to good, from injustice to justice, from the false to the true, from night to day, from appetite to conscience, from rottenness to life, from brutality to duty, from Hell to Heaven, from nothingness to God. Starting point: matter; goal: the soul; hydra at the beginning, angel at the end.[16]

The musical does not provide such a clear teleology or sense of progress. Its depiction of the sweep of history and the march of events is cyclical rather than linear, as exemplified by the considerable use of the revolving circular stage, the note of weary resignation sounded in 'One day more' and the depressing conclusion of the chorus 'Turning':

> Nothing changes. Nothing ever can.
> Round about the roundabout, and back where you began.
> Round and round and back where you began.

It is significant that in its first French conception *Les Misérables* was described as a *tragédie musicale*. It is depressing as well as uplifting, not least in the emphasis which it gives to the shattering and breaking of human dreams. The three main female characters, Fantine, Eponine and Cosette, are all portrayed as dreamers but only for the third do dreams come true. The collapse of Fantine's dreams is given the most extensive treatment. Her song, 'I dreamed a dream' totally contradicts

Hugo's insistence that *Les Misérables* is about the march from evil to good, night to day and hell to heaven. For her the movement has all been in the other direction. The tigers of the night have torn her hopes apart and turned her dreams to shame:

> I had a dream my life would be
> So different from this hell I'm living,
> So different now from what it seemed.
> Now life has killed the dream I dreamed.

Here is a total reversal and rejection of the dream theme as it had been expounded in musical theatre. This bitter reflection is the antithesis of the Mother Abbess's advice to Maria to find 'a dream that will last for as long as you live' or the promise in *Carousel* that 'at the end of the storm there's a golden sky'. The reality which Fantine has experienced is that the dream will evaporate, like the young man who spent a summer by her side and left her with a baby, and that the end of the storm will bring only misery and depression. For some critics, the power of the anguished message of this song is diminished by the lush romantic melody to which it is set. I have heard it argued that it would have had much more power with a discordant, unresolved musical accompaniment. Yet its pastoral and representative significance, which I think is considerable, would surely have been diminished had it been set to a forbidding, angular and unmemorable tune.

'I dreamed a dream' has a significant spiritual as well as pastoral dimension. Among Fantine's shattered dreams are that 'God would be forgiving', a concept which was significantly introduced in the English version of the libretto. There is no mention of God in the original French version of this song which instead gets straight into Fantine's disillusion in its second line, 'J'avais rêvé d'une autre vie/ mais la vie a tué mes rêves'. The killing of her dreams is all too graphically displayed in the musical as she sinks into the degradation of abject poverty and prostitution. She is redeemed partly by Valjean's loving care of her in her dying hours but perhaps even more by her own sacrificial life and death, as is suggested in the novel in an exchange between Cosette and Valjean:

> 'Father, I saw my mother in a dream last night. She had two great wings. My mother must have attained to sanctity in her life.'
> 'Through martyrdom,' answered Jean Valjean.

Fantine is not the only character in *Les Misérables* who is portrayed as a martyr. So, too, is Eponine who is given a much more self-sacrificial persona in the musical than in the novel. She is also someone whose dreams never come true – in her case the dream that Marius will return her love. Yet she acts selflessly as messenger between him and Cosette and heroically returns to join him on the barricade where she is shot and dies reflecting on the mysterious power of sacrifice and life through death as she sings 'a little fall of rain will make the flowers grow'.

Cosette is the only one of the trio of principal female characters whose dreams do come true and even with her there is an aura of wistfulness and unfulfilled longing. This is expressed most strongly in her song 'Castle on a Cloud' in which she dreams of a place where no one is lost and no one cries, a place where she can only go in her sleep. Critics are divided as to whether this is a song of aching need or brattish desire. It seems to me to represent an unhappy child's view of heaven reminiscent of those contained in Victorian hymns. The reference to the 'lady all in white' suggests an angel or perhaps even the Virgin Mary. In the musical Cosette's dreams provide an escape from the misery of her effective imprisonment and enslavement in the Thenardier household. In Hugo's novel, they arise in a quite different context, that of her convent education:

> Nothing prepares a young girl for passions like a convent. The convent turns the thoughts in the direction of the unknown. The heart, thrown back upon itself, makes for itself a channel, being unable to overflow, and deepens, being unable to expand. From thence visions, suppositions, conjectures, romances sketched out, longings for adventures, fantastic constructions, whole castles built in the interior obscurity of the mind, dark and secret dwellings where the passions find an immediate lodging as soon as the grating is crossed and they are permitted to enter.[17]

If Valjean, Fantine, Eponine and Cosette all stand in some sense as types of martyrdom and sacrifice, the other principal figures in *Les Misérables* also embody clearly drawn values – cynical nihilism in the case of the Thenardiers, stern judgementalism in the case of Javert and misguided idealism in the person of Marius and his fellow students.

The Thenardiers have a much more prominent role in the musical than in Hugo's novel. That is partly because they provide much-needed comic relief. Thenardier is also cast as something of a philosopher, albeit of a very cynical and negative kind. His solo, 'Dog eats dog', sung as he robs the corpses in the Paris sewers, carries something of the message of Hugo's reflection on the importance of this hidden part of the city's anatomy:

> The sewer is the conscience of the city. All things converge into it and are confronted with one another. In this lurid place there is darkness but there are no secrets. Everything has its real form, or at least its definitive form. This can be said for the garbage-heap, that it is no liar . . . A sewer is a cynic. It tells all.[18]

In his song the truth which Thenardier finds revealed in his subterranean den is a bleak one:

> It's a world where the dogs eat the dogs
> Where they kill for the bones in the street
> And God in His Heaven
> He don't interfere
> 'Cos He's dead as the stiffs at my feet.

If Thenardier acts as the apostle of Neitzsche and the death of God school, he also represents the likeable rogue with whom the audience laughs along and identifies. With his wily determination to take 'here a little slice, there a little cut', he is more human than the heroic Valjean or the tragic Fantine and Eponine. For all their cruelty to Cosette and their selfishness, the Thenardiers, singing together from a manhole in their final song, do acknowledge the basic decency of ordinary people:

> Everywhere you go,
> Law-abiding folk
> Doing what is decent,
> But they're mostly broke!
> Singing to the Lord on Sundays
> Praying for the gifts He will send.

In several productions of *Les Misérables* that I have seen the biggest cheer of the evening has gone to Thenardier's parting line 'Jesus, won't I see you all in Hell'. Is this simply because it is the funny man who is singing it or does it reflect the audience's identification with his roguish honesty amidst so much sacrifice and sanctity?

Javert is far from being a cynic. He is in fact as much an idealist and dreamer as Fantine and Eponine, though in his case they are stern unrelenting dreams of justice, order and vengeance. He is also like them a tragic figure, indeed more so in that his descent into darkness and despair which mirrors Valjean's ascent into hope and purpose seems to offer no possibility of ultimate redemption. Javert's final lonely descent into the murky waters of the Seine as he commits suicide parallels Valjean's final ascent to heaven led on by the spirits of Fantine and Eponine. Unlike Judas in *Jesus Christ Superstar*, a character whom in several ways he resembles, Javert has no resurrection scene. His tragedy is total, his fall unstoppable.

The novel provides important background to the character of Javert which there is inevitably not time for in the musical. We are told that he was born in a prison of gipsy stock and that he has always felt an outsider and beyond the pale, hating the background from which he came. This is the context for his obsession with rectitude, order and morality and for his entry into the police force through whose ranks he rose rapidly to the rank of inspector. In Hugo's words:

> This man was a compound of two sentiments, very simple and very good in themselves, but he almost made them evil in his exaggeration of them, respect for authority and hatred of rebellion . . . He was stoical, serious, austere: a dreamer of stern dreams, humble and haughty, like all fanatics. His stare was cold and as piercing as a gimlet. His whole life was contained in these words: waking and watching.[19]

In the musical, Javert's costume, bearing and make-up suggest a cold, sinister figure of darkness. His narrow obsession with order and judgement is well conveyed. So is his belief in 'a vengeful, Old Testament God' of the kind described by Trevor Nunn. This is, of course, a distortion of the God of the Hebrew Bible who is as much a God of grace as a God of vengeance and who is in a covenant relationship with his people Israel. Javert's God has no room for grace and deals entirely in judgement and vengeance, having a relationship with his people which is contractual, conditional and legalistic. There are no grey areas, and therefore no room for grace or forgiveness, in Javert's world-view, as clearly expressed in the original French version of his soliloquy which is entitled 'Noir ou blanc':

Il n'y a que deux sortes d'hommes et pas d'autre,
Une pour subir et une autre pour sévir,
Noir et blanc, hors la loi ou dedans.

Javert's rigid and fixed view of life, with no room for *metanoia* or forgiveness, is clearly expressed in his Act I confrontation with Valjean where he sings: 'Men like me can never change. Men like you can never change'. His solo 'Stars', specially written for the English version of the show, conveys superbly his dream of a black-and-white ordered world where the stars keep watch in their night and always return to their place. It also articulates very clearly his concept of divine grace as a conditional state from which one essentially falls rather than as a quality of continual overflowing forgiveness which one can always accept. The fugitive out in the darkness is running and fallen from grace:

He knows his way in the dark,
But mine is the way of the Lord
And those who follow the path of the righteous
Shall have their reward.
And if they fall
As Lucifer fell,
The flame,
The sword!

The soliloquy which precedes Javert's suicide deliberately mirrors Valjean's first song, 'What have I done?' Both songs are about forgiveness. While Valjean is able to accept the Bishop of Digne's pardon and let it change his life, Javert cannot cope with Valjean's failure to kill him when they met on the barricades:

I should have perished by his hand
It was his right.
It was my right to die as well.
Instead, I live – but live in hell.

The mirroring of Valjean's and Javert's soliloquies – they share the same tune and the same structure – reinforces the opposing theologies which the two men embody. Valjean embodies the triumph of grace and the power of forgiveness, Javert the rule of law. It is his inability to accept unconditional love and forgiveness which leads him into the hell from which he can only escape by suicide. In Hugo's words:

> An entire new world appeared to his soul; favour accepted and returned, devotion, compassion, indulgence, acts of violence committed by pity upon austerity, respect of persons, no more final condemnation, no more damnation, the possibility of a tear in the eye of the law, a mysterious justice according to God going counter to justice according to men. He perceived in the darkness the fearful rising of an unknown moral sun; he was horrified and blinded by it. An owl compelled to an eagle's glare.[20]

Marius and his fellow students are dreamers of a more appealing but perhaps equally misguided kind. They provide another more subtle counter to Valjean, in this case by standing for sacrifice to a cause. For them suicide can be a noble expression of self-dedication rather than a statement of utter despair as it is for Javert, yet the parameters need to be strictly drawn as Combeferre reminds his fellow revolutionaries as they wait to die on the barricades: 'Suicides like those which will be accomplished here are sublime; but suicide is strict, and can have no extension; and as soon as it touches those next you, the name of suicide is murder.'[21] With this in mind, Combeferre orders all those who have wives, mothers, daughters and sisters to go away. For those who remain, the prospect of dying a sacrificial death for the cause of freedom and justice is one which Enjolras extols in a speech which uses the language of religion and metaphysics:

> Whence shall arrive the shout of love, if it be not from the summit of sacrifice? O my brothers, here is the place of junction between those who think and those who suffer; this barricade is made neither of paving stones, nor of timbers, nor of iron; it is made of two mounds, a mound of ideas and a mound of sorrows. Misery here encounters the ideal. Here day embraces night, and says: I will die with thee and thou shalt be born again with me. From the pressure of all desolations faith gushes forth. Sufferings bring their agony here, and ideas their immortality. This agony and this immortality are to mingle and compose our death. Brothers, he who dies here dies in the radiance of the future, and we are entering a grave illuminated by the dawn.[22]

This extraordinary hymn to sacrifice echoes the language of religious martyrdom throughout the ages and across the world's faiths. It is in the spirit of Irenaeus' enthusiastic embrace of the prospect of being torn apart by the lions and Tertullian's oft-quoted statement that 'the blood of the martyrs is the seed of the Church', which finds its own echo in the musical in the line 'the blood of the martyrs will water the meadows of France'. It is also the language and sentiments of the suicide bombers of Hamas and Al Qaida.

Inevitably the novel deals much more subtly and deeply with the profound ambiguities of sacrifice for a high ideal. In the musical these are only touched on in the two songs 'Red and Black' and 'Empty Chairs at Empty Tables'. The first of these conveys something of the regenerating power of sacrifice suggested in Enjolras's speech in its picture of the colour of the world changing day by day:

> Red – the blood of angry men!
> Black – the dark of ages past!
> Red – a world about to dawn!
> Black – the night that ends at last!

I have sung these lines more than once from church pulpits in the context of sermons seeking to expound the difficult and forbidding Christian doctrine of sacrifice. They resonate for me with the closing line of George Matheson's great hymn 'O love that wilt not let me go' which proclaims that 'from the ground there blossoms red life that shall endless be' and with Matheson's explanation of that choice of imagery: 'I took red as the symbol of that sacrificial life which blooms by shedding itself.'[23]

In the musical, the song 'Red and Black' is also used to contrast two different kinds of sacrificial passion. While for the students red symbolizes the blood of angry men and black the night of oppression which is about to end, for Marius, head over heels in love with Cosette, the colours have altogether different connotations, red being the colour of desire and black his world when she's not there. To some extent the contrast here is between Marius the dreamer, who in Hugo's words 'preferred an idea to a fact, a poet to a hero, and admired a book like Job still more than an event like Marengo' and the other students who, while equally idealistic, are more men of action and focused on winning the battle for freedom than on pursuing a love affair. There is, too, a deeper dimension to this contrast, underlined in

Enjolras's impatient dismissal of Marius's self-indulgent 'oohing' and 'aahing':

> Who cares about your lonely soul?
> We strive towards a higher goal,
> Our little lives don't count at all.

Does this affirmation point to the nobility of communal sacrifice for a great cause in which the interest of the individual is subordinated to the common and higher good? Or is it rather the terrible blasphemy uttered by the suicide bomber who disregards the lonely soul and the little life – not just his own but those of others – in his fanatical zeal for the cause?

'Empty chairs for empty tables', Marius's lament for his comrades killed on the barricades, has been taken up internationally as an anthem for those suffering from HIV/Aids. It has clear pastoral value as an articulation of the grief and guilt felt by those left alive when others have died. It also expresses the spiritual and almost sacramental bonds which unite those drawn together in the fellowship of suffering and tragedy. Marius reflects of his dead comrades that 'the very words that they had sung became their last communion on the lonely barricade at dawn'. There are echoes here of the students' earlier song 'Drink with me to days gone by' with its plea 'May the wine of friendship never run dry'. 'Empty chairs at empty tables' also returns to the vexed question of the nobility or futility of sacrifice for a cause when Marius disturbingly and despairingly cries to his lost companions:

> Oh, my friends, my friends, don't ask me
> What your sacrifice was for.

The other student song, the show-stopping anthem, 'Do you hear the people sing?' has a more communitarian feel than the anthems from mid-twentieth-century Broadway shows. Essentially a secular hymn of political liberation, its reprise at the very end of the show includes two biblically inspired couplets:

> They will live again in freedom
> In the garden of the Lord.
> They will walk behind the plough-share,
> They will put away the sword.

Several American television networks played 'Do you hear the people sing' as an accompaniment to their coverage of the pro-democracy protests at Tiananmen Square in Peking in 1989. It was also turned into an international anthem for freedom at the end of the *Les Misérables* tenth anniversary concert at the Albert Hall when it was sung in 16 different languages by some of those who had played Jean Valjean in productions around the world while their national flags were paraded through the auditorium.

Alongside the individual characters who so powerfully represent conflicting values and approaches to life, *Les Misérables* is, of course, as its title implies, a story about the starving, hungry masses at the bottom of the pile of humanity. In Hugo's novel they are a constant presence. They first appear when Marius suddenly awakes from his own dreamings to the plight of those around him and refers to them as 'his brothers in Jesus Christ'. In the musical they are also ubiquitous, not least in terms of merchandizing and publicity. It is the lithograph of the waif-like Cosette created by the mid-nineteenth-century French illustrator, Emile Bayard, which appears on posters, T-shirts, programme covers and CDs. In the musical the reality and presence of *Les Misérables* is evoked through the crowd scenes and through songs. In their first appearance they sing 'At the end of the day you're another day older/And that's all you can say for the life of the poor'. Towards the end of the show they apparently endorse Thenardier's sense of the death or absence of God as they reflect ruefully in 'Turning':

Nothing changes. Nothing ever will.
Every year another brat, another mouth to fill.
Same old story. What's the use of tears?
What's the use of praying
If there's nobody who hears!

This pessimism and nihilism is countered by the character of Gavroche, the irrepressibly perky little street urchin who injects a note of hope and humour into the musings of *Les Misérables*. Gavroche has a more central role in the musical than in Hugo's novel, particularly in the original French concept album where he is made something of a philosopher, reflecting in one of his three songs on the extent to which the blame for his condition of life can be laid at the feet of Rousseau and Voltaire. In the English-language version, his role is reduced and altered. He becomes a spokesman and apologist for all 'little people' and what they can do against the strong and mighty, significantly taking one of his main examples from the Bible:

Goliath was a bruiser who was tall as the sky
But David threw a right and gave him one in the eye
I never read the Bible but I know that it's true
It only goes to show what little people can do.

Les Misérables the musical may extol the virtues of little people but it is essentially a show about big themes. This is why it has so much theological resonance and provides so much meaty material for sermons and discussion groups. It raises important ethical and philosophical issues, some of which feature in the study guide on the official website which asks, inter alia, whether there is a place for mercy in the law and if there are things worth fighting and perhaps even dying for. There is also a significant pastoral dimension to *Les Misérables*. Several people I know have been helped by lines from songs in the show when confronted with difficult personal situations. In one case, a wife coped with her husband's unfaithfulness by reflecting on the lines from the song 'In Life' where Cosette quizzes Valjean about her origins and he replies:

There are words
That are better unheard
Better unsaid.

Susan Sutherland makes the claim that

with the power to communicate its theme across cultural boundaries, this musical has provoked countless acts of charity, rekindling the flame lit by its French author, Victor Hugo, whose nineteenth-century images of the struggle against oppression and social iniquity have real resonance for the audience of today.[24]

It would be interesting to know exactly what she has in mind here. The only act of charity directly inspired by the musical of which I am aware were collections for Amnesty International made by the Vienna company in the wake of the Tiananmen Square massacre but I am very willing to believe that there have been many others. The song 'Bring him home' (one of three that Kretzmer wrote from scratch for the

English version, the others being 'Stars' and 'Dog eats dog') has undoubtedly helped grieving parents and is increasingly requested at funerals. It was used by the US State Department in promotional material about US troops engaged in the Gulf War. *Les Misérables* has political as well as pastoral appeal. The song 'One day more' was used by Bill Clinton at the final New Jersey rally in his 1992 presidential campaign.

Alain Boublil and Claude-Michel Schönberg have followed up *Les Misérables* with one other mega-hit and one flop. The hit, *Miss Saigon* (1989), has little if any theological or spiritual resonance, and, for me at least, not much to commend it dramatically or musically either. It is relentlessly intense and angst-ridden with everyone singing at the very edge of their vocal range and capacity. There is a pastiche gospel number at the beginning of the second act, 'They're called *Bui Doï*', when a gowned choir sings about the world's orphans being our children as pictures of Vietnamese babies are flashed up on screen. There is also a nod to indigenous Vietnamese religion (it is not clear which variety) in the scene where Kim kneels before a little altar in her room. But the religion most clearly celebrated in *Miss Saigon* is that of western materialism, enthusiastically extolled in Engineer's song 'The American dream' and in the Act 1 number 'The Last Night of the World' where Kim sings 'Dreams were all I ever knew' and Chris responds 'Dreams you won't need when I'm through', implying that the United States is the land where dreams are fulfilled. There is none of the romantic idealism of Rodgers and Hammerstein here. Rather the dream theme is firmly and unashamedly focused on conspicuous consumption.

Boublil and Schönberg's other major musical post-*Les Misérables* is much more interesting and significant, at least from a theological point of view, although it has had little success commercially. *Martin Guerre* opened in 1996, was drastically revised after five months and then almost completely rewritten again in 1998. It is based on a true story and set in the French village of Artigat during the sixteenth-century wars of religion between Huguenots and Catholics. Many of its central themes are similar to those in *Les Misérables*. There is the same emphasis on broken dreams, with the Act 1 ballad for the heroine, Bertrande ('When will someone hear' in the original 1996 version and 'How many tears' in the 1998 rewrite), very clearly echoing the sentiments of Fantine's 'I dreamed a dream':

All that I've begun
All that I believe
Is just another broken dream.

There is also a similar emphasis on the redemptive power of sacrificial
love, in this case represented by Martin Guerre who is stabbed
while shielding his friend Arnaud in a battle against the Protestants.
Believing that Martin is dead, Arnaud steals his wife, Bertrande.
Martin forgives him and, realizing the depth of their love for each
other, helps Arnaud and Bertrande escape from prison. In the end,
Arnaud is stabbed, shielding Martin from an assassination attempt by
the odious Guillaume. Martin feels a sense of redemption and leads
the villagers in their traditional task of working the land.

What distinguishes *Martin Guerre* from *Les Misérables* and indeed
from most other musicals is that it is primarily about religious warfare
and conflict between Christians. It is fiercely partisan – the Catholics
are on the whole made out to be bigots, while the Protestants are
portrayed as generally peace loving. In the original version the
Protestants are given one of the nearest approximations to a straight
Christian hymn in any musical score. Entitled 'Bethlehem', it is sung to
a harp accompaniment and has distinct echoes of 'Silent Night':

There a stable was the altar table
For the feast, a manger
For the priest, a stranger
Braying cattle for the choir
Singing praises to the Messiah

Guillaume, the villain of the story and a Catholic bigot, is cast very
much in the mould of Javert. In his view order and justice will only be
achieved by rooting out Protestants:

Look around! Can't you see
What the world has become?
It is time we were cleansed
Of this Protestant scum.
By the blood of the martyrs
We will take up the sword
We will root out this cancer
In the name of the Lord!

Everywhere is chaos,
Everywhere is doubt.
Everywhere are heretics
The time has come to burn them out.

The original version offers a slight counterbalance to the prevailing anti-Catholic tone in its sympathetic portrayal of the priest, Father Dominic, who sings in the context of a song about imposters:

The imposters are you and I
Look inside and you'll see
It is we who are dying

The villagers respond with a prayer to Jesus to end the savage sectarian fighting:

Who are the imposters here?
Christians who would hunt and seize us,
Worshipping the bloodied spear
Killing in the name of Jesus.
Only love will see us through
Only faith in you, Lord, frees us.
Jesus. Save us, lead us, free us.
Lead us out of mortal fear.

The 1998 version of *Martin Guerre* is, if anything, even more pro-Protestant than the original. While the Catholics are given a chorus entitled 'God's Anger' which is all about apportioning blame and punishment, the Protestants sing in 'The Holy Fight' of the love of God. Both versions of the show have an unresolved and somewhat pessimistic ending. Despite the Catholics' pleas to be forgiven for their massacres, the Protestants depart from the village of Artigat, leaving the Catholics to till the land. The show ends with a plea for forgiveness which is particularly powerful in the 1998 version:

Can we try to rebuild all we lost in the night?
Please forgive us our sins, now we pray to God's love
And to you where you live in the Heavens above.

Perhaps one of the reasons why *Martin Guerre* failed to emulate the success of *Les Misérables* and *Miss Saigon* is the nature of its subject matter. It epitomizes a new style of musical which appeared in the 1990s dealing with difficult and unappealing issues with which many theatre-goers would perhaps rather not be confronted. The rise of the issue-based musical drove another nail into the coffin of the old Broadway dream theme. Increasingly, in the post-*Les Misérables* world of musicals, dreams were made to be shattered and wasted rather than to be found and followed.

6

Dreams don't die –

musicals of the last 25 years

The last two decades of the twentieth century saw the musical achieve its dominant position in the theatres of London and New York and establish itself as a truly global phenomenon. Critics expressed concern at the eclipse of legitimate straight theatre in the face of the seemingly relentless march of Lloyd Webber's ever more elaborate creations and the 'gloomy, doomy blockbusters' that followed in the wake of *Les Misérables* and looked askance at the increasing flirtation with musicals on the part of the subsidized National Theatre and Royal Shakespeare Company. A handful of musicals, including *Les Misérables*, *Cats* and *The Lion King*, showed themselves to be as much part of the phenomenon of globalization as McDonald's and Starbucks, moving out of the traditional Anglo-Saxon orbit of musical theatre and playing to capacity audiences in cities as diverse as Beirut, Beijing and Tokyo.

The dream theme remained strong. It is there very clearly in one of the first major musicals of the 1980s, Stephen Sondheim's *Merrily We Roll Along*. This show, which opened on Broadway in 1981 and has never had the success which it deserved, is important on a number of counts. It is one of the few musicals to take musical theatre as its subject matter. Its central characters, Franklin Shepherd and Charles Kringas, are respectively a composer and lyricist who achieve considerable success with their shows but whose private lives and relationship with each other disintegrate over their twenty years of working together. At one level, *Merrily We Roll Along* is a tribute to the whole genre of the musical. As they set out together, composer and lyricist dream of changing the world through their words and tunes, telling people things that they don't know. Echoing Hammerstein, they reflect 'musicals are popular. It's a great way to state important ideas.' Yet their youthful idealism soon turns to cynical opportunism.

The song 'Franklin Shepard Inc.', which brilliantly encapsulates the business of writing a musical with its alternating phrases of piano chords and typewriter keys, plays up the commercial aspects of the genre with constant telephone calls from agents, impresarios, secretaries and lawyers. When a television interviewer asks Charley 'Which generally comes first, the words or the music?', he replies 'Generally, the contract.' In the end the two men go their separate ways, Frank to write a hit film musical and Charley a Pulitzer-prize winning play.

If Sondheim plays up the fragility and commercialism of musical theatre, he is also concerned to explore the nature of human dreams and aspirations and the way they are lost sight of and compromised through life. *Merrily We Roll Along* runs backwards rather than forwards in time. It begins in 1979 with Frank professionally successful but personally disillusioned, and ends in 1957 with he and Charley embarking on their collaboration. The last song in the show, chronologically the first, is the most optimistic. Entitled 'Our Time', it speaks of the limitless possibilities of youth and ends with the two men singing of 'our dreams coming true'. The transition numbers which mark the gradual rolling back of the years through the show speak not so much of the fading of dreams as their discarding and disappearance in the muddle and compromise and unexpected twists and turns of life – 'When did you let things slip out of gear, when did the road behind disappear?'

Merrily We Roll Along has been described as telling the story of how the American dream turned into a nightmare, following the cast back from the sordid infidelities and disillusionment of their mid-life crises in the late 1970s to their undergraduate days in the late 1950s, the pre-Vietnam, pre-sixties era when it was possible to grow up in America devoid of either guilt or anxiety. Yet for all the cynicism there is still a faith in the dream. The college anthem 'The Hills of Tomorrow' which originally opened and closed the show, but was later removed, is both a hymn to idealism and a cynical lament for what has gone wrong in the lives of those who sang it so earnestly at their graduations. The dream theme recurs again and again in the transition numbers which repeat the refrain of the opening title song:

Yesterday is done.
See the pretty countryside.
Merrily we roll along, roll along, bursting with dreams.
Travelling's the fun, flashing by the countryside,

Everybody merrily merrily following dreams.
Rolling along! Rolling along!
Dreams don't die, so keep an eye on your dreams
And before you know where you are, there you are.
Time goes by and hopes go dry
But you can still try for your dream.

Know what you want to do,
Where you're willing to go.
Keep an eye on your dream while you're travelling.
Soon enough you're merrily merrily practising dreams.
Dreams that will explode,
Waking up in the countryside,
Making you feel merrily, merrily,
What can go wrong?

In reprises of this song, mention is made of 'gathering dreams' and 'catching at dreams'. Even for the cynical Sondheim in the 1980s, the message is still essentially what it was for the idealistic and optimistic Rodgers and Hammerstein in the 1940s and 1950s – following your dreams.

For the arch-romantic and spiritual yearner, Andrew Lloyd Webber, who dominated the world of musical theatre throughout the 1980s and much of the 1990s, the dream theme was still very much alive, although sometimes in danger of being swamped in lavish glitziness and special effects. There is an intriguing theological undertone to *Cats*, which opened in 1981, enjoyed a non-stop run in London for the next 21 years and has so far been seen by over 50 million people around the world. Indeed, this is another musical which has a considerably more theological and indeed overtly Christian message than the original work on which it is based. Despite the fact that T. S. Eliot wrote *Old Possum's Book of Practical Cats* in the same year as *The Idea of a Christian Society*, there is nothing very theological in his collection of verses about different kinds of cat. Indeed, the work gets very little critical attention in the numerous books devoted to Eliot's poetry and is normally dismissed as a series of charming but largely inconsequential verses for children.

In the hands of Lloyd Webber, Richard Stilgoe and Trevor Nunn, however, *Cats* becomes a parable of resurrection and rebirth. Seeking something to give a narrative structure to what would otherwise be a series of unlinked character sketches, they hit on an intriguing phrase in an unpublished letter of Eliot's which his widow, Valerie, showed to Lloyd Webber. It spoke of 'the Heaviside Layer' a kind of animal heaven to which worthy and deserving cats might be transported. The musical centres on the choosing of a cat who is to be transported to this layer. In the event, it is Grizabella, the glamour cat, who is chosen to be reborn because she has discovered the meaning of what true happiness is. The theological implications of this story with its echoes of the doctrines of election and resurrection are not pursued in the musical but there are at least two significant spiritual moments in this most commercial of all box offices successes. The first comes in the prologue, 'Jellicle Songs for Jellicle Cats', where a series of organ chords announce a dramatic change of pace and theme as the company go into 'churchy' mode to sing:

> The mystical divinity of unashamed felinity
> Round the Cathedral rang 'vivat'
> Life to the everlasting cat.

If the message here is of feline divinity and immortality, the second spiritual moment, which occurs near the end of the show, seems to be speaking rather of redemptive feline apotheosis and resurrection as Old Deuteronomy and Grizabella are carried up to the Heaviside Layer on a flying saucer-like object with dry ice pouring out of every orifice. A stairway descends from the skies and Grizabella walks up it as if to another realm and another life.

Phantom of the Opera (1986), Lloyd Webber's lushest and most operatic score with lyrics by Charles Hart, explores a much darker side of the dream theme. The phantom first comes to Christine in a dream. As she glides across the underground lake in his boat, she sings: 'In sleep he sang to me, in dreams he came'. Luring her into his subterranean lair with that extraordinarily bewitching song 'The music of the night', he commands her: 'close your eyes and surrender to your darkest dreams'. The ravishing, seductive music here suggests dreams of an intoxicating and bewitching kind. We are a world away from the strenuous, wholesome outdoor dreams to be found by climbing every mountain and fording every stream – the atmosphere here is claustrophobic and overpowering. There is a deep ambiguity too in Christine's surrender to these darker dreams and in the character of the phantom, 'the loathsome gargoyle, who burns in hell but secretly yearns for heaven . . . this repulsive carcass who seems a beast but secretly dreams of beauty'.

Phantom is also significant for containing one of the show songs which is most frequently requested at funerals. It comes in the fifth scene of the second act when Christine visits her father's grave:

Wishing you were somehow here again,
Wishing you were somehow near,
Sometimes it seemed, if I just dreamed,
Somehow you would be here.

Wishing I could hear your voice again,
Knowing that I never would,
Dreaming of you won't help me to do
All that you dreamed I could.

This song develops into a remarkably accurate run through the various stages of mourning as they have been classically described by Elizabeth Kübler-Ross in her book *On Death and Dying*. It ends with the crucial and poignant words 'Help me say goodbye', a sensitive acknowledgement of the importance of letting go. There is a pastorally very helpful development of the dream theme in this song – from the initial wishful thinking that you can dream up the presence of someone who has died to the realization at the end that one has to accept what has happened.

While Lloyd Webber's romantic extravagance and spectacular special effects set the tone for musical theatre, a very different type of show began to emerge in the mid-1980s. *Blood Brothers* (1983), with book, lyrics and music by the Liverpool beat poet Willy Russell, had no glamorous sets or soaring melodies. It recounted in a depressing and utterly realistic way the story of an impoverished Liverpool housewife deserted by her husband and unable to afford the cost of bringing up her twin baby sons, Mickey and Eddie. Keeping Mickey, she gives Eddie away as a surrogate son to the rich lady for whom she works as a charlady. The very different lives of the two boys as they grow up provide the basis for a biting commentary on the English class system. Mickey is sent to prison for seven years for his part in an armed robbery. In gaol he suffers severe depressive illness, which is harrowingly portrayed on stage. On his release, he sees Eddie with the girl that he had married before he was imprisoned and shoots him dead. Mickey is then shot by the police. Ironically, the day that the two men die is also the day that they discover they are brothers. There is no glimmering of a happy ending in this tragic tale set in the grim back-to-back terraces of depressed post-industrial urban Britain. The dream theme is certainly there, but only to point to its futility. Mickey and Eddie's mother dreams hopelessly and absurdly of being Marilyn Monroe. It is left to the narrator, a somewhat sinister figure who provides a commentary on the unfolding tragedy, to reflect on its depressing message: 'If only we didn't live in life as well as in dreams.'

The gritty realism of *Blood Brothers*, which despite its drab set and depressing theme became a major hit, was picked up by several subsequent British musicals in the increasingly gloomy atmosphere of the late 1980s and 1990s. There was a similar move away from lush romantic escapism in American musical theatre. The defining Broadway show in this respect came more than a decade after its British equivalent. If *Blood Brothers* made a hit musical out of the subjects of social inequality and mental illness, *Rent* (1996) did so out of the scourge of HIV/Aids. The action is set in similarly grim surroundings – in this case a seedy industrial loft in East Village, New York, in which a group of HIV-positive, drug-taking and homeless young people are squatting. Such a setting was all too familiar to *Rent*'s creator, lyricist and composer, Jonathan Larson, whose loftspace apartment in downtown Manhattan had a leaking roof, worn-out furniture and a doorbell which did not work. He died there at the age of 35 from an aortic aneurism on the day of the final dress rehearsal. In the four months before his own death he had lost two close friends to Aids.

Despite its grim subject matter, *Rent* is a much more hope-filled and life-affirming musical than *Blood Brothers*. Its treatment of the dream theme is much less cynical and despairing. There is a nobility in the dream of the central character and narrator, Roger, a struggling rock musician, that he will write one great song before he is carried off by the Aids virus:

One song
Glory
One song
Before I go
Glory
One song to leave behind . . .

Find
The one song
Before the virus takes hold
Glory
Like a sunset
One song
To redeem this empty life.

Essentially, however, *Rent* is not about dreaming but rather about facing reality and making the most of life. The life which it celebrates may be rackety and raunchy but it is filled with human companionship and sharing – much more so than is the case in Puccini's opera *La Bohéme* on which it is based. Its most exuberant song, 'La Vie Boheme', is a wonderfully infectious anthem to wild, authentic, alternative living. It also contains the one and only biblical quote in the show: 'Let he among us who is without sin be the first to condemn.' There is no attempt to hide or cover over the nasty side of life for those suffering from a terrible and terminal illness. It is starkly expressed in the haunting song 'Will I lose my dignity?' *Rent* is ultimately a hopeful show, however, because it recognizes and acknowledges the power of love and especially of love in adversity. Without any explicit Christian or other theological underpinning it identifies the truth that the deepest human fellowship is to be found in human suffering, in Christian terms at the foot of the Cross. This is demonstrated especially through the figure of Angel, the transvestite street drummer who radiates love and expresses his creed as he covers the man whom he has rescued from a mugging with his own coat:

I think they meant it
When they said you can't buy love
Now I know you can rent it

Rent's great hit song, the anthem-like 'Seasons of love', proclaims that love is the only way you can really measure out your life. The ultimate message of the show is a reiteration of the familiar theme that we first encountered with Gilbert and Sullivan of *carpe diem*. The meeting of the HIV self-help support group concludes with everyone singing:

No other road
No other way
No day but today.

This becomes a central theme and constant leitmotif throughout the musical with the cast reiterating the message 'There's only now, there's only here'. The final song ends with the words 'No day but today.'

At one level, *Rent* stands as a musical representation of contemporary urban living. Anthony Rapp, the gay actor who created the role of Mark, the show's narrator, in the original Broadway production, has written: 'We recognize this play is a theatricalization of something, but we feel like we're being represented. My friends and I, we want something alive, something relevant, something meaningful, and thrilling, and sexy and sad.'[1] But it also stands in a long line of musicals which, from Gilbert and Sullivan onwards, have essentially celebrated and extolled living in the here and now. To that extent, it counters the theme of dreaming and yearning for a different and better life found in so many musicals of the mid-twentieth century. Rather it echoes the 'live for today' philosophy of Jerry Herman, articulated in 'Before the parade passes by' in *Hello Dolly!* (1964) and 'The best of times' in *La Cage aux Folles* (1983). *Rent* has other echoes of *La Cage*, which broke a significant barrier as the first Broadway show to major on the theme of homosexuality. It picks up the theme of non-judgementalism and being easy with your own sexuality and that of others so well expressed in Herman's song 'I am what I am'. But *Rent* is emphatically not a self-consciously gay musical, nor a preachy one. It is a moving and exhilarating testimony to human warmth and connectedness and to both the earthiness and vitality of human existence. In some ways uncompromisingly secular, its concern entirely with the here and now and living for today, it is also profoundly spiritual and fundamentally incarnational in its rootedness and testimony to the fellowship of suffering.

While the last three decades have seen no biblically based musicals coming close to the popularity of *Joseph*, *Godspell* or *Jesus Christ Superstar*, the Scriptures have continued to provide inspiration and subject matter for mainstream lyricists and composers. This has been particularly the case for Stephen Schwartz although, in keeping with the title of his first CD song album, *The Reluctant Pilgrim* (1997), he insists 'I have not chosen religious material. It has chosen me' and that the biblically-based projects on which he has worked have been, like *Godspell*, ones which he was asked to do and which he 'would not have dreamed of saying no to for professional reasons'.[2] The one exception to this general principle is his 1991 musical, *Children of Eden*, which he himself pursued after the idea was suggested to him.

Children of Eden deserves much greater success than it has so far had on either side of the Atlantic. It is a fairly straight retelling of the story contained in the first nine chapters of Genesis from the creation of the world to God's covenant with Noah following the flood. Schwartz has told me that he has always considered this musical 'a story about families, the relationships between parents and children, and generational conflicts, not a story about religion'.[3] It is certainly true that much is made of Adam and Eve's relationship with Cain and Abel but there is also a good deal in it about the parenthood of God who is portrayed in a long white coat as a benevolent father perplexed by the disobedience and bickering of his children. *Children of Eden* also and fascinatingly portrays God as a dreamer. Indeed, the opening number of the show, introduced by the words 'And God said "Let there be"', portrays him dreaming the world into creation:

I woke up from a curious dream,
I dreamed a perfect garden
And there were whirling shapes and swirling sounds,
And I wasn't lonely any more.

I woke up from a wonderful dream,
A world full of emptiness and hunger
And now this hunger will be stilled
And this emptiness be filled
As I set about to build my dream.

This rather attractive presentation of the idea that in the beginning was not so much the Word as the dream is accompanied with the refrain 'Let there be, let there be'. The dream theme is continued through the show. Eve is portrayed as a habitual dreamer – she sings the title song 'Children of Eden' in which she laments the loss of innocence that cannot be regained. This theme is picked up after her death when Noah asks his children, 'Can we give Eden back to you?' Overall, the theme of this rock opera is the yearning for the lost Eden of primal innocence and purity.

In 1998 Schwartz wrote both words and music for another biblically based musical, *The Prince of Egypt*, a 97-minute animated film on the life of Moses. Described as 'the first spiritual animated film', it had the prominent evangelical Jerry Falwell as its religious adviser. It has neither the freshness, vitality and sense of fun of *Godspell*, nor the epic quality of *Children of Eden*. Rather portentous arrangements hype up every song with soaring ethereal choirs and strings. There are occasional attempts to introduce a more authentic Middle Eastern flavour, as in the engaging rendition of verses from Moses' great song to the Lord in Exodus 15, 'I will sing to the Lord for he has triumphed gloriously'. For the most part, however, it is American to the core and as pre-packaged and predictable as a Chicken Macnugget. Produced by the intriguingly named DreamWorks Pictures, it sometimes feels like a self-consciously evangelistic Christian musical, as in the main hit, 'When you believe', sung by Miriam and Tzipporah:

> There can be miracles
> When you believe
> Though hope is frail
> It's hard to kill
> Who knows what miracles
> You can achieve
> When you believe
> Somehow you will
> You will when you believe.

Schwartz originally wrote the first line of this song as 'You can work miracles when you believe'. However, he was asked to change it because some of the more conservative Christian leaders vetting the film objected that only God can work miracles.

> I was asked to change it to something like 'God will work miracles when you believe' and needless to say, I declined for both aesthetic and philosophical reasons. But ultimately, it was so important to DreamWorks to have the imprimatur of approval from these religious leaders or at least not have them urge their followers to boycott the film as had happened with other films in the past, that I acceded to the request to change the line and came up with the more innocuous 'There can be miracles when you believe' that was used in the film.[4]

A rather more substantial and original musical of 1998, certainly in its subject matter and lyrics if not perhaps in its music, was *Sophie's*

World, written by two Norwegians, Oystein Wilk and Gisle Kvern-dokk, and based on Jostein Gaarder's best-selling novel. Premiered at the Schlossfestpiele in Ettlingen, Germany, it has so far come to neither Britain nor the United States despite being written in English. It has the surely unique distinction of being a commercial musical almost entirely based on the exploration of philosophical concepts. Among its more intriguing and original numbers are a love song in which Plato tells Sophie that together on the wings of love they will fly to the world of ideas, an exposition of Darwin's theory of evolution by Noah and a duet between Kierkegaard and Hegel (who sounds remarkably like Noel Coward on the original cast recording) about the competing merits of existentialism and dialectic which is reminiscent of Jesus and John the Baptist's counter-duet in *Godspell* and involves such tongue-twisting lines as 'To blazes then with this Hegelian historicism' and 'Truth for everyone of us is existentially defined'. Freud and Hildegaard of Bingen also have solo songs and there is a brisk tutorial on medieval theology:

Well along came old Aquinas
Putting Ari on his feet
Joining up this thing of faith with natural reason
Well he says it's just a matter of thoughts crossing the street
And Aristotle is no longer out of season.

In the end, the message of *Sophie's World* is similar to that of *Rent* – forget the philosophy and go with your instincts. It is belted out by Freud in his song 'Libido', with its distinct echoes of the Phantom of the Opera's call on Christina to follow her darker dreams:

Let, let our murky desire
Let, let us burn up in its fire
Let us go searching in the darkest of dreams
Let us go wallow in the underground streams.

The year 1998 also brought a new musical from Andrew Lloyd Webber which departed from the lush romanticism and spectacular effects of most of his work over the previous two decades and harked back rather to the angst-ridden angularity of *Superstar*. His lyricist on *Whistle Down the Wind* was Jim Steinman, a songwriter memorably described by the *Los Angeles Times* as 'the Richard Wagner of Rock' and best known for his Meat Loaf album, *Bat out of Hell*. Their collaboration, based on Mary Hayley Bell's 1958 short story about a group of children who shelter a murderer on the run in the conviction that he is Jesus, had a reasonable run in London but has yet to make it to Broadway despite breaking box-office records during a nine week try-out in Washington in 1997. Critics, especially in the United States, were generally dismissive but in theological terms it is perhaps the most interesting and significant musical of the last ten years.

Whistle Down the Wind has close affinities with *Jesus Christ Superstar* in its subject matter as well as its tone. It also resembles *Les Misérables* in having a noticeably more Christian and spiritual focus than the original story on which it is based. *Whistle Down the Wind* has, in fact, had three incarnations. Mary Hayley Bell's original story is set in Sussex and centres on the arrival of a convict on the run, referred to as The Man, who takes refuge in a barn on a farm. A trio of children, Swallow, Brat and Poor Baby, discover him and are convinced that he is Jesus, largely because they have been drilled at Sunday School in the doctrine of his imminent second coming. They care for The Man and protect him when the police come looking for him. He manages to escape and leaves a little black cross etched on to the wall of the barn. The book leaves the question open as to whether The Man could, in fact, have been Jesus. It is certainly clear that the children believe he was and there is a slight suggestion that they persuade their father although for the most part he stands for adult scepticism, not knowing how to react when Brat asks him 'Grown ups don't believe much in Jesus, do they?'

In the 1961 film of *Whistle Down the Wind* made by Richard Attenborough and Bryan Forbes The Man is portrayed in a rather more menacing light and there is a much clearer sense that he is not Jesus but simply an escaped convict. It introduces the idea, taken up in the musical, that the children think he is Jesus because his first words when they see him in the barn are 'Jesus Christ'. It also makes much of the fate of the kitten whom Charles, the youngest of the three children, entrusts to The Man, having previously tried to give it to a Salvation Army officer who tells him that 'Jesus will look after it'. The Man lets the kitten die and Charles is heartbroken and perplexed as to how Jesus could let this happen. His eldest sister, who is called Katy in the film, takes this question to the local vicar who flannels about the need for all of us to die in order to make way for new babies to come into the world.

Steinman and Lloyd Webber's musical changes the mood and dynamics of the story told in the original book and film in a number of ways. By transporting the setting from sleepy Sussex to 1950s Bible-belt Louisiana in the throes of a religious revival, it creates an atmosphere of steamy intensity and revivalist fervour. It also takes away some of the innocence of the earlier versions. Swallow, who is just 12 in Mary Hayley Bell's short story, is made 16 and there is an element of sexual tension in her relationship both with The Man and the local boy Amos. A racial element is also introduced by giving Amos a relationship with a black girl, Candy. More than either the book or the film, the musical explores the nature of religious faith by pitching the children's trust and credulity against the sceptical cynicism and harsh judgementalism of the adults. It also introduces a new essentially theological element by having The Man explore the implications of the identity which the children insist on giving him. He becomes a figure not unlike the angst-ridden Jesus of *Superstar* wrestling with the question of his identity and with such deep subjects as the nature and value of prayer.

Like *Les Misérables*, the libretto of *Whistle Down the Wind* makes copious use of religious language and imagery. Prayer and praying are mentioned 39 times (they do not receive a single mention in Mary Haley Bell's short story), Jesus 24 times, the Devil 20 times, Heaven 10 times and the Saviour 7. The religious emphasis in the musical is apparent from its very first song, 'The keys to the vaults of heaven', a revivalist hymn introduced by crashing organ chords and sung by the preacher and congregation of a typical Bible-belt meeting house who roar out their need to find the keys which will open the vaults of heaven. This opening number sets up one of the musical's key themes – the contrast between the dark, suspicious world of adults and the faith and optimism of children. While the adults sing 'The nights have been growing darker, even darker now than sin', the children counter with 'One sweet day when the whole world's ready, we'll awake to a glorious sight'.

The subject of prayer which bulks so large in this musical is introduced significantly by the children, who ruminate about all the things they pray for, worthy, unworthy, significant, trivial, altruistic and selfish, but none of which ever seem to be answered or come true. Swallow sums up their perplexity in her song 'I never get what I pray for':

I want to be baptised and I want to be saved
I want to see my saviour face to face
I want to feel the rapture
Feel the fire
I want to be taken to some place higher
But I never get taken to some place higher.
I never get what I pray for
I could pray for less
Or a whole lot more
It don't ever matter
It's a sure bet
That I never get
What I pray for.

The Man identifies himself to the children by shouting out 'Jesus Christ' when they first disturb him in the barn and ask him who he is. Poor Baby is initially sceptical, saying 'He's not Jesus. He's just a feller', but he is won round by Brat's response: 'But don't you see. Every Sunday the Preacher keeps tellin' us . . . "He will return! And those who fail to recognise him will burn in a fiery hell." Besides, why should he lie?' The children see The Man as the answer to their prayers and vow to save him. His first big song, 'Unsettled scores' picks up the theme of prayer:

There's a prayer for the living and the dying,
There's a prayer to soothe the savage sea.
There's a prayer, it seems, for almost everything
But you, you haven't got a prayer for me.
And I, I haven't got a prayer.

This song takes the form of a shrieked catalogue of humanity in all its varied forms, the good, the bad and the merely ordinary. 'Say a prayer for all of these and more but there's still no prayer for me', bewails The Man. Is he saying that there is no prayer for the outcast, the despised and rejected, those on the run? Or could this in fact be a song about the unique plight of Jesus, the anguished, tortured figure, betrayed and the scapegoat for the world's sins who does not quite know who he is himself? Is it reflecting the fact that we pray to and through Jesus but never for him? There are distinct parallels with the Gethsemane song from *Superstar* in both the words and musical style of 'Unsettled Scores' and it raises fascinating questions about the nature of prayer and the identity of Jesus which could make a good starting point for theological discussion groups.

Whistle Down the Wind picks up the inevitable dream theme. In keeping with the mood of musicals in the 1990s, it is very much the theme of dreams not coming true, summed up in Swallow's lyrical song of yearning 'If only':

> If all our dreams were golden
> And never black or grey
> If all our dreams came true
> Then we'd never have to say
> If only it was so
> These are the loneliest words I know.

For the children of the area, among whom word gradually spreads of the arrival of Jesus in their midst, however, there is a real expectation that their dreams are about to come true:

> Wow! If we got Jesus on our side
> That'll make us awful strong
> Imagine that if it all came true
> We're long overdue
> Long overdue for a miracle.

The sense that Jesus is particularly the friend of children, and that when and if he does return he will work predominantly if not exclusively through them and not through adults is reinforced in the marvellously exuberant chorus 'When children ruled the word' which could without virtually any rewriting be transported into a popular carol book or church nativity play:

> Doves and kings and shepherds and wise men
> Came together and followed the star
> They all gathered down in the manger
> They came from so very far.

> Midnight is clear
> Our Saviour is here
> He's gonna guard each boy and girl
> No hunger or thirst
> The last shall be first
> The night that children rule the world.

In the original West End version of the musical, this chorus was followed by The Man telling the children a strange and inconsequential song about a wild woman called Annie Christmas, who had a necklace made with a bead for every year of her life and a nose she had bitten off. This song seemed almost deliberately unclear in its purpose or message and ended with the children repeatedly asking the question 'And the moral is?' to which The Man was finally forced to reply: 'I don't know'. For the 2001 UK tour, this number was replaced by a song in which Jesus describes himself as 'The Leader of the Gang', a gang which includes Elijah, Godzilla, Doris Day, John the Baptist, Abraham and Perry Como. It provides a much lighter atmosphere, more in keeping with *Joseph*, and reflects a general re-working of the figure of The Man in the 2001 revival to make him less disturbing and angst-ridden and more laid-back.

Whistle Down the Wind's great hit song, 'No matter what', sent soaring into the charts by the boy band, Boyzone, comes towards the end of the first act. As a hit single it appealed and came over as a fairly straight love song with a nice catchy, lilting tune. In the musical it carries a rather different and more profound message about the primacy of faith over reason and scepticism. As the children bring The Man their touchingly original and heartfelt gifts, a plastic flower that will never die, a seashell which he can put to his ear, a glass of fireflies and a four leaf clover, they assure him:

No matter what they tell us
No matter what they do
No matter what they teach us
What we believe is true.

This contrasts with the adults' harsh words:

No matter what he's scheming
No matter what he's got
We'll tear him limb from limb
That's all that matters
No matter what.

The second act, in which substantial cuts were made in the 2001 revival, does not have the strength of the first. A relationship develops between Swallow and The Man and with Amos also pursuing her she is caught in a maze of desire, fear and uncertainty. The protagonists in this three-way relationship sing a trio which is full of intimations of tragedy – 'so many cries in the night . . . so many unanswered prayers' – and returns to the theme of dreams not coming true:

> If you listen in the night
> You can hear your plans fall through
> One more fight you'll never win
> One more dream that won't come true.

Where the musical version of *Whistle Down the Wind* does clearly follow the original short story is in its insistence that if this is, indeed, Jesus who has come back, then it is not to give answers. Mary Hayley Bell makes this point by having The Man respond to all the children's questions:

> I don't really know what to say to you people . . . I'll just say this, Brat, and don't you forget it ever. We're all on our own, see? Every man jack of us is on our own. We've got our own lives to live and no one can live it for us . . . We're all responsible for ourselves. Me for myself – you for yourselves. No one can really save anyone else.[5]

In the musical there is a very touching scene where the children reflect that what they asked for from Jesus they did not get, not even answers to the questions as to why their mother died or why the cat that they had been nursing so carefully did not survive. It does not cause them to lose their faith, however. Rather Swallow reflects:

> Even Jesus didn't give me an answer
> Although he must have known
> So I've been thinking the answer is
> Comin' up with answers of our own.

Towards the end of the musical The Man tries to disabuse Swallow of her fantasies about him.

> If you go deep down inside my eyes
> Do you see a Saviour?
> A prophet?
> Or even a priest?
> Or do you see only the blackness there.
> That's the nature of the beast

The ones that you should fear the most
May be the ones you fear the least
If you know me
Then you'll have to know
The nature of the beast.

Swallow, however, persists in her faith:

I don't know why
You try to make me doubt you
Don't know why
When I believe my spirit soars.

She goes on believing even when he tells her that he can't bring her
mother back, admits that he has been in prison and sings about his
utterly wasted life, but she does seem to have a moment of doubt at the
end. In many ways *Whistle Down the Wind*, certainly in the original
1998 West End version, does seem to have a very disturbing and
ambiguous message. Is the children's faith in fact dangerous credulity
and are the adults right all along in their suspicion and scepticism?
Why is The Man so deliberately destructive of Swallow's belief in him?
It is all rather puzzling and unsatisfactory. The revisions made for the
2001 tour make The Man a much less threatening figure. Even though
Swallow does not want to leave him, he throws her out in an act of
selfless love before torching the barn. He is more touched than in the
earlier version by the children's faith and their ability to see the good
in him that he was so sure he didn't contain. Is there even a sense that
he has in some way been redeemed by the children's faith in him and
by Swallow's love which has released some latent goodness in him? He
is certainly not in a Valjean situation although the revised version does
end in a slightly similar way to *Les Misérables* with Swallow, Brat and
Poor Baby singing 'Whistle down the wind' with The Man joining in
off-stage and apparently from heaven to where they seem to look up.
Two girls come on and say 'have we missed him?' to which Swallow
replies: 'Yes, but he'll come again.' The earlier version ended simply
with an empty stage and a spotlight focused on the symbol of the
Cross etched on the charred wall of the barn.

Whistle Down the Wind is an extremely interesting musical from
the theological and spiritual point of view. Charles Spencer welcomed
it as 'a commercial musical with the courage to take Christian faith,
mortality, racism and the problem of suffering as its subject matter',

while for Michael Coveney it signalled that Lloyd Webber had 'come full circle to the primal questions of faith, belief and friendship that he and Tim Rice had first, and more flippantly, addressed in *Superstar*'.[6] It provides a powerful treatment of the phenomenon of religious revival and the fundamentalism and judgementalism that so often accompanies it, epitomized by the snake handling and 'wrestling with the devil with a heartbeat'. Then there is its significant analysis of prayer and the persistent contrast between children's faith and adult scepticism. The overall message and moral is far from clear. At one level, it seems to be that of the closing couplet of John Drummond Burns's hymn, 'Hushed was the evening hymn': 'that we may see through child-like eyes/Truths that are hidden from the wise'. Yet there is an ambiguity about whether the children's faith in The Man is deluded and dangerous and there is also a strong counter-theme to the religious emphasis which suggests that life in this world is more important than any concerns about the next one. This is well expressed in the frenetic song 'Tyre tracks and broken hearts' where Amos sings:

Well I don't give a damn
About life after death
But I gotta get some proof
That there's some life after birth.

Perhaps what this musical shows more than any other in the Lloyd Webber canon is the theme which Michael Coveney has identified as running through all the composer's work, 'a quest and a yearning for the spiritual dimension in life'.[7] Significantly, perhaps, it was just after he had written *Whistle* that Lloyd Webber talked about prayer on 'Songs of Praise', indicating that he did pray but that he did not know to whom. At the end of his biography, published in 1999, Coveney goes so far as to describe Lloyd Webber in terms of the central character of *Whistle*, 'the hunted, haunted Man . . . no longer a superstar, nor even a superstore, but a transparent shop-soiled window of lost opportunity, unfulfilled potential and spiritual yearning'.[8] In that respect, he was the perfect muse for the uncertain hopes that accompanied the dawning of the second millennium.

While Lloyd Webber was expressing his spiritual yearnings in collaboration with an American rock expert, his old partner, Tim Rice, was teaming up with Elton John, the king of popular music, to create a Disney spectacular. *The Lion King*, which had begun in 1994 as an animated film, opened as a stage show on Broadway in 1997 and in London in 1999. As well as having spectacular sets, it had an exciting sound with much use of African drums and chant overlaying the soft rock music. It had its corny Disneyesque moments and characters, like Timon the meerkat and Pumbaa the warthog, but it also had a pulsating spiritual message in its celebration of creation, primal religion and sacred kingship brought to life through the thrill of sunset and shadow, the shaman and the focus on Simba's dawning realization of his responsibility to succeed to his father's throne.

It is tempting to identify *The Lion King* as the first distinctively post-Christian show, drawing on the religions of animism and ancestor worship. The compelling opening song 'The circle of life' takes us into the primal realms of regeneration and rebirth, sacrifice of one for the many, reinforced by Mustafa's profound statement to Simba as he shows him the lands which he will one day inherit: 'Life rises from death. Everything is connected in the great circle of life. As a king you will have to understand it.' As I have pointed out elsewhere, I take *The Lion King* to be a celebration and affirmation of the doctrine of sacred kingship.[9] Its three leading characters are the good, wise king Mustafa, the evil usurper, Scar, and the reluctant heir to the throne, Simba, who eventually comes to realize that he must follow his hereditary duty and destiny and assume the crown in order to rescue his land from famine and anarchy. The musical underlines the theme of cosmic order and sacrifice so central to primal notions of sacred kingship and emphasizes the intimate relationship between the character of the sovereign and the well-being of his land. It also underlines the hereditary aspect of monarchy and explores the theme of ancestor worship. It is when Simba sees the reflection of his dead father's face in a pool that he realizes his royal destiny and responsibility. The song 'He lives in you' sung by the shaman Rafiki conveys the sense of the departed spirits of the ancestors living on in their descendants and the especially strong continuing presence of the departed king:

He watches over
Everything we see
Into the water
Into the truth
In your reflection
He lives in you.

Critics have been divided about the extent to which *The Lion King* does, in fact, carry a philosophical message. For Sarah Sands, while it is 'a perfect millennium show – multicultural, slightly PC, full of hope and delight', it is 'over-sold and over-invested with philosophical significance'.[10] Matthew Parris, by contrast, found it almost wholly lacking in deep meaning.

> What did *The Lion King* mean philosophically? The musical was not without a moral, but the moral was, to our whole rich hinterland of Western philosophy, what Grandma Moses is to the heritage of European art. The moral was that good will triumph over evil in the end, the souls of the dead live on in the living, we must respect the natural world (whatever that is) and there's a place for every creature under the sun. Absurd, I realise, to expect Hegel or St Augustine in a family show, and the trite can move to tears. It moved me to tears. But trite is trite. A century which has lost its Christian confidence has found no new moral confidence beyond a sort of Hollywood-sanitized primitivism. Natural Law, by Walt Disney, out of Rousseau. If the cast did not quite break into 'Search For the Hero Inside Yourself' to the backing of skin drums, that's probably because it's copyrighted. Halfway through the century now complete, Rodgers and Hammerstein, in *Carousel*, were still capable of drawing upon moral ambiguity in a family show. We seem to have lost even that degree of philosophical literacy.[11]

That seems to me an unfair verdict. We are not going to get deep moral ambiguity from a Disney musical – I am not at all sure we got it in *Carousel*. *The Lion King* can be reasonably criticized for providing a Disneyfication of Africa but it does provide food for thought and it does have spiritual resonances. Its message about the pleroma and diversity of creation, and how life can only thrive on the basis of sacrifice and death, is not to be taken lightly. There is also surely some significance in this highly packaged and hyped musical from the most commercial of all entertainment stables returning to the values of primal religion. Is this a new kind of postmodern primitivism?

The closing of the twentieth century seemed to see musicals carrying everything before them, swamping the West End and crowding out straight plays. Under the headline 'Musicals turning drama into a crisis', the *Independent* devoted its main home news page in August 1999 to a story by its media and culture editor which began 'an unprecedented invasion of musicals into the West End of London is harming the quality of British drama, say producers and playwrights'. It pointed to the fact that 19 musicals were currently playing in the West End with a dozen or more due to open within a few months, and contrasted this glut with the huge difficulties faced by those trying to stage serious plays in London. Peter Shaffer, author of *Amadeus* and *The Royal Hunt of the Sun* was quoted as saying 'The quasi-immortality of today's musical shows fills me with dismay.'[12]

In fact, the fate of the new shows which opened in the first year of the new century suggested that very little was immortal in the new crowded world of musical theatre. Short runs seemed to be the norm, whether for shows at the glitteringly romantic or the grittily realistic end of the spectrum. None of the four significant new West End shows which opened in 2000 did very well. Picking up the gritty northern realism of *Blood Brothers*, Steve Brown and Justin Greene's *Spend, Spend, Spend*, retold the true story of a Yorkshire housewife, Viv Nicholson, who won the pools in 1961. The show's moral and message is all too predictable and is essentially told in its opening line: 'I know what you're thinking – What's it like having everything? – Well, you still want something'. This leads into an opening song 'I want it' which is reminiscent of Sondheim's 'I wish' from *Into the Woods* and expresses the theme of eternal yearning and never being satisfied. Viv Nicholson ends up reflecting back to the time before she won the pools, when she was in her little terraced house in love with her second husband, as the happiest time of her life. *Spend, Spend, Spend* is a classic example of a musical based on a subject which would previously have been treated via a kiss-and-tell biography or a television documentary. At the end I was left asking the question what was added to the story by making it a musical?

At the other end of the spectrum, *The Witches of Eastwick*, John Dempsey and Dana Rowe's adaptation of a novel by John Updike, was billed as 'a musical comedy' and offered a throwback to the pre-Rodgers and Hammerstein days of light, air-headed musicals without much message. Centred on the character of an ageing roué, Darryl Van Horne, who seduces three middle-aged ladies in a small American town and also practises magic, it provided the excuse for lots of special effects and razzle-dazzle production numbers. It is worth a mention in a book on the theology of the musical for being the only musical that I know of which accords a prominent place to Unitarianism. The opening scene features the dedication of the Unitarian

Church at Eastwick, prompting the line 'This is not a real church. You guys are all Unitarians.' This church is the venue for Van Horne's marriage at the end of the show to a young college girl, Jennifer Gabriel. The three ladies whom he has seduced and strung along, and to whom he also taught magic, now turn the tables on him in their revenge, and cast spells with the result that in the midst of the marriage ceremony he is struck with terrible pains, falls over the Communion table and ends up hanging from the roof while the church itself goes up in flames, its clock spinning backwards and its steeple toppling off.

The third major musical to open in 2000, *La Cava*, represents a romantic throwback of a slightly different kind, more full-blooded and portentous. Set in eighth-century Visigothic Spain at the time of its invasion by the Moors, it deals with the rivalry between Christians and Muslims and also has a subplot involving the expulsion of Jews from Spain. Religious references and imagery bulk large in the musical. It begins with the waving of the crescent flag and a call to Allah and at various points in the action a large crucifix descends and features as a focal point on stage, allowing various characters to strike attitudes and pray to God. The leading spokesman for and representative of Christianity, Archbishop Oppas, is portrayed as a deeply unattractive and duplicitous figure obsessed with converting everyone in sight. King Roderic tells him 'You're hunting souls instead of saving them.' The king takes a tolerant attitude towards Jews, Muslims and Christian heresies, telling the Archbishop: 'The Moor allows the Jews religious freedom as people of the book. We should do the same.' Oppas, by contrast, prays piously in Latin as his henchmen kill Ezaak the Jew on his orders and flits between the rival Christian and Muslim camps on the eve of their great battle, offering both his help and whipping up their hatred of each other. The spiritual build-up to the battle is powerfully conveyed with the Christians singing the 'Agnus Dei' and 'Kyrie' in Latin and both Muslims and Christians praying. When King Roderic is killed, the Muslims join in the 'Agnus Dei' and 'Kyrie'. It is a pity that the music is so weak and unmemorable. Although *La Cava* is first and foremost a romantic love story – the focus here being the king's love for Florinda, the young daughter of the governor of the Spanish colony of Ceuta in North Africa – it does explore, albeit in a fairly superficial way, issues of multi-culturalism, religious tolerance and pluralism and provides through the character of Archbishop Oppas a chilling portrayal of religious bigotry.

Religious bigotry is also the theme of the fourth major musical of

2000, *The Beautiful Game*, on which Andrew Lloyd Webber collaborated with Ben Elton in exploring the subject of sectarianism in Northern Ireland in the early 1970s. The first Lloyd Webber work to tackle a near-contemporary subject, it belongs firmly in the camp of gritty realistic musicals alongside *Blood Brothers* and *Rent*. *The Beautiful Game* is based on the true story of Bobby Sands, who played as a teenager in the 1960s for the Belfast-based Star of the Sea football team, which had both Catholic and Protestant players. He went on to become a member of the IRA and deliberately starved himself to death in the Maze Prison in 1981. Another player in the team became a loyalist paramilitary and also ended up in prison. Lloyd Webber and Elton had both been captivated by a BBC television documentary about the non-sectarian football team which showed how a shared love for the game of football eclipsed sectarian rivalries until the onset of 'the troubles' in Northern Ireland in the early 1970s broke up the squad.

The Beautiful Game provides a chilling insight into the strange combination of idealism and utter cynicism which makes up the terrorist mentality and into the power of violence to corrupt and deaden all those caught up in its spiral. There is not much sense of redemption in it and the overall mood is one of bitterness, despair and the needless waste of so many young lives. In many ways the strongest and most attractive character is the football-mad Catholic priest who coaches the non-sectarian soccer team and tells the players that 'there are just three things you need to know about God – he's Irish, he's Catholic, he plays the Beautiful Game'. He vainly seeks to restrain the more fervent Republican lads from joining the IRA. The dream articulated in this particular musical is the touchingly simple yet unattainable one of 'an ordinary day' when there will be no more violence and bombs and Del and Christine will be able to 'love in peace' despite the fact that they come from different sides of the religious divide. Their song begins with the dream:

> Dream about a day when we'll be
> Calm, serene, completely carefree.
> Just for fun. Think of one. Ordinary day.

It ends with a heartfelt prayer:

> Sometimes I get
> Down on my knees and pray

For that one
Ordinary day
When all the pain will fin'lly cease.

'Let us love in peace' was sung at President Bush's inaugural gala and at the first major inter-faith service at Ground Zero remembering the victims of the terrorist attack on the World Trade Center. It has also been movingly recorded by the Omagh Community Choir, a cross-community body set up in the wake of the bombing in Omagh in 1998.

It is sadly significant that the dream in this particular musical is expressed early on and that its realization becomes ever less of a possibility as the action progresses and we witness the progressive brutalization of John, the most talented and promising footballer in the team who is selected to play for Everton on the same day that he is imprisoned for his complicity in an IRA attack. In prison he finds that the only way to survive among the IRA hard men in 'the dead zone' where 'Satan sits on the throne' is to learn how to be angry and to hate. The musical ends with the boys who once played 'the beautiful game' together either dead, in prison, in rival paramilitary organizations or far away from Ireland and its seemingly endless cycle of sectarian hatred and violence. Their girlfriends are left to grieve and to reflect bitterly on:

Holy wars. Settling scores.
Ancient debts to call in.
We just loved to kill and we always will.
If hatred's all we're fighting for then I don't want to win.
I don't want to win.

Both composer and librettist insisted that although *The Beautiful Game* was set very specifically in Northern Ireland between 1969 and 1972, its theme was universal. Lloyd Webber revealed that he had been moved to write it by more recent events in the Balkans, the Middle East and the Indian subcontinent and that 'it was a story that could just as easily have been set in Kosovo, Beirut or Jerusalem'. For him, 'it deals with the issues of bigotry and hatred and what religions can stir up'. He also confessed to another motivation for writing a work so different from his usual output: 'I've been worrying, too, about where musicals are going. This one will tackle issues and will very much have a contemporary feel and sound.'[13] Although he did not expand on this last remark, it suggests that he, too, had become a convert to the issue-based musical and was seeking a change of direction from the romantic escapism of some of his earlier work. In the programme he thanked his socialist collaborator for 'steering me well away from, say, the Bloomsbury world of David Garnett or Holywood ageing divas' and coming up with 'a story about young people on the verge of adulthood, young people wanting to love, to play football and to lead lives in a city dominated by violence and hatred', although he characteristically felt obliged to locate his latest work in the great tradition of twentieth-century musical theatre, noting: 'It was the kind of story that Rodgers and Hammerstein in their early days would have seriously thought about setting.'[14]

Ben Elton similarly emphasized the universal and the political dimensions of the musical:

> We don't take sides. I don't have solutions. But it doesn't shirk the politics. It's a Catholic team, though there's a lad from the other side. One boy joins the IRA. One Republican becomes alienated from them. It ain't *The Sound of Music*, that's for sure.[15]

While less happy than his collaborator to make comparisons with Rodgers and Hammerstein, however, he went on to define the underlying message of *The Beautiful Game* in terms which would certainly have struck a firm chord with the mid-twentieth-century American pioneers of musical theatre with a moral message:

> Although this is an Irish story, taking place in Belfast, I hope that the themes and sentiments of *The Beautiful Game* are universal. All over the world communities are challenged by violence and hatred. This musical is dedicated to all those innocent and defenceless people who every day are forced to struggle simply to be left alone. Simply to be allowed to live and love in peace.[16]

I suspect that the heavy message and moral content of *The Beautiful Game* may have been major contributors to its failure at the box office. Its relatively brief West End run of just 12 months and its failure to transfer to the United States confirms that musical theatre audiences want entertainment rather than political comment and moralizing. *Les Misérables* gets away with it because it is so intensely human and the deep theological resonances are carried along and sweetened by tremendous spectacle and soaring songs. It also helps that it is so firmly historical and not contemporary. *The Beautiful Game* failed because it was set too near home and simply demanded too much of an audience who expected when they paid their £30 or more for an evening out at a Lloyd Webber musical to have big romantic tunes and glorious sets. When I saw the show, several of those sitting around me chatted throughout the performance, clearly either bored or unprepared to engage with the substantial dialogue which makes it very different from the usual through-sung Lloyd Webber score and with its serious attempt to grapple with the mentality of a terrorist mind – something that one might expect from a late-night television documentary or a feature in the *Guardian* but not from a musical by the creator of *Starlight Express* and *Sunset Boulevard*.

If the new more serious and issue-laden Lloyd Webber musicals were failing to find an audience, then some of his seemingly unstoppable earlier creations were also showing signs of running out of steam in the early years of the new century. *Starlight Express* closed in January 2002 after 17 years and 10 months, making it the second-longest running musical in the history of the West End. Among those at the last night performance was Karyna Thorne Booth, administrator of Jersey's alcohol and drugs advisory service, who had seen it more than 800 times and spent over £30,000 flying to London weekend after weekend and staying in a hotel in order to be able to take in the Friday and Saturday evening performances and the Saturday matinée. Asked to explain her addiction to the musical inspired by *Thomas the Tank Engine* in which the main character is a steam engine, Rusty, bullied by bigger engines, she said: 'The story is about how if you believe in yourself, even when things look black, you can really reach for your dreams. Watching it always makes me feel better and cheers me up.'[17]

Within days of the closure of *Starlight Express*, it was announced that *Cats* would finally end its record-breaking run in the New London Theatre in May 2002, after 21 years and over 9,000 performances seen by a total audience of over eight million. Hailed by the press as marking the end of an era, the end of these two exceptionally long runs seemed to confirm the feeling of critics like Charles Spencer and Mark Steyn that the reign of the big blockbuster musical was nearing an end. Cameron Mackintosh announced in 2000 that he would be producing no more new musicals, just revivals.

What is the state of musical theatre in the opening decade of the twenty-first century? There is a sense of the great shows being in the past. The twenty-year-old *Les Misérables* and *Phantom of the Opera* are still the surest box-office successes. Revivals are much in the air – *Joseph* returned to the West End in a brand new production in 2003, the same year that saw the launching of a singalong version, and *Oklahoma, My Fair Lady, South Pacific* and *Anything Goes* have all been successfully revived at the National Theatre. Another kind of revival, hinting perhaps at the end of the plot-led musical, is represented by the shows which basically string together hit songs from the 1950s, 1960s and 1970s with minimal story, the most successful being *Mama Mia* based on the music of Abba.

This backwards-looking mood is evident even in some of the few major new musicals to make a significant impact. Mel Brooks's *The Producers*, launched on Broadway in 2001, in many ways represents a throwback to the days of vaudeville, its songs a pastiche of 1930s' and 1940s' style and its central character a washed-up producer who teams up with an accountant to write a musical about Hitler.

If nostalgia is booming, so too is the wordless musical. Dance shows, first made popular in the mid-1990s with *Riverdance* and Broadway shows like *Dancin'* and *Fosse* are becoming increasingly dominant. *Contact*, which opened in New York in 2000 and came to London in 2002, is a compilation of three ballets danced to pre-recorded soundtracks which range in musical style from classical to pop and swing. Despite having no original score or live singing, it won the Tony award for best musical in 2000.

Do these trends suggest that the word-driven musical was an essentially twentieth-century phenomenon and has now finally outgrown its life or is being transmogrified into something very different? It is too early to say. The genre is far from being dead. The West End and Broadway remain full of musicals, short-lived new ones as well as old stagers. The dream theme remains strong and people are still writing issue-based musicals. As I was finishing this book, I learned of a fascinating new one based on the relationship between Freud and Jung. Entitled *Sabina* and based on a play by Willy Holtzman, it recounts the real-life story of Jung's first private patient, a Russian Jew called Sabina Spielrein, who went on to become a psychoanalyst herself. Jung's work with her attracted the attention of Sigmund Freud and led to the two men meeting. The book for the musical is by Holtzman and the lyrics by Darrah Cloud. As one might expect given its subject matter, the dream theme looms large in the score which includes such delights as a waltz song for Jung and his patient and an analysts' dance. Early on in the show, Jung tells his patients that they will have to choose between the dream world and the real world that he occupies. Sabina, with whom he becomes infatuated, comes to embody the message that dreams are the reality and that it is through understanding and sharing our dreams that we are saved. The show's theme of salvation through dreams is presented very much as an alternative to salvation through religion or some other external force. As Sabina sings to the patients:

> There's no God to cherish
> The sick and the lame.
> No one to punish you
> No one to blame.
> No one who can master your pain
> There is no one to watch over you.
>
> Lay down your head and dream, my son.
> Your dreams are the light that will help you to see.
> Don't wait for an angel who'll never come
> It's the mortal who'll set you free.

The finale develops this humanist message as Jung sings in the final song:

> We all dream the same dream
> We are all part of one soul.

Perhaps the most interesting recent development is Lloyd Webber's move into non-western musical idioms in his production of *Bombay Dreams* (2002) with music by A. R. Rahman, Bollywood's most famous composer with more than 50 Indian film scores to his credit. It is tempting to categorize this as the first 'ethnic minority' musical. More than half of the audience during its opening run in London was made up of members of Britain's Asian communities. The programme includes an invitation to those of 'South Asian origin or appearance' to consider auditioning for roles. There is a significant celebration of Indian religious tradition and ritual in the show, especially in the Second Act procession marking an important Hindu festival in which effigies of sacred elephants are carried through the auditorium and on to the stage.

Like *The Lion King*, *Bombay Dreams* presents a westernized version of a non-western culture. Its tunes may be eastern in flavour but they still have a pumping bass line and disco beat. It relies heavily on spectacle – in this case water fountains and stunning dance routines – and has the glitzy, over-the-top feel of earlier blockbuster musicals. Lloyd Webber has been quoted as saying that it has captured the imagination of people who do not usually go to musicals – 'We wanted to make people feel that musicals are hip and cool again. Musicals were losing the younger audience.'[18] In many ways, however, it represents a return to the classic Broadway dream theme transported to an exotic location. The underlying message is proclaimed in the second song, 'Anything is possible in Bombay dreams', and by the observation of the philosophically inclined eunuch, Sweetie, reflecting on the life of his fellow slum-dwellers, 'what else have we got but these foolish dreams?' For Akaash, the central character, the dream of escaping from the slums and becoming a Bollywood star comes true, although it is only when he returns to the slum and reflects that 'every dream I had began here' that he finds true happiness. The essential evil of the mafia boss, JK, the show's key baddie, is summed up in Akaash's comment, 'you turn every dream into a deal'.

Perhaps the brief experiment with gritty realism and documentary-style musicals was an aberration and, after all the angst and pessimism of the gloomy-doomy blockbusters of the 1980s and 1990s, musicals are back to offering what they do best – dreams. After attending a rehearsal of *Bombay Dreams* the journalist Chloe Fox noted:

> Musical theatre's job, it could be argued, is not to hold a mirror to society but rather to depict it as it would like to be – with not a note out of place. The fact that it has reached popular heights at times of political, social and economic unrest (the all-singing, all-dancing Hollywood of the Twenties and Thirties being a case in point) confirms its status as the most escapist of all forms.[19]

Is it escapism or is it rather their strangely spiritual, almost sacramental quality which makes musicals deal in dreams, possibilities and visions of what might be if only we lived in a better world? Nostalgia, retreat from reality and sheer simple uncomplicated entertainment value, as well as massive commercial calculation and hype, all undoubtedly play their part in the continuing appeal of musicals but perhaps they also speak to that deeper sense of yearning which is part of the human condition, particularly in times like our own where so much seems frightening, uncertain and hopeless.

7

Catching God's dream –

the message for the Church

This book has sought to show that musicals are the vehicle through which a significant number of people now gain much of their philosophy of life and their spiritual and theological perspectives. It is increasingly to songs from shows and films rather than to hymns that people are turning to express and represent their feelings at significant rites of passage such as weddings and funerals. Musicals are no longer just offering escapist dreams and 'happy ever after' endings as they once did. While continuing to celebrate and affirm the vitality and variety of human life, they now tackle gritty realities and are as likely to focus on the shattering as the fulfilment of dreams. Does the continuing power and the changing face of the musical have any message for today's churches, as they see their congregations dwindle and seek to connect with contemporary culture?

One of the main reasons why musicals connect so powerfully with so many people is that they appeal to all the senses and offer a total rather than just a one-dimensional experience. They gain their impact through being performed. The same is surely true of religion, and especially of religious worship. In Victor Turner's seminal words, 'religion, like art, lives in so far as it is performed'.[1] There is, rightly, much debate as to the extent that Christian worship is, or ought to be, a performance and much unease about the importation of the performance culture of contemporary popular music into modern liturgy. At a fundamental level, however, it is surely true that worship does involve enacted and performed ritual. Ronald Corp, who is both a choral conductor and an Anglican priest, sees close parallels between his two vocations:

A priest is rather like a conductor. He is a director, he has to interpret and, like a conductor, he has to be faithful to the text; yet inevitably adding his own slant to the reading of it. He is also responsible for a performance, for making an often repeated service sound fresh and new.[2]

The worship of God is the most important and distinctive work of the Christian Church. The word liturgy derives from the Greek word *leitourgia* which originally meant a public duty. It is important to hold on to both these aspects. Worship is a duty and an obligation, not a voluntary leisure activity or form of entertainment. But it is also a public and popular activity which must connect with and inspire people as well as offering a sacrifice of praise suitable and acceptable to God. Too often the Church's worship is dull, formulaic and static. People come to worship with many different expectations. They hope to be refreshed, challenged, uplifted, consoled, moved, instructed, cheered, assured and perhaps also disturbed. Too often they leave bored, deflated and unchanged.

John Bell, one of most innovative contemporary practitioners of liturgical reform, sees five components standing at the heart of worship: sound, silence, symbol, movement and colour.[3] All too often, it has to be said, only the first of these is present in church services, and before and after them as well, given the babble of conversation which precedes and follows most acts of worship. The sound of silence is conspicuously lacking from much modern worship. It is also lacking in most musicals, whose heavily amplified sound is certainly not something which I would advocate churches seeking to emulate. In other respects, however, going to a musical can often involve engaging far more of the senses than attending a church service. There is the experience not just of sound but of symbol, movement and colour. It can also for some people offer a more communal and transforming experience. This is the conclusion of Paul Glass, reflecting on his ten years as a theatre chaplain:

> In a society where traditional means of worship are being shunned I strongly believe that the basic needs that worship fulfils are still present in people and are met for some by a visit to the theatre. A communal experience where people are transported via the means of language and vision to a place where they can understand themselves and their place in the world better. A place where they can feel something together as a group and leave, as a group, having had their spirits lifted, or been aided in examining a common issue.[4]

It is, of course, true that attending a performance of a musical is in many ways an essentially passive experience, albeit often less passive than in the case of a straight play. There may be some clapping or singing along, perhaps some standing up or dancing at the end, and occasionally moments of more direct involvement like the sharing of the interval glass of wine in *Godspell*, but on the whole the audience remain in their seats throughout the show, focused on what happens on the stage. This is, of course, broadly similar to the experience of congregations in most church services, apart from when they stand up to sing hymns or perhaps go up to the altar to receive Communion. Relevant here are the three models of Christian worship outlined by Robert Warren during his time as officer for evangelism in the Church of England. The first and most familiar, which he calls the passive audience model, involves the congregation remaining seated for most of the time and focused on what is being said or read in the pulpit and at the lectern and prayer desk. In the second or spectator sport model, there is more colour and liturgical movement to engage the eye and perhaps a praise band performing but the congregation, while being encouraged to clap along, remain essentially spectators rather than participants. The third model, which Warren wishes to see adopted much more widely, is that of participative drama where the congregation are themselves involved in acting out the liturgy and do not remain rooted to their pews.[5]

Many churches, especially those touched in some way by the charismatic movement, are engaging in worship which conforms closely to Warren's desired participative-drama model. Significantly, there have also been more specific attempts at or proposals for liturgical reform in this direction which consciously seek both to emulate and integrate elements from the world of musical theatre. One of the most detailed is put forward by the North American Lutheran minister Tex Sample in his book *The Spectacle of Worship in a Wired World*. As the title suggests, Sample is concerned as much with the spectacle of worship as with the need for it to be more participatory. Describing worship as 'the celebration and dramatization of God's story', 'the crucial practice of bonding and commitment in the church' and 'the major entry point for people into the faith', he also regards it as 'the practice of the church closest to spectacle, though I'll admit that more often than not it does not show it'.[6] For him the element of spectacle is crucial if worship is to be relevant and truly incarnational in a culture which is dominated by visual images.

I want to design worship for an electronic culture that is fleshy and pitches tent with the indigenous practices of that culture. I want to design worship that has as a basic characteristic 'the construction of experience'. Worship will learn from spectacle. It will make use of the pacing, rhythm, and participation of performance. It will work with the soul music of the people gathered. And it will engage people in movement and dance.[7]

Sample goes on to 'set the stage' for his worship experience. He envisions a contemporary praise band with keyboard, guitars, bass, drums and other available instruments and four to six singers each of whom has a microphone. He notes, 'it will be helpful also to mike the congregation, provided sufficient technology is available so that a fuller voiced singing can be encouraged'.[8] He calls for a performance area cleared of pulpit and other furniture, 'except what is necessary for the enactment of the liturgy' and suggests that the room being used for worship should be one that can be filled to at least 80 per cent capacity – 'don't get thirty people lost in an auditorium built for several hundred'. Colourful banners 'which bespeak God's story' are hung or projected on the walls and the lighting reflects the liturgical colours of the season in the Church year. He notes: 'In this setting careful attention is given to image, beat, visualization, spectacle, performance, soul music, dance, convergence, meaning in experience, bonding and commitment.'[9]

For Sample,

attention to the construction of the liturgy as an experience requires focus on the basic integrity of Christian worship – gathering, pro-clamation and response, thanksgiving, sending forth – and on spectacle and the practice of performance with its characteristic of pacing, rhythm and participation.

He suggests beginning with a 'warm up period of extended invocation of the Spirit' when the band and singers offer songs and prayers in which the gathering congregation will be encouraged to participate through singing, clapping or other movement. Key phrases from the lections can be projected on one screen as the songs are sung from another – 'the point is to create a sense of expectancy and readiness about the morning and the themes of faithful life to be addressed'. He is keen to avoid anything that impedes the flow of worship and takes his cue from the model of the through-sung musical:

Stop and start movements need to be eliminated. The service will be designed to flow from one point to the next without such instructions as 'Now we are going to pray' or 'Now we are going to sing'. These can be clearly indicated without such intrusion into the experience. Moreover, music will be virtually continuous throughout the service, though silence can be very important. Prayers, litanies and responses can be done as voice-overs and they can be sung. The flow of the mood of the service can be suggested by the movement of the music, especially in transitions.[10]

Sample goes on to provide a specific example of the kind of service he has in mind. It begins with the praise band playing a fast-paced version of 'Will the circle be unbroken?' while lights flash across the congregation in a layered way. The tempo of the movement of the lights increases during the singing of the chorus, encouraging the congregation to join in more fully. A dance group moves into the aisles during the singing of the song, encouraging the congregation to move with them. Selections from Psalm 98 and Isaiah 52 are flashed on the different screens throughout the gathering time. With the ending of this first song the music modulates towards the next phase and changes in mood and pace. The next song is 'Just a closer walk with Thee', sung more slowly and in a more pensive mood possibly by a soloist. A prayer invoking the Holy Spirit and giving thanks for God's presence is offered as a voice-over. The lights now focus steadily either on the soloist and the one offering the prayer or on the Cross or other symbol. As the prayer ends, the music modulates again into an upbeat, faster paced song, 'I saw the light', accompanied by visuals capturing special events of the previous week in the Church or community. A time of confession is introduced by Frank Sinatra's 'My way' and a voice-over confessing that we all seem to want to live life our way and on our own terms. For the pardon or absolution Sample suggests using a song like 'People' ('People who need people are the luckiest people in the world'). He also offers an alternative musical accompaniment for this part of the service which underlies the dream theme.

Another popular music variation on this is the song 'I'm always chasing rainbows' where we find the line 'all my schemes are just like all my dreams ending up in the sky'. This nuances the confession differently since it owns up to the fact that one's schemes and dreams evaporate and do not take on any kind of reality, but it does address the widespread desire to live life on one's own terms. In the pardon a popular song like 'Somewhere,' which proclaims that there is 'a place for us, a time and place for us' offers hope. Here the proclamation of forgiveness in a voice-over can base this hope in what God has done for us.[11]

The service continues with Joan Osborne's song 'What if God were one of us' introducing the Scripture readings, read by a man and woman together in 'duet' fashion, followed by a ten-minute sermon most of which is given over to a story. Members of the congregation are then invited to talk amongst themselves about the story and its implications for them. Some of their thoughts are briefly shared with the congregation as a whole before the music sets the scene for the transition into the Eucharist, a highly dramatized event in which six young people are positioned on the stage, each representing someone with a different and desperate condition – deep depression, suicidal thoughts, a profound handicap, abject loneliness, acute hunger and poverty. Another youth represents Christ coming to their aid and healing them – 'Each time this happens, Christ took on the condition of that person and, after doing so, was crucified by those who had been healed.'[12] The enactment of this scene is accompanied by a soloist singing 'Pie Jesu' from Andrew Lloyd Webber's *Requiem*. The scene then goes completely dark, the music stops and the congregation sit in silence for a full minute or two. Then a light shines from the point above where Christ was crucified, symbolizing the Resurrection.

> This light has a very small aperture but can cast a beam across the room. With this light a soprano sings, at first quietly and without accompaniment, 'Prepare ye the way of the Lord'. As she sings, the light expands its sweep and magnitude and the volume of the song increases. Instruments join in on the third verse and the congregation is cued in to sing as the words appear on the screen. The volume of the song continues to increase with the growing volume of light in the sanctuary. In a room full of sound and light the elements are then received in this celebration of the Resurrection.[13]

However contrived, manipulative, over-elaborate and over-prescriptive it may seem, this specimen act of worship does represent a real attempt to engage with and utilize contemporary culture, and especially the culture of the musical. It is significant that in his apologia for such liturgical innovation, Sample makes clear that he is not so much uncritically hijacking or buying into the ubiquituous dream theme but seeking to critique it:

> Because popular music provides the narratives of so many people's lives, I want them [*sic*] in the liturgy and placed in the framework of the larger story of God's work in Christ. This placement involves not only an appreciation for certain forms of yearning and narrative display in popular music, but also calls into question claims from this music that will not stand the scrutiny of a prophetic faith.[14]

Sample's proposals represent the most radical and comprehensive blueprint that I have come across for importing not just the material but the whole feel of musical theatre into church worship. However, as far as I know, they have remained at the theoretical level and not actually been put into practice although some elements of his proposed service are based on a dramatized Eucharist performed by young Russians at an international peace camp in Alabama. Less radically but more practically, several churches and worship leaders have imaginatively built services around musicals. For ten successive Sundays in the autumn of 2001 the Cathedral of Hope in Dallas, Texas, based both its 8 a.m. and 10 a.m. services, which between them attract a congregation of around 1200, on specific musicals in a programme described as 'Odyssey Down Broadway'. Items from the featured show were performed by soloists, sanctuary choir and orchestra and used for the prelude, anthem and offertory. The musicals chosen were *Les Misérables* ('Bring him home' and 'I dreamed a dream'), *Beauty and the Beast* (this was the featured show for the service which followed the September 11th terror attack so in the event no songs from it were used but the sermon reflected on its theme), *La Cage Aux Folles* ('We are what we are' and 'The best of times' with Sondheim's 'No one is alone' being used for the offertory), *Cats* ('Memory', 'It's alright, it's Okay' and 'We are each other's angels') *Joseph* ('Potiphar', 'Close every door' and 'Any dream will do'), *Annie Get Your Gun* ('I've got the sun in the morning and the moon at night' and 'Anything you can do, I can do better'), *West Side Story* ('America' and 'Somewhere'), *Phantom of the Opera* (Toccata in D minor, Phantom medley and 'Music of the night'), *The Lion King* ('Circle of life' and 'Can you feel the love tonight') and *Man of La Mancha* ('To each his Dulcinea' and 'To dream the impossible dream').

The orders of service, drawn up to look like playbills with the logo of the featured musical on the front, included appropriate reflections by members of the Cathedral staff. For the service based on *Les Misérables*, for example, the director of counselling wrote on the theme of loss and pointed out how it can come through the loss of a job, the loss of a loved one by death or divorce or, as in the case of Fantine, the loss of a dream. She went on to reflect on the musical's 'miracle moments' which 'come from the soul as an act of compassion and faith'.[15] The sermons preached at each service were similarly focused on a theme from the chosen musical of the week. The Cathedral's dean and senior pastor, Michael Piazza, bracketed *Les Misérables* with the parable of the prodigal son and compared Javert to the older brother with his narrow view of love and inability to comprehend the mystery of grace and the power of forgiveness. Valjean, by contrast, accepted forgiveness and resembled the person that the younger brother became. *The Lion King* was featured on All Saints' Day with a sermon linking Mustafa's message to Simba about the meaning of the stars looking down with the Christian doctrine of the communion of saints. The sermon on *Phantom of the Opera* contrasted the phantom's words to Christine, 'Close your eyes, for your eyes can only show the truth and the truth isn't what you want to see', with Jesus' invitation to come out of the dark and into the light and know the truth that make us free.[16]

Another North American church which has made creative use of show songs in its services is Crescent Heights Methodist Church, West Hollywood, mentioned earlier on page 7. Among those who have started attending the church since it introduced songs from musicals rather than hymns is Sarah Wright, who stopped going to church 30 years ago but says she has now found a spiritual home: 'I think you can identify with a lot of these songs. I think everyone can.' John Griffin, the pastor, who has several HIV/Aids sufferers in his congregation, cites 'Empty chairs at empty tables' as having particular pastoral benefit. Asked what show tunes have to do with religion, he responded: 'They have everything to do with God. God is in our midst and God is experienced in community.'[17]

I have come across several examples of churches in Britain using songs from musicals both in worship services and in concerts. Mary Henderson, minister of Martyrs' Church in St Andrews, sent me details of a morning service which she based on Sondheim's *Into the Woods* following a performance of that work in the town's Byre

Theatre. Presented in two acts with an epilogue, the service reflected on the way the musical deals with fairy tales and particularly on the disillusionment which so often follows on from emotional highs and the way things don't end happily ever after. The service ended with an injunction from the minister to 'pick ourselves up, dust ourselves down and start all over again'. St Paul's Church in Covent Garden, London, regularly invites a performer from a current West End show to present a song and reflect on its message. Robert Saunders, a Methodist minister who formerly worked in the theatre, holds a monthly Sunday evening event in the studio theatre of the Theatre Royal, Plymouth, where he is chaplain. It often involves some of those performing in the theatre at the time and can include anything from stand-up comic routines, acting exercises and extracts from plays and musicals to communal singing and storytelling. Described by Saunders as 'a mix between cabaret, a show and a service', these Sunday evening events, which sometimes but not always include prayers and readings, attract many regulars who 'would never come to a conventional church service but regard this as their church'.

St Richard's Church in Hanworth, Middlesex, has included show songs in a number of its concerts. One held in 2000 to celebrate the opening of a new extension to the church building featured 'Day by Day' from *Godspell* and 'Gethsemane' from *Jesus Christ Superstar*. Paul Hughes, the church's music co-ordinator, has written:

> In concert situations, using songs from musicals with Christian themes seems a good way of telling non-Christian members of the audience what we are about and what we believe, but in a way that is not overly 'cosy Christian'. A lot of non-Christians will have seen *Jesus Christ Superstar* and *Godspell* in theatres all over the world and will have probably enjoyed them for the entertainment value. Whether the actual meaning and relevance of what took place on the boards will be retained (or even taken in at all) is a different matter. Taking the songs out of the theatre and into the church in some ways removes the pieces from their theatrical context but may cause people to take a second glance at their meaning, sitting in a church rather than a theatre. Another good reason for programming songs from musicals is that most appeal to a very wide age group and they also appeal to audiences of varying musical tastes.[18]

The children's music group at St Richard's Church, which caters for those aged between 6 and 12 and goes by the name of STRUM (St Richard's Unique Musicians), regularly sing songs from musicals such as *Oliver!*, *Grease* and *The Sound of Music* alongside contemporary worship songs and hymns. They have also performed a Christian musical, *Resurrection Rock*, during a service. Paul Hughes has only once used a song from a 'West End' musical during an actual worship service. 'All Good Gifts' from *Godspell* was sung as a performance item by the praise group at a harvest service. He says 'I would be less likely to ask my group to perform anything during a service now, due to the debatable implications of performance in a worship setting.'

A number of clergy and worship leaders have no such inhibitions and are given to breaking into song from the pulpit. At the Millennium Conference of the Methodist Music Society, I was delighted to encounter a lay preacher who confessed to singing 'Love changes everything' as a sermon illustration, and at a weekend conference at St Deiniol's Library on the theology of the musical I met a retired Anglican priest who for the last 40 years has sung to his congregation 'a bell is no bell till you ring it' from the *Sound of Music* and gone on to share with them the profoundly theological and grace-centred message of the subsequent song 'You are sixteen, going on seventeen' with its lines:

Somebody kind, who touches your mind
Will suddenly touch your heart.
When that happens, after it happens,
Nothing is quite the same.

I myself have sung from the *Sound of Music* while preaching in an Anglican cathedral and from *Les Misérables*, *Godspell* and *Whistle Down the Wind* in school chapels. I have also included songs sung by choirs in sermons – notably 'Hosanna, Heysanna' from *Jesus Christ Superstar* for a Palm Sunday service in a university chapel and 'Try we lifelong' from *The Gondoliers* for a Gilbert and Sullivan Festival service. In 2003 I used songs from musicals in a Sunday morning act of worship for BBC Radio 4 which took the form of a meditation on dreams and visions. The numbers featured were 'To dream the impossible dream' and 'To each his Dulcinea' from *Man of La Mancha*, the prologue to *Joseph*, 'I dreamed a dream' from *Les Misérables*, 'Let us love in peace' from *The Beautiful Game*, 'When you walk through a storm' from *Carousel* and 'Climb Ev'ry Mountain' from *The Sound of*

Music. To my surprise, there was not a single complaint to either myself or the BBC about the use of show songs as hymns in this broadcast act of worship and I received some very moving and heartfelt letters of appreciation which reinforced for me just how powerfully songs from musicals can touch people spiritually and speak to their deepest and most intimate feelings and concerns. It further convinces me that we could and should be using show songs much more in church services and meetings as worship songs in their own right as well as triggers for prayer, sermons and reflection. I have come across several examples of the imaginative use of well-known items from musicals to highlight liturgical, pastoral and evangelistic themes. One United Reformed Church organist regularly plays 'Memory' from *Cats* during the distribution of the elements in Communion services. Members of a Church of Scotland Kirk Session sang 'I have often walked down this street before' from *My Fair Lady* following a Communion service to underline their commitment to mission in their own streets and greater involvement in the local community.

I know that such gestures will strike some readers as cheesy and cringe-making and I am not advocating a universal move to belting out musical show-stoppers from the pulpit and accompanying every liturgical action with a contrived show tune. I am all too conscious of the negative effect produced on the unfortunate Katie in Nick Hornby's best-selling novel, *How to be Good*, when, seeking refuge in religion after her husband falls in with a faith-healing sect, she goes to a North London church run by a lady vicar who sings 'Getting to know you' from *The King and I* from the pulpit in a cringe-making way. Plenty of people are allergic to musicals and their sensibilities should be respected. When, however, the Church is seeking to connect with contemporary culture and with where people are now, I do believe that musicals have at least as much relevance as the films and novels of which so much is made in contemporary theology and missiology.

It is clear that a good many people find that lines and songs from musicals speak to them of ultimate values and help them devotionally as well as pastorally by providing reference points and resources of a kind that for previous generations might have come from familiar prayers or biblical references. I think of the bereaved parents who wanted to inscribe on their daughter's tombstone the line from the Abba song: 'I believe in angels, something good in everyone I see'. I think of the middle-aged woman who sang 'His love makes me beautiful' from *Funny Girl* with its line 'You are a beautiful reflection of his love's affection' and told me that she found it a wonderful summation of the Christian understanding of Jesus' love for us which accepts us as we are and accepts and transforms us. I think of the man who said that he learned more about the way that prejudice is inculcated into us from our youth from 'You've got to be taught to be afraid' from *South Pacific* than from any number of sermons and homilies.

The growing use of songs from musicals at weddings and funerals has already been mentioned. In fact, it is not a new phenomenon. An entry in the July 1974 edition of the parish notes faithfully compiled by Oliver Willmott during his 34-year incumbency in rural West Dorset, mentions a wedding in Loders Church where 'the bride entered the church to the pealing of bells and Purcell's *Trumpet Voluntary* and left to *The Sound of Music*'.[19] 'Love changes everything' and 'His love makes me beautiful' are two songs requested for weddings which, particularly when explained either to the couple or the congregation, can add to rather than detract from the theological and spiritual significance of the occasion. With funerals, the impact of songs from films and musicals can be particularly powerful. I was recently told of the funeral of an 18-year-old boy who had tragically committed suicide and where the only music played were recorded versions of 'Bring him home' from *Les Misérables* and 'Wishing you were somehow here again' from *Phantom of the Opera*. The latter number, as we have already noted, is a remarkably sensitive and pastorally helpful treatment of the theme of grief which goes through the stages to the need to let go. I would like to think that there are rich resources from the world of musicals for weddings and funerals, which maybe those of us who conduct such services are not always open to as we might be.

There is another way in which musicals are profoundly affecting the character of Christian worship. The musical style in which many contemporary worship songs and hymns are cast owes a great deal to the 'soft rock' idiom which characterizes most of the successful musicals of the last thirty or more years. I have myself talked and written of the 'Lloyd Webber effect' on church music. This is not so much a direct influence – aside from his *Requiem* Lloyd Webber himself has written next to no liturgical music – but rather a highly pervasive style and approach which informs much contemporary Christian music. There is, of course, nothing new about musical theatre being a dominant influence on church music. Victorian hymn tunes, not just those of Sullivan but others written by other more 'churchy' composers like J. B. Dykes and John Stainer, were regularly criticized for being over-theatrical and vulgar in their emotionalism and sentimentality. In the 1960s members of the Twentieth Century Light Music Group produced hymn tunes which owed something to the style of Richard Rodgers and perhaps even more to the influence of the British musical comedy composer, Sandy Wilson, best known for *The Boy Friend* and *Salad Days*.

Thomas Gieschen has identified ten different styles in contemporary Christian music which he describes variously as Contemporary Esoteric, Church Modern, Neo-Romantic, Pop Chord Romantic, A Touch of Broadway, Popular Triumphalism, Holy Pop, Pseudo-Folk, Clever Casual and Trivial.[20] There are doubtless other identifiable influences and styles as well but the 'soft rock' sound of *Jesus Christ Superstar*, *Les Misérables* and other blockbuster musicals of the last 35 years has surely been one of the major influences on popular contemporary Christian music. John Frame has described it as a 'touchy-feely' kind of style in terms of both melody and harmony which is 'seeker friendly' and primarily evangelistic rather than liturgical in orientation and purpose. For him, it expresses a theology of immanence and a God to whom we can draw near, as exemplified in the very popular worship song, 'Draw me closer, Lord'.[21]

A good number of popular contemporary worship songs and hymns could have come straight out of musicals in terms of their harmonic and melodic structure. In contrast to traditional foursquare, metrical hymns, they have a more irregular metre, with long held notes and much use of modulation and abrupt changes of key and rhythm. They are generally sung in unison rather than four-part harmony and often have an accompaniment which is more suited to instrumental praise band than to organ and which can often involve obbligatos and bridging passages between verses. Their tone is often personal rather than communal or congregational and their impact emotional rather than intellectual.

Responsible for some of the most enduring examples of this genre is a group of singer-songwriters who are very much of the Lloyd Webber generation – Graham Kendrick, Dave Bilborough, Garth Hewitt, Ian White and the slightly younger Matt Redman. They are evangelists as much as if not more than they are liturgists and they are performers as well as lyricists and composers. Their material is heard not just in churches but in concert halls and at huge gatherings like Greenbelt and Spring Harvest. In many ways these pioneers of contemporary Christian music have, consciously or unconsciously, brought the atmosphere of musical theatre into Christian worship. They have given worship music a much broader *locus* than the church building or sanctuary and have made it something to be performed before an audience as well as joined in by a congregation. In large part, of course, this latter achievement is a reflection of the wider performance culture which dominates modern popular music. It is not just the influence of musicals which is leading more and more worship songs to be written for performance by praise band, choir or soloist rather than sung by a congregation. It is a natural response to a whole range of cultural and technological trends. In the words of Brian Wren, 'Congregational song is in trouble nowadays, not because authority frowns on it, but because our culture undermines it, through social mobility, performance-oriented popular music, electronic discouragement and over-amplification.'[22]

In fact, as we have already noted, musicals may be supplying some of the new communal hymns and anthems of our age. Although they belong to the heavily performance-orientated and amplified world of contemporary musical culture, they also supply songs with strong melodies and stirring words which can be sung along to and are being picked up as community chants and finding their way into hymn books and church services. The quality of these songs is often very much better in terms of both words and music than that of much contemporary Christian worship song, justifiably described by Raymond Gawronksi as 'spiritual Wonder Bread: it utterly lacks roots, depth, sustenance'.[23] Where is the worship song which reflects as realistically and powerfully on the experience of shattered dreams as 'I dreamed a dream' from *Les Misérables* or laments for lost loved ones as movingly as 'Empty chairs at empty tables'? What contemporary Christian songs tackle the themes of Aids or sectarian hatred so directly dealt with in *Rent* and *The Beautiful Game*? The fact is that not only is the music in commercial musicals much better than in contemporary Christian worship songs but the topics addressed and the language used are often more serious, spiritually profound and theologically challenging.

How can the quality of contemporary Christian worship songs be improved? In respect of the music, it is tempting to suggest that leading composers from the world of musical theatre should be commissioned to write for the Church. Arthur Sullivan perhaps stands as the supreme example of a composer who successfully straddled the worlds of musical theatre and church music and wrote prolifically for both genres. More recent composers have also combined theatrical and liturgical work with striking results. Leonard Bernstein, almost certainly best known for his musicals *Candide, On the Town* and *West Side Story*, composed two significant religious works, *The Chichester Psalms* (1965) and his *Mass* in 1971. The first work, commissioned by Chichester Cathedral, involves a setting of the Hebrew text of parts of Psalms 2, 23, 100, 108, 131 and 133, and lasts for less than twenty minutes. It is in three parts, the first strongly percussive with much use of drum rolls, the second gentler and more lyrical with echoes of the English choral tradition but punctuated by sudden angry interruptions and the third dreamy and lushly romantic. The *Mass*, which Bernstein described as 'a theatre piece for singers, players and dancers', was commissioned for the opening of the new John F. Kennedy Center for the Performing Arts in Washington, DC. A straight setting of the Roman Mass with significant additional material written by Stephen Schwartz, it is a spectacular work which blends worship and theatre, enhances the element of performance in the celebration of the Eucharist and provides the kind of total liturgical experience for which Sample calls.

The staging for Bernstein's *Mass* involves a continuous path originating in the orchestra pit and rising as stairs on to the stage apron. The path leads to a central playing area and then up to a raised circular altar space from which stairs further ascend to a distant summit point. There are two orchestras – one in the pit with strings and percussion and one on stage with brass, woodwind, electric guitars and keyboards – as well as both a concert and a rock organ. The instrumentalists on stage are costumed. A chorus of street people consists of singers and dancers, the latter dressed in hooded robes acting as acolytes and assisting the celebrant in the ritual of the Mass. A 60-member robed mixed choir fill pews which appear upstage in the third sequence. The libretto stipulates that the celebrant should be 'a young man in his mid-twenties dressed in blue jeans and a simple shirt'.

The music is an eclectic mixture of highly percussive carnival and jazz rhythms reminiscent of *West Side Story* and more reflective and romantic orchestral meditations. Following the opening 'Kyrie Eleison', the celebrant sings a gentle lyrical solo, 'Sing God a simple song'. The powerful confession sequence is introduced with the celebrant speaking over an oboe solo reminiscent of birdsong. The choir cuts in with a crashing discordant chant of 'Confiteor Deo omnipotenti' which moves into swing time for 'mea culpa' with rhythmic bass and guitar accompaniment. Then a soloist offers a haunting vamp-like rock song:

> If I could I'd confess
> Good and loud, nice and slow
> Get this load off my chest
> Yes, but how, Lord – I don't know.
>
> What I say I don't feel
> What I feel I don't show
> What I show isn't real
> What is real, Lord – I don't know,
> No, no, no – I don't know.
>
> I don't know why every time
> I find a new love I wind up destroying it.
> I don't know why I'm
> So freaky-minded, I keep on enjoying it –
> Why I drift off to sleep
> With pledges of deep resolve again,
> Then along comes the day
> And suddenly they dissolve again –
> I don't know.

This leads into a trope for three blues singers expressing the ease of superficial confession contrasted with the pain of really opening up one's heart. The *miserere nobis* is sung as the chorus to a song written by Paul Simon and sent to Bernstein as a Christmas present:

> Half of the people are stoned
> And the other half are waiting for the next election.
> Half the people are drowned
> And the other half are swimming in the wrong direction.

The reading of the Scriptures is introduced by an operatic-style aria sung by the celebrant, 'You cannot imprison the Word of the Lord'. For the Gospel–Sermon sequence, the preacher reflects in a Gospel song style on the 'God said' passages in the Genesis account of creation, proclaiming the message that for all we have done to it,

God's creation and the world are basically good. The 'Credo' is followed by a 'Non Credo' in which a soloist wrestles with his difficulties over the humanity of Jesus, human mortality and the general perils of human life. This is followed by a solo urging Christ to 'hurry and come again'. The second part of the recitation of the Creed in Latin is followed by another questioning solo:

> I believe in God,
> But does God believe in me?
> I'll believe in any god
> If any god there be.
> That's a pact. Shake on that. No taking back.

The theme of the shattering of human dreams is picked up more than once in the Bernstein *Mass*. The 'Gloria' is followed by a soprano solo recalling that 'There once were days so bright/And nights when every cricket call seemed right' but reflecting that now, 'though nothing much has really changed, I miss the *Gloria*, I don't sing *Gratias Deo*. I can't say quite when it happened but gone is the thank you'. The 'Lord's Prayer' leads into a trope which begins:

> When the thunder rumbles
> Now the Age of Gold is dead
> And the dreams we've clung to dying to stay young
> Have left us parched and old instead.

The most dramatic moment in the *Mass* comes during the fraction when the celebrant suddenly hurls the raised elements to the floor and angrily asks the whole company, who have dropped to their knees in shock, 'What are you staring at? Haven't you ever seen an accident before?' This leads to a long meditation on the theme 'Things get broken' which seems to revel in the fun of shattering things and to question the whole meaning of the liturgy, 'that mumbo and jumbo I've heard for hours'. The celebrant then rips the coverings off the altar, leaps on to it and dances, tearing off his vestments and throwing them to the congregation while telling them that they should not be waiting and depending on him:

> Take a look, there is nothing
> But me under this,
> There is nothing you'll miss!

Put it on, and you'll see
Any one of you can be
Any one of me!

What?
Are you still waiting?
Still waiting for me,
Me alone,
To sing you into heaven?
Well, you're on your own.

The celebrant cries out, 'Lord, don't you care if it all ends today?' and disappears into the pit. The *Mass* concludes with the *Pax* and Communion, the 'Lauda, Lauda, Laudate Deum' being repeated tenderly and reverently by a boy soprano and all voices combining in a gentle and lyrical blessing. The directions indicate that the celebrant enters and joins in unobtrusively, dressed as in the beginning in his simple clothes. The boys' choir descend into the auditorium, bringing the touch of peace to the audience and saying with each touch 'Pass it on'.

It is extremely hard to know quite what to make of this work. Is it a grotesque parody and mockery of the most sacred Christian ritual or an honest interpretation of the Mass in which the liturgical niceties are interspersed with what people really think in a way which is truly incarnational and emphasizes the priesthood of all believers while at the same time acknowledging the reality of doubt? It is tempting to draw parallels between the celebrant in Bernstein's *Mass* and the Jesus of *Jesus Christ Superstar*, which dates from the same year. Each finds everyone pinning their hopes on him, yet deep down is confused, scared and tortured with doubts. It is not surprising that both works provoked similarly strong reactions. When it was first performed, many critics found the *Mass* nasty, cheap and vulgar. The Archbishop of Cincinatti called it 'blatant sacrilege'. A performance at St David's Hall, Cardiff, in 2000, however, brought warm praise from the *Church Times* music critic Roderic Dunnett:

It is, in fact, a wonderful work: vibrant, alive, visceral, challenging: a piece about faith and trust, and disillusion, and trust (seemingly) betrayed . . . This may be let-it-all-hang-out Christianity, but it doesn't date. The problems were much the same for St Augustine or Villon or Tippett or Tillich.[24]

Dunnett's verdict is that overall Bernstein's *Mass* is 'theatre, perhaps, but Christian theatre'. The huge range of resources required mean that it is unlikely to get more than a very occasional performance, although an excellent CD version conducted by the composer (CBS M2K 44593) conveys much of the work's atmosphere. It is probably not appropriate, let alone feasible, for liturgical use although some of Schwartz's songs and Bernstein's individual settings might well be worth using in the context of worship and the work as a whole does serve to show what exciting things can happen when a lyricist and composer from the world of musical theatre are set loose on a liturgical text.

Andrew Lloyd Webber's *Requiem* resembles Bernstein's *Mass* in being a setting of a liturgical text by a composer working predominantly in the world of musical theatre. Unlike Bernstein, Lloyd Webber had grown up steeped in church music and particularly in the English choral tradition which he had imbibed from his church-musician father and from his education at Westminster School. As a 13-year-old he had crossed the yard to Westminster Abbey in thick fog to hear the first London performance of Britten's *War Requiem* which had deeply impressed him. In 1978 he was approached by Humphrey Burton, then director of arts programmes at the BBC, about writing a requiem for the victims of the troubles in Northern Ireland. When he did get round to writing his *Requiem* in 1983–4, it was inspired partly by his father's death, partly by the murder in the IRA bomb attack at Harrods of Philip Geddes, a young journalist whom he knew and who had just been interviewing him, and partly by a story which he had read about a Cambodian boy who was faced with the choice of killing his mutilated sister or killing himself. This last incident gave him the idea of scoring the work for a boy soprano, youngish female soprano and tenor. In his words, 'the whole idea was that the boy was the innocent, the girl a sort of girl child, and the tenor the voice of the adult'.[25] The *Requiem* was tried out at the Sydmonton Festival in 1984 and recorded later that year with Lorin Maazel conducting and Placido Domingo, Sarah Brightman and Paul Miles-Kingston as soloists. The same team were brought together for the world premiere given in St Thomas' Episcopal Church, New York, in February 1985. Lloyd Webber insisted on the choir of Winchester Cathedral being flown out to join them in order to get the unique sound of the English choral tradition.

The critical reaction to the work was predictably mixed. Edward

Heath, who reviewed it for the *Financial Times*, loved it. For the *Los Angeles Times* critic 'it aspires to the pure fragrance of churchly incense, but ends up reeking of cheap perfume', and the *New York* magazine simply dismissed it as 'a pretentious and crushingly trivial hunk of junk'.[26] The 'Pie Jesu' which, following Fauré, Lloyd Webber inserted into the work in place of the more usual 'Dies Irae' shot into the British top ten, the only Latin liturgical text ever to reach the pop charts and the only single ever issued by the classical department of HMV records. Like Bernstein's *Mass*, Lloyd Webber's *Requiem*, although in many ways a more conventional and conservative piece, was as much a theatrical as a liturgical work. It was turned into a ballet by Kenneth MacMillan and at the Omaha Opera House Anthony van Last staged it in a double bill with the composer's *Variations*, turning the *Requiem* into a story about a car crash.

Apart from the *Requiem* and his setting of the millennium prayer, Lloyd Webber has not written any church music. It remains to be seen whether he will ever be persuaded to turn his hand to liturgical settings, hymn tunes or worship songs. He is fascinated by churches, their architecture and ambience and set up the Open Churches Trust to allow people to visit those of particular architectural interest. According to his biographer, Michael Coveney, 'if there is one theme running through all of Lloyd Webber's works, it is a quest and a yearning for the spiritual dimension of life . . . I hear church bells in the rock and roll, the liturgy in the levity and the agony in the ecstacy'.[27] The composer's own religious beliefs are ambiguous. Interviewed on *Songs of Praise* he admitted that he prayed but found it impossible to say to whom he felt he was praying – 'I don't know. I do believe there's something we don't understand and it's impossible to contemplate infinity.'[28] Maybe this is not solid enough ground on which to provide tunes for worship songs and choruses but it would certainly qualify him to follow Sullivan in setting some of the great texts of doubt-filled faith.

The truth is that Sullivan composed for the Church largely to make money. Today's musical theatre composers do not need the money and they would not get any from the Church even if they did. Instead of commissioning leading composers and lyricists, the Church has had to make do with its own home-grown musicals produced at a fraction of the cost of Broadway and West End shows. Christian musicals form a distinct species within the genre of Christian music and they really deserve a study in themselves rather than the very cursory treatment they are about to receive in the next few paragraphs. Given the lack of funding and the lack of hype which surrounds them, they do their primarily evangelistic work very well and also provide considerable fun and community-building opportunities for congregations putting them on. However, they generally lack both the quality and the spiritual and emotional power and reach of commercial musical theatre. Most are based on either biographical or biblical subjects. Alan Thornhill, an Anglican priest and playwright, based his first musical *The Crowning Experience* (1957) on the life of Mary McLeod Bethune, founder of the first African American college. His *Ride!Ride!* (1976) with music by Penelope Thwaites told the story of John Wesley and has recently been revived. The popular biblical cantatas for schools and youth groups like Herbert Chappell's *Daniel Jazz* (1963) and Michael Hurd's *Jonah-man Jazz* (1966) have already been mentioned as precursors of *Joseph and the Amazing Technicolor Dreamcoat*. Hurd went on to write other biblically based cantatas, including *Swingin' Samson* (1973). In 1973 a Jesus Rock musical *Lonesome Stone* toured the UK.

A significant clutch of Christian musicals came out of the Salvation Army in the 1970s and 1980s. John Gowans and John Laarsen, who both went on to become generals, were responsible for *Takeover Bid* (1968), *Hosea* (1970), *Jesusfolk* (1972), *Spirit* (1975), *Glory* (1977), *Blood of the Lamb* (1979), *Man-Mark II* (1985), *The Son of Man* (1988) and *The Meeting* (1990). Other Salvationist musicals include *Chains of Gold* (1982) and *Ruth* (1984), both by Gwyneth and Robert Redhead, *Beyond the Stars*, by Len Ballantine and Frank Reynolds, and 17 unpublished musicals written by Major Joy Webb. Most of these musicals were written for special occasions and congresses but several are still performed today, although Keith Turton, the Army's drama coordinator, tells me that 'not many musicals are being written these days'.

The single most prolific composer of contemporary Christian musicals is undoubtedly Roger Jones, a graduate of the Birmingham School of Music who began writing songs while teaching in Birmingham in the early 1970s. His first cantata *Jerusalem Joy* was followed by *Stargazers: The Story of the Wise Men*, *Apostle* and *A Grain of Mustard Seed* (about the Sunday School pioneer Richard Raikes). In 1984 he gave up teaching to concentrate on full-time Christian music ministry and has since written *From Pharaoh to Freedom* (1985), *Jairus' Daughter* (1992), *David* (1992), *Angel Voices* (1993), *Pharisee*

(1996), *Snakes and Ladders* (1999) and *Wildfire* (2002), which have been performed widely in the United Kingdom and elsewhere. Three significant new Christian musicals celebrated the millennium in 2000 – Paul Banderet's *AD*, which was designed to tell primary school and youth groups about Jesus, Garth Hewitt's *Feast of Life*, written for Christian Aid, and Rob Frost and Paul Field's *Hopes and Dreams* which included the setting of the Lord's Prayer to 'Auld Lang Syne' written by Stephen Deal and recorded by Cliff Richard. New Christian musicals are regularly featured in the annual Greenbelt Festival of Christian arts and music. Their dependence on commercial musicals is underlined by a report in the *Church Times* on the 2001 festival, which commented 'Theatre was largely represented this year by *Strange Kind of Hero*, a musical on the conversion of St Paul that was a little too Andrew Lloyd Webber for many.'[29]

Perhaps more fruitful and artistically more satisfying are the community musicals increasingly being written and performed by local groups on social and religious themes. A good recent example of this is *Freedom Sings* which traces the journey of the African American people from the slave gathering areas of West Africa to the cotton plantations of America and then on to emancipation and the civil rights movement. Written by Jenny Bowen and focusing particularly on the character and message of Martin Luther King, the musical, which includes slave chants, spirituals, gospel songs, blues, jazz and more contemporary styles, was first performed by a cast drawn from the local black and church communities in Leeds, West Yorkshire, as part of the 'Together for Peace' festival in November 2003. Another prominent Christian figure in the struggle for racial equality, Bishop Trevor Huddleston, is also soon to be the subject of a musical which is currently being written by the African jazz trumpeter, Hugh Masekele.

Putting on Christian and community musicals is one way that the churches are now modelling themselves on musical theatre and its great success. But how far should this go? Not quite as far, I may say, as I have been quoted as suggesting by some of the journalists reporting my enthusiasm for exploring the theology and spirituality of modern musicals and the lessons that the Church can learn from them. Among headlines in the Scottish press following the publication in the Church of Scotland's magazine, *Life and Work*, of an article by me about the spiritual power of musicals were 'Musicals show church the world', 'Kirks told to be more theatrical', 'Kirk urged to catch West End beat' and 'Stage set for religious conversion to musicals'. One reporter, who did not bother to interview me, declared that 'he urges priests to introduce the theatrical methods of the music hall to make their message more palatable to modern worshippers'.[30] Not surprisingly, I received a shoal of letters accusing me of wanting to dumb down worship by bringing the wholly inappropriate values of music hall into church. Confronted with the views attributed to me, John Bell, leader of Iona Community's Wild Goose Group, commented quite reasonably, 'the job of churches is not to entertain. If you have to deal with serious moral issues, such as the reality of evil, you cannot do that in an entertainment and expect people to change.'[31]

I was forced to write to the paper which had carried this story pointing out that I had never made any reference to music hall in my original article and had certainly not suggested that clergy and worship leaders should seek to emulate its methods or practices. Indeed I had specifically said in my *Life and Work* piece that I hoped the churches would not turn their services into light entertainment turns. In my letter to the paper which had so misrepresented my views I wrote: 'I can think of nothing worse than church services based on music hall turns and this was certainly not what I was advocating in my article, which looked rather at the significant spiritual dimension in several contemporary musicals.'[32]

Let me attempt to sum up what I have been saying in this book about musicals and what I feel the message is for churches and the Christian community today. I began this book by giving ten reasons for taking the subject of the theology of the musical seriously. Let me end it with ten messages that musicals might have for the churches.

1. Musicals are introducing millions of people to theological and philosophical themes, speaking to them of spiritual truths and ultimate values and helping them pastorally. The churches should be aware of and acknowledge this. It does not necessarily mean incorporating show songs into worship or quoting from musicals in sermons. It might well involve exploring how scenes, themes and characters from musicals can be used as a basis for prayer and meditation in the way that Edward McNulty suggests be done with scenes from films such as *Star Wars* and *Dead Men Walking* in his book *Praying the Movies* (2002).

2. Recognizing the benefits of putting on musicals. Increasingly, churches, youth groups and community groups are putting on their

own musicals and discovering that this is one of the best ways to weld community and bring young people into encounter with God. These may be home-grown musicals, specially written for the group or the occasion, or performances of tried and tested hits like *Joseph* or *Godspell*. I have met with a number of very enterprising clergy and youth leaders, especially in inner city areas, who have put on musical productions involving young people and enthused about their effect in building community and raising morale. Putting on a musical develops skills of commitment, discipline and cooperation as well as more obvious performance-related dramatic and musical skills. In some areas the church is the only building with a stage and a hall and can become the focus of the creative and corporate life of the local community by producing and staging a musical.

3. Making churches more like theatres. This is a controversial subject but one which may well be worth exploring in some situations and in some of its aspects. Already there is a welcome trend to build new churches as multi-purpose community centres. St Martin's Church in Stockport, for example, is essentially a theatre with a sacred space, a single building which incorporates an arts and performance area as well as housing a neighbourhood health centre. Many recently built churches resemble theatres in their interior layout with comfortable raked seats, large performance areas at the front and state-of-the-art sound and lighting systems. Many older churches are creating larger and more flexible worship spaces and performance areas by taking out pews, making previously fixed fittings like pulpits and fonts moveable and generally freeing up their space. There are pros and cons in these developments. Churches are not primarily places of entertainment, and worship is as much about participation as performance. However, there may well be lessons that the churches can take from the layout as well as the total experience of the theatre, and musical theatre in particular.

On Broadway, the decline of the blockbuster musical has provided one large evangelical church with a permanent base in a theatre. When David Wilkerson founded Times Square Church as a gospel ministry with a particular outreach to the poor, hungry, destitute and addicted in New York City in 1987, he was offered six empty theatres in which to stage his services. He chose the 1600-seater Nederlander but it was soon too small and in 1989 he moved to the Max Hellinger Theatre on 51st Street where Rex Harrison and Julie Andrews had starred in *My*

Fair Lady and Tim Rice and Andrew Lloyd Webber had made their New York debut with *Jesus Christ Superstar*. The church's first service at the Hellinger featured a live performance on stage by Jeff Fenholt, who had created the title role of *Superstar* in 1971. Wilkerson, whose congregation now numbers more than 7,000 and who holds six services every week in the theatre, describes his church as 'the hottest show on Broadway'.

4. Recovering the power of story. There is a general move in worship today to recover the theme of narrative and story. This goes back, of course, to the way that Jesus presented his message – not through abstract propositions and concepts but through parables which drew on everyday situations familiar to his listeners and characters with whom people could identify. Musicals tackle big themes in a similar way through fleshing them out in the form of strongly drawn characters facing situations and responding to them. In this respect, musicals are highly incarnational and they perhaps prompt us to make our worship more incarnational. Story can also be a very good medium through which to enable people to focus on their fears and insecurities. Educational consultant Shelley Marsh runs workshops for parents on how they can use *The Wizard of Oz*, of which, like the *Sound of Music* and *Joseph*, there is now a hugely popular sing-a-long version, to prompt discussions with their children:

> Everyone has at least one thing that they feel is not right about themselves. I look at each character and get people to talk about how they feel about themselves and how they might be helped to feel better. Some say they feel like the scarecrow, who doesn't think he's smart, or the tin man, who doesn't think he is loving or loved enough, or the lion, who doesn't think he has courage. Most teenagers say they feel like the wizard, a big-talking fraud.
>
> Self-confidence, *The Wizard of Oz* says, comes from recognizing our own good qualities and from others acknowledging them in us. The wizard makes the scarecrow, tin man and lion feel better about themselves by giving out certificates and medals proclaiming that they are indeed clever, loving and brave. Parents might remember to acknowledge their children's good qualities more often. Parents, too, need to be appreciated.[33]

5. Paying more attention to the atmosphere and experience of worship. One of the most striking characteristics of musicals, as we

have already observed, is that they offer a total experience which engages all the senses and leaves audiences moved, uplifted and perhaps even transformed as well as entertained. Worship is, or should be, an experience, and this aspect is increasingly important to those engaging in it. Writing about the post-1964 generation, Timothy Wright has observed 'people value experience-oriented services. They want to know that God is present.'[34] There are various dimensions to this experiential aspect of worship. One is the extent to which worship allows people to release their emotions. Performances of musicals often move audiences to laugh and weep. Should worship similarly allow and even encourage people to release their emotions, sorrowful as well as joyful? This already happens to some extent in charismatic worship. Some people are very understandably concerned about the dangers of manipulation and playing on people's emotions. Yet Jesus himself both expressed his own emotions, including shedding tears, and wanted others to express theirs, complaining 'We piped to you, and you did not dance; we wailed, and you did not mourn' (Matthew 11.17).

There has long been a school of thought that the worship of the Church and especially its music should be passionless and eschew emotion. It lies behind the measured regularity and restraint of Gregorian chant and Calvin's insistence that secular music should never invade the sanctuary and that only dedicated four-square metrical unaccompanied melodies were suitable for the Psalms of David. Musicals are full of passionate melodies, deliberately contrived to heighten emotion. But this has also been true of much church music – nothing could be more carefully constructed and contrived to heighten emotional tension and a sense of eager expectancy than the opening bars of Handel's *Zadok the Priest* or Vivaldi's *Gloria*. Victorian hymn tunes are supreme examples of melodies deliberately constructed to heighten and enhance the emotional impact of the words. J. B. Dykes was just as much a master as Andrew Lloyd Webber of the art of creating highly emotional and eminently hummable tunes.

Worship, like musical theatre, is essentially a communal experience. Robert Warren has suggested a new framework and paradigm for worship services to replace the traditional structure of adoration, confession, thanksgiving and supplication. He calls rather for a new dynamic of celebration-lament-hope.[35] This seems to me to be close to the way many musicals move and develop in their plot and overall theme. From Rodgers and Hammerstein, through *Fiddler on the Roof* to *Rent* and *The Lion King*, the elements of celebration, lament and hope are worked through and expressed, often in the form of communal anthems.

Another important lesson that the Church can perhaps learn from the musical is the importance of engaging with all the senses and picking up on non-verbal forms of communication. Brian Wren, a Protestant hymn writer deeply steeped in the tradition of the primacy of the word, has increasingly come to see the importance of other aspects of worship:

> My journey has shown me how hard it is to avoid the nonverbal arts in worship. When reformation traditions banished paintings, carvings, and banners, their architecture, pulpit, table, and seating still conveyed powerful nonverbal messages. The most determinedly word-centred congregations are heavily engaged in nonverbal art whenever they sing. The music they sing has its own inescapable autonomy: even unaccompanied unison song needs strong, memorable melodies to be singable for any length of time.
>
> Today, words still matter, but in different ways from even the recent past. In emerging electronic culture, whether or not we have the desire or resources to create worship spectaculars, we need to use our worship speech (including song lyrics) more economically and more vividly, in a seamless unity of words, visual images, drama, dance and music.[36]

I am not sure myself that the answer is simply to have more 'through-sung' worship which is a seamless unity of words, visual images, drama, dance and music. This is the way that worship has gone in many of the house churches and charismatic churches and it is increasingly the norm in many more mainstream congregations. It is surely equally possible for highly experiential worship to be very simple and to involve a great deal of that sound which is not heard very much in musicals, the sound of silence. Relatively simple but highly atmospheric services like Tenebrae and Compline are becoming increasingly popular. The most dramatic service in which I have ever participated was a Maundy Thursday Communion held in the upper room of a city-centre church in Glasgow. It was very simple but it abounded in atmosphere and experience. We walked up a flight of stairs to a small room where we sat at tables covered with cloths and lit by candles, and celebrated the Eucharist. As I recall, there was no music at all apart from our unaccompanied unison singing of a simple chant as we went up the stairs.

6. Taking worship seriously – rehearsal and discipline. I suspect that one of the important lessons that the Church can take from musical theatre is the huge importance of meticulous planning, rehearsal and discipline. Putting on a musical is a very complex exercise in team-work and corporate discipline. There is a considerable amount of dull slog and repetitive rehearsal. One member of the team can let everyone else down. It is a communal effort. Worship can too often be hugely casual by comparison, poorly planned, under-rehearsed and often not really a corporate, communal effort but all in the hands of one person.

7. Giving the audience what they have come for – a good night out. Worship is not a branch of the entertainment industry. Yet it takes its place in our society where choice is king as one of a huge range of voluntary leisure activities which all have to compete for custom among a bewildering variety of alternatives. People come to worship with all sorts of expectations and too often come away from it let down and unmoved. Too much worship is simply boring. People feel they have got their money's worth from an evening out at a musical if it moves them and if they spend the next week singing or humming at least one of the show-stopping numbers. How many worshippers carry in their head the words and tune of a hymn, a phrase from the sermon, a prayer or a reading the week after a service? We need to think more about giving worshippers their money's worth in terms of feeding them, engaging them and giving them something to keep them going. It may very well be a song. Research which I have conducted suggests that what people are likely to retain from a service of worship is much more likely to be a hymn or worship song than the sermon, readings or prayers. Brian Wren argues that for many people it is only through contemporary music that they will hear or experience the gospel message:

> For great numbers of people in our culture, especially those born since the late 1940s, music with a beat, and the integration of music, visual images, and dance are so deeply embedded in consciousness that they constitute the only cultural format in which they are likely to hear, sing and experience the good news of Jesus Christ. Thus understood, using contemporary worship music is both evangelical opportunity and evangelical obligation.[37]

That statement seems to me to underrate the other ways in which people can hear, sing and experience the Gospel. But it does remind us of the importance of speaking to people in a language to which they are attuned and of giving them the equivalent of their money's worth when they come to church.

8. Being true to oneself and remembering the importance of authenticity and honesty. This is a cautionary message rather different from the others in this concluding list. Services of worship are not carefully manufactured commercial products. They are rather offerings to God, sacrifices of praise which represent the honest intentions of those taking part. There is a great deal to be said for authenticity and honesty in worship, and also a great deal to be said for simplicity. Nothing is worse than worship which seeks to emulate the techniques and standards of professional musical theatre where the resources are simply not up to it. A recent letter in the *Church Times* described two over-elaborate Nativity services held in adjoining parish churches which were packed to the brim with congregations full of eager anticipation for a simple retelling of the story of Jesus' birth. In both cases people walked out feeling cheated and let down.

> Both these services, aimed at families with children, lasted for an hour and a half – a great deal longer and much less enjoyable than a Disney cartoon. If the church wants to set up an entertainment, the clergy need to remember how much stunning, high-tech entertainment (films, theatre, computer games) we are used to seeing in the space of an hour. They can't compete – and they shouldn't be trying.
>
> Next year – if those parents and children bother to return – I hope they will find a service which will last half an hour at maximum. I hope it will consist of a timeless story of wonder and marvels, delivered in the magic of candlelight, told in some of the most beautiful words and music ever written; and that they go out with a message of hope and joy in their hearts.[38]

There is much wisdom in this letter. Simplicity, brevity and sincerity are all important in worship. I fully accept that authenticity is a commodity that is often not very much to the fore in modern musicals. They can be highly contrived and commercial, part of a globalized westernized culture which Disneyfies Africa as in the *Lion King* and distorts India as in *Bombay Dreams*. It is salutary to read what Martin

Neary, the former organist of Westminster Abbey, wrote about his experience in attending a world festival of sacred music at the Holywood Bowl in 1999:

> I was intrigued to discover that what really moved the vast throng most was the chanting of some Buddhist monks, who had come together from three separate monasteries to make a 'symbolic offering of the cosmos for the purification of the Universe'.
>
> The Bowl was hushed as this extraordinary multi-phonic singing, combining the low overtone and the high tone (falsetto) heralded the arrival of the Dalai Lama. The sight of the monks, splendidly attired in orange robes, was almost as striking as their singing – but apart from that, there was no razzmatazz.
>
> This contrasted sharply with the negro spirituals and gospel songs which ended the concert. Deliberately preying on the emotions, these Christian songs of praise seemed to me rather an anticlimax, primarily because of the westernizing influence of so many of the arrangements.
>
> Clearly my neighbours disagreed as they cheered and clapped in the best 'happy clappy' tradition. What I longed for, selfishly, was to hear the spirituals in their original form, rather as I had ten years ago in South Africa.[39]

Here is a plea from a classically trained western musician for simplicity, authenticity and not westernizing other cultures. The musical more than many art forms could stand accused of rendering everything in a bland, palatable, easy-listening soft rock format. This is the sound that is increasingly predominant in Christian worship. Is it altogether too smooth and not dissonant and rough-edged enough? Worship, like theatre, has perhaps been dumbed down by the influence of musicals and other contemporary cultural phenomena so that it tends to be judged in terms of its spectacle, accessibility and hummable tunes. We need to guard against this tendency.

9. The twin-track approach – performance and participation. Not all musicals are hugely spectacular through-sung blockbusters costing millions to stage. There are others which are simpler and more minimalist – indeed, they may represent the way the genre is going in the twenty-first century. At the moment, the two styles coexist and complement each other. There is room for a similar variety of styles

and approaches in worship. In my book *Colonies of Heaven*, which explored Celtic models for today's Church, I suggested that perhaps the crucial lesson that we have to learn from Celtic Christianity in respect of worship is the importance of balance and rhythm.

There needs to be room for both awe and intimacy, silence and celebration, relevance and transcendence, order and spontaneity. But how can we hold these apparent opposites together and not lean so far towards one that we lose the other? I suspect that the answer may lie in adopting the twin-track approach that I am more and more convinced characterised the Celtic Christian model of worship. This might take some of the sting out of the rather unedifying and sometimes ill-tempered debates between traditionalists and modernizers, élitists and populists, proponents of timeless transcendence and apostles of relevance. The austerity, awe and formality of monastic liturgy existed alongside popular devotions in homes and at outdoor gatherings which may well have had pagan elements and certainly had an earthy simplicity and intimacy. There was no attempt to merge the two and create blanket all-age, inclusive services which mixed the formal and the informal, the timeless and the contemporary, the clerical and the popular.

We should likewise not be trying either to merge or to set against each other traditional church services and contemporary, praise-filled worship. There is no call to snipe at cathedral choral evensong for being élitist and inaccessible to many. So was the worship in Celtic monasteries. Nor is there any call to condemn modern worship songs and choruses as simplistic repetitive ditties. So were many of the prayers and charms used by Hebridean crofters and fishing folk in their homes and places of work. Both styles of worship are equally honest and valid expressions of the deep-seated human instinct to communicate with God and voice petitions and praise. They reflect the fact that people are on different stages of their faith journeys and express their worship in radically different ways.[40]

I suspect that the future of worship lies in adopting this two-tier approach, which is both/and rather than either/or. Let us cherish and resource centres of liturgical excellence, whether they be cathedrals offering highly traditional liturgy with superb choirs, monasteries with austere chant or state-of-the art worship spaces with complex sound and lighting and high quality praise bands. Let us have liturgical performances of Bernstein's *Mass*, Tex Sample's 'worship as spectacle' Eucharist and Lloyd Webber's *Requiem*. But let us also cherish and affirm churches and congregations where the worship is much simpler, more rough and ready and above all participatory – where everyone is singing even if it is not of cathedral standard.

Perhaps particularly important is to recognize and acknowledge the balance between performance and participation. This is not a new phenomenon. There is a long tradition in Anglican church music especially of putting a premium on technical excellence and precise enunciation of the lines. For its critics this amounts to a 'tyranny of excellence', creating a sound which is altogether too perfect and has emotion drained out of it. In the United States there is a current fad for turning hymns into chorales with elaborate instrumental preludes and bridging passages between verses which similarly puts professional performance above congregational participation.

We live in a performance culture, especially in terms of music. Despite the advent of praise bands, soloists and choirs, the Church has in many ways held out as one of the last bastions of communal singing. In doing so, it makes an important theological point about all of God's people coming together to unite in praise. In its own way, as we have seen, musical theatre is also encouraging communal singing by producing some of the few songs in contemporary popular culture which are singable. They may even be becoming our new corporate hymns and folk anthems.

10. Responding to the dream theme. This book has argued that the dream theme has dominated musical theatre over the last hundred years. It has many facets – the Pelagian dimension, the theology of immanence, the expression of human yearning, the desire to build a better world and also the increasing acknowledgement of the fragility of human dreams and how easily and often they are shattered by the tigers of the night. Somehow the Church needs to connect more with people's dreams and with the reality of their disillusionment. There is a huge interest in and yearning for dreams in our society. On a recent visit to a major bookshop in an English cathedral city I was amazed to discover two shelves of the religion section given over to books on dreams and dreaming – rather more than was devoted to mainstream Christianity.

We need even more to connect people with God's dreams for us, his creatures. The distinguished theatre director, Peter Brook, has written that

> in everyday life, 'if' is a fiction, in the theatre 'if' is an experiment. In everyday life, 'if' is an evasion, in theatre 'if' is the truth. When we are persuaded to believe in this truth, then the theatre and life are one.[41]

However that 'if' may be sought – whether at the end of the rainbow, by climbing every mountain, dreaming the impossible dream or recalling that brief and long-lost moment that was Camelot – it is vital to the human condition that it exists as a possibility, transforming, redeeming and ever presenting new possibilities. It allows us to believe that things can be different from what they are, that it is a question of 'if' rather than of 'if only'.

Musicals may over-romanticize and encourage escapism but they also point to deep spiritual truths. We all need to find our God-given and God-implanted dreams to live by – perhaps we all need like Don Quixote in *Man of La Mancha* to 'dream the impossible dream'. More than forty years ago the American civil rights leader Martin Luther King dared to dream of a society where all were treated equally – what must have seemed then and still seems today an impossible dream. His phrase 'I have a dream' has gone into folklore and inspired a modern hymn. It encourages us to dream our dreams and sing our songs but never to be content nor to rest until we see God's dream fulfilled and his love throughout humanity uniting us in peace. For Christians, for the Church, for all humanity, as for Lieutenant Cable, 'you gotta have a dream – if you don't have a dream, how you gonna have a dream come true?'

Notes

Introduction

1 M. Wolff, 'Now and what seems like forever', *The Times*, 11 May 2001, p. 8.
2 *Daily Telegraph*, 14 December 1999.
3 *The Times*, 23 June 2000.
4 The answers are as follows: (1) *The Witches of Eastwick*; (2) *Les Misérables* – James Fenton, initially chosen as the English librettist, is the son of John Fenton, former Principal of St Chad's College, Durham, and author of the Penguin commentary on St Matthew's Gospel; John Caird, the co-director, is the son of W. B. Caird, former Principal of Mansfield College, Oxford, and author of the Penguin commentary on St Luke's Gospel; (3) *Guys and Dolls*; (4) *Sweet Charity*; (5) *Chicago* – the Old Testament character is Methuselah who is mentioned in the song 'Give 'em the old razzle dazzle' and the hymn tune played during the trial scene in Act 2 is 'Rock of Ages'; (6) The Lord's Prayer set to the tune of 'Auld Lang Syne'; (7) Lutherans; (8) 'When you walk through a storm' also known as 'You'll never walk alone'; (9) 'Edelweiss' – the doxology is 'May the Lord, mighty God, bless and keep you for ever'; (10) 'Let us love in peace' from *The Beautiful Game*.
5 *Daily Telegraph*, 8 April 1998.
6 Manuscript copy of Don Lewis's sermon given to me by his widow, Ann, and quoted with her permission.
7 A. Barr, *Songs of Praise*, Oxford: Lion Books, 2001, p. 108.
8 'Building for God', Huntcliff Recordings Services, Redcar (HRSCD 372), 1997.
9 Sleeve note for 'Climb every mountain', CBS Masterworks (M30647), 1969.
10 *The Times*, 1 April 1967.
11 H. I. Khan, *The Music of Life*, Santa Fe, NM: Omega Publications, 1983, pp. 335–6.
12 See D. Campbell, *The Mozart Effect*, New York: Avon, 1997; T. Verney, *The Secret Life of the Unborn Child*, Warner Books, 1993.
13 K. Kimball (ed.), *The Music Lover's Quotation Book*, Toronto: Sound & Vision, 1990, p. 31.

14 Kimball, *The Music Lover's Quotation Book*, p. 92.

15 R. Rastall, *The Heaven Singing*, Woodbridge: D. S. Brewer, 1996.

16 S. Sutherland, *Teach Yourself about Musicals*, London: Hodder Headline, 1998, p. 3.

17 *Operatic Prayers*, Decca Record Company, 1997.

18 P. Glass, 'Chaplaincy at the West Yorkshire Playhouse', *Epworth Review*, April 2001, pp. 10, 12.

19 *Scotsman*, 1 July 1998.

20 Charles Spencer in the *Daily Telegraph*, 23 December 2000.

21 I. Bradley, *The Power of Sacrifice*, London: Darton, Longman & Todd, 1995, p. 19.

22 S. Miller, *From Assassins to West Side Story*, London: Heinemann, 1996, p. 220.

23 *Daily Telegraph*, 14 August 2001.

24 R. Christiansen, 'Opera over easy', *Daily Telegraph*, 1 June 2000, p. 28.

25 *Spectator*, 16 January 1999.

26 C. Wall, 'There's no business like show business: A Speculative Reading of the American Musical', in R. Lawson-Peebles (ed.), *Approaches to the American Musical*, Exeter: University of Exeter Press, 1996, p. 38.

27 Wall, 'There's no business like show business', p. 40.

28 A. J. Bergesen and A. Greeley, *God in the Movies*, New Brunswick, NJ: Transaction Publishers, 2000, p. 45.

29 D. Self, 'We need theatre, to ask difficult questions', *Church Times*, 20 April 2001.

30 A. Blackwell, *The Sacred in Music*, Cambridge: Lutterworth Press, 1999, p. 233.

31 M. Steyn, *Broadway Babies Say Goodnight*, London: Faber & Faber, 1997, p. 137.

32 *Daily Telegraph*, 19 September 2001.

33 G. Jones, *Christian Theology*, Cambridge: Polity Press, 1999, p. 131.

34 C. Marsh and G. Ortiz (eds), *Explorations in Theology and Film*, Oxford: Blackwell, 1997, p. 2.

35 Marsh and Ortiz, *Explorations in Theology and Film*, pp. 32–3.

36 *New York Times*, 21 May 2000.

37 P. Westmeyer, *With Tongues of Fire: Profiles in 20th Century Hymn Writing*, St Louis, MO: Concordia Publishing House, 1995, p. 118.

38 Westmeyer, *With Tongues of Fire*, p. 114.

39 *Daily Telegraph*, 20 October 2001.

40 E-mail to the author, 30 December 2003.

41 Essay written by Catherine Riggs for first practical theology class, St Andrews University, April 2001. Quoted with permission.

42 I take these definitions from R. Grimes, *Ritual Criticism*, Columbia: University of South Carolina Press, 1990, p. 14.

43 S. Purdie, 'Secular Definitions of "Ritual": The Rocky Horror Show', in S.

Levy (ed.), *Theatre and Holy Script*, Brighton: Sussex Academic Press, 1999, pp. 171–90.

44 *Guardian*, 5 March 2003.

45 *Daily Telegraph*, 12 November 1999.

46 *Center Line*, Wheaton, IL: Billy Graham Center, Spring/Summer 2000, p. 1.

47 *Coracle*, October 1999, p. 6.

48 N. O'Donoghue, *Patrick of Ireland*, Wilmington, DE: Michael Glazier, 1987, p. 53; A. Long, *Listening*, London: Darton, Longman & Todd, 1990, p. 15. For recent treatments of the dream theme in the Bible, see J.-M. Husser, *Dreams and Dream Narratives in the Biblical World*, Sheffield: Sheffield Academic Press, 1996, and S. Bar, *A Letter That Has Not Been Read: Dreams in the Hebrew Bible*, Cincinnati: Hebrew Union College Press, 2001.

49 D. Bonhoeffer, *Life Together*, London: SCM Press, 1954, pp. 15, 16.

50 *Daily Telegraph*, 13 February 2001.

51 H. Carpenter, *Dennis Potter: A Biography*, London: Faber, 1998, p. 348.

52 Carpenter, *Dennis Potter*, p. 350.

53 Carpenter, *Dennis Potter*, p. 350.

54 J. B. Cook, *Dennis Potter: A Life in Screen*, Manchester: Manchester University Press, 1995, p. 164.

55 Carpenter, *Dennis Potter*, p. 352.

56 Cook, *Dennis Potter*, p. 164.

57 Cook, *Dennis Potter*, p. 179.

58 Cook, *Dennis Potter*, p. 181.

1 *So ends my dream – the theology of Gilbert and Sullivan*

1 S. Morley, *Spread a Little Happiness: The First Hundred Years of the British Musical*, London: Thames & Hudson, 1987, p. 9.

2 D. Cannadine, 'Gilbert and Sullivan', in R. Porter (ed.), *Myths of the English*, Cambridge: Polity Press, 1992, p. 18.

3 Steyn, *Broadway Babies*, p. 68.

4 J. B. Jones, *Our Musicals, Ourselves: A Social History of the American Musical Theater*, Hanover: Brandeis University Press, 2003, p. 11.

5 Cannadine, 'Gilbert and Sullivan', p. 17.

6 (1) *The Gondoliers*, Act 1, line 311; (2) Castle Adamant, the all-female university in *Princess Ida*, Act 1, line 315; (3) Thomas Aquinas is listed as one of the elements essential to creating a Heavy Dragoon in the song 'If you want a receipt of that popular mystery' in *Patience*, Act 1, line 145.

7 J. Stedman, *W. S. Gilbert*, Oxford: Oxford University Press, 1996, p. 8.

8 A. Fischler, *Modified Rapture: Comedy in W. S. Gilbert's Savoy Operas*, Charlottesville: University Press of Virginia, 1991, pp. 51–2.

9 Miller, *From Assassins to West Side Story*, p. 3.

10 P. Stone, *The Musical Comedy Book*, New York: Random House, 1974, p. 15.

11 A. Jacobs, *Arthur Sullivan, a Victorian Musician*, 2nd edn, Aldershot, Hants: Scolar Press, 1992, p. 410.

12 E. Routley, 'Hymn Tunes of Arthur Sullivan', *The Hymn Society Bulletin*, 2.7, July 1949, p. 7.

13 These remarks were made in a talk at the Sullivan Society Festival at Ely in June 1994.

14 S. Rogal, 'The Hymn Tunes of Arthur Sullivan', in J. Helyar (ed.), *Gilbert and Sullivan*, Lawrence: University of Kansas Press, 1971, p. 179.

15 A. Sullivan, *The Prodigal Son*, London: Boosey & Co., 1869, preface. I owe this reference to Will Parry.

16 Sullivan, *The Prodigal Son*.

2 'Til you find your dream – the golden age of Broadway

1 E. Mordden, *Beautiful Mornin': The Broadway Musical in the 1950s*, Oxford: Oxford University Press, 1999, p. 89.

2 Stone, *Musical Comedy Book*, p. 8.

3 *Daily Telegraph*, 24 April 1998.

4 D. Horn, 'Who Loves You, Porgy? The Debates surrounding Gershwin's Musical', in R. Lawson-Peebles (ed.), *Approaches to the American Musical*, Exeter: University of Exeter Press, 1996, pp. 119–20.

5 M. Hertsgaard, *The Eagle's Shadow*, London: Bloomsbury, 2002, pp. 126, 128.

6 Mordden, *Beautiful Mornin'*, p. 21.

7 E. Mordden, *Opera in the Twentieth Century*, Oxford: Oxford University Press, 1978, p. 312.

8 A. J. Lerner, *The Street where I Live: The Story of 'My Fair Lady', 'Gigi' and 'Camelot'*, London: Hodder, 1978, p. 34.

9 Lerner, *Street where I Live*, p. 220.

10 Lerner, *Street where I Live*, p. 34.

11 C. Brahms and N. Sherrin, *Song by Song*, Bolton, Lancs: Ross Anderson, 1984), p. 89.

12 W. G. Hyland, *Richard Rodgers*, New Haven: Yale University Press, 1998, p. 205.

13 R. Kislan, *The Musical*, Tonbridge, Kent: Applause Books, 1995, p. 141.

14 H. Fordin, *Getting to Know Him: A Biography of Oscar Hammerstein II*, New York: Random House, 1977, p. 36.

15 Hyland, *Richard Rogers*, p. 216.

16 Brahms and Sherrin, *Song by Song*, p. 89.

17 Steyn, *Broadway Babies*, p. 72.

18 S. Citron, *Sondheim & Lloyd Webber: The New Musical*, Oxford: Oxford University Press, 2001, p. 30.

19 Steyn, *Broadway Babies*, p. 97.

20 Miller, *From Assassins to West Side Story*, p. 55.

21 Jones, *Our Musicals, Ourselves*, p. 146.

22 Fordin, *Getting to Know Him*, p. xiii; D. Rodgers, *A Personal Book*, New York: Harper & Row, 1977, p. 32.

23 E. Norton, 'Broadway's Cutting Room Floor', *Theatre Arts*, 36, April 1952, p. 80.

24 Mordden, *Beautiful Mornin'*, p. 95.

25 K. Ganzl, *The Musical: A Concise History*, Boston, MA: Northeastern University Press, 1997, p. 259.

26 See, for example, G. Block, *Enchanted Evenings: The Broadway Musical from Show Boat to Sondheim*, Oxford: Oxford University Press, 1997, pp. 292–3, and Miller, *From Assassins to West Side Story*, p. 45.

27 Hyland, *Richard Rogers*, p. 255.

28 F. Nolan, *The Sound of their Music: The Story of Rodgers and Hammerstein*, New York: Walker & Co., 1978, p. 220.

29 Nolan, *The Sound of their Music*, p. 220.

30 Nolan, *The Sound of their Music*, p. 225.

31 Fordin, *Getting to Know Him*, p. 349.

32 Hyland, *Richard Rogers*, p. 254.

33 Fordin, *Getting to Know Him*, p. 350.

34 *Church Times*, 22 June 2001.

35 Jones, *Our Musicals, Our Selves*, p. 313.

36 E. Mordden, *Coming Up Roses: The Broadway Musical in the 1950s*, Oxford: Oxford University Press, 1998, p. 34.

37 M. Druxman, *The Musical: From Broadway to Holywood*, New York: Yoseloff, 1980, p. 58.

3 To dream the impossible dream – the rhythm of life and the brotherhood of man

1 Miller, *From Assassins to West Side Story*, p. 220.

2 Lerner, *Street where I Live*, p. 221.

3 Lerner, *Street where I Live*, p. 222.

4 Lerner, *Street where I Live*, p. 174.

5 Miller, *From Assassins to West Side Story*, p. 102.

6 Miller, *From Assassins to West Side Story*, p. 103.

7 Block, *Enchanted Evenings*, p. 209.

8 Brahms and Sherrin, *Song by Song*, p. 202.

9 These extracts come respectively from the song 'At the Basilica of St Anne' and the song 'Heredity-Environment' in the musical *Smiling the Boy Fell Dead*.

10 M. Pinsky, *The Gospel according to the Simpsons: Leader's Guide for Group Study*, Louisville, KY: Westminster John Knox Press, 2001, p. 111.

11 D. Wasserman, *Man of La Mancha*, New York: Random House, 1966, p. ix.
12 Wasserman, *Man of La Mancha*, p. ix.
13 Miller, *From Assassins to West Side Story*, p. 61.
14 Miller, *From Assassins to West Side Story*, p. 56.

4 Any dream will do – the biblical superstars of the 1970s

1 M. Coveney, *Cats on a Chandelier*, London: Hutchinson, 1999, p. 212.
2 Citron, *Sondheim & Lloyd Webber*, p. 400.
3 *Sunday Times*, 19 May 1968.
4 T. Rice, *Oh, What a Circus*, London: Hodder & Stoughton, 1999, p. 134.
5 R. W. L. Moberly, 'Solomon and Job: Divine Wisdom in Human Life', in S. C. Barton (ed.), *Where Shall Wisdom be Found?*, Morton Kelsey, 1999, p. 9.
6 Rice, *Oh, What a Circus*, p. 141.
7 Rice, *Oh, What a Circus*, p. 141.
8 Dimbleby Lecture, 19 December 2002. The full text can be found on both the *Guardian Unlimited* and *Church Times* web pages.
9 T. Copley, 'Children "Theoligising" in Religious Education', *Education Today*, 51, April 2001.
10 E. Nassour, *Rock Opera: The Creation of Jesus Christ Superstar*, New York: Hawthorn Books, 1973, p. 21.
11 Rice, *Oh, What a Circus*, p. 177.
12 Nassour, *Rock Opera*, p. 190; K. Richmond, *The Musicals of Andrew Lloyd Webber*, London: Virgin, 1995, p. 28.
13 *Christian Century*, 27 June 1973; *Christianity Today*, 12 October 1973; *Time*, 30 July 1973; *Newsweek*, 9 July 1973.
14 S. Morley, *Spread a Little Happiness*, London: Thames & Hudson, 1987, p. 176.
15 Nassour, *Rock Opera*, p. 81.
16 Nassour, *Rock Opera*, p. 200.
17 Nassour, *Rock Opera*, p. 164.
18 R. C. Stern, C. N. Jefford and G. Debona, *Savior on the Silver Screen*, New York: Paulist Press, 1999, p. 185.
19 Nassour, *Rock Opera*, pp. 37–8.
20 Nassour, *Rock Opera*, pp. 39–40, 41.
21 Stern, Jefford and Debona, *Savior on the Silver Screen*, p. 181.
22 *Church Times*, 23 February 2001.
23 R. Ellis, '*Godspell* as Medieval Drama', *America*, 23 December 1972.
24 S. Schwartz, '*Godspell* Script Notes and Revisions', 1999, on www.geocities.com/sloanpeters/scriptnotes.htm.
25 Schwartz, '*Godspell* Script Notes and Revisions'.
26 J. Barton, 'The *Godspell* Story', *America*, 12 December 1971.

27 *New York Times*, 20 March 1973; *New Republic*, 12 May 1973; *America*, 14 April 1973; *Saturday Review*, 28 April 1973; *Christianity Today*, 10 April 1973.

28 'Godspell – the Ultimate Blasphemy', on www.av1611.org/crock/godspell.html.

29 Barton, 'The *Godspell* Story'.

30 Schwartz, '*Godspell* Script Notes and Revisions', p. 1.

31 Ellis, '*Godspell* as Medieval Drama'.

32 E-mail sent to Rebecca Howard, 3 June 2002.

33 The history of 'Beautiful City' is well covered in Shawn McCarthy's article 'Understanding the Song and Its History' on www.musicalschwartz.com/godspell-beautiful-city.htm

34 Programme for 2002 UK tour of *Godspell* (John Good Holbrook, 2002).

5 Now life has killed the dream I dreamed – Les Misérables

1 S. Morley and R. Leon, *Hey Mr Producer*, London: Weidenfeld & Nicolson, 1998, p. 91.

2 E. Behr, *Les Misérables: History in the Making*, London: Pavilion, 1996, p. 78.

3 Behr, *Les Misérables: History in the Making*, p. 160.

4 Miller, *From Assassins to West Side Story*, p. 167.

5 V. Hugo, *Les Misérables*, London: Everyman's Library, 1998, p. xxi.

6 Hugo, *Les Misérables*, p. 36.

7 Hugo, *Les Misérables*, p. 64.

8 Hugo, *Les Misérables*, pp. 107, 109.

9 Hugo, *Les Misérables*, p. 112.

10 D. Bonhoeffer, *The Cost of Discipleship*, London: SCM Press, 1959, p. 15.

11 Hugo, *Les Misérables*, p. 202.

12 Hugo, *Les Misérables*, p. 1431.

13 Hugo, *Les Misérables*, pp. 873–4.

14 On this, see I. Bradley, *The Power of Sacrifice*, London: Darton, Longman & Todd, 1995, pp. 166–9.

15 www.lesmis.com/inspiration/creation

16 Hugo, *Les Misérables*, p. 1220.

17 Hugo, *Les Misérables*, p. 876.

18 Hugo, *Les Misérables*, p. 1239.

19 Hugo, *Les Misérables*, p. 174.

20 Hugo, *Les Misérables*, p. 1298.

21 Hugo, *Les Misérables*, p. 1164.

22 Hugo, *Les Misérables*, p. 1172.

23 I. Bradley, *O Love That Wilt Not Let Me Go*, London: Fount, 1990, pp. 39–40.

24 S. Sutherland, *Teach Yourself about Musicals*, London: Hodder & Stoughton, 1998, p. ix.

6 Dreams don't die – musicals of the last 25 years

1 Quoted in G. Beals, 'The World of *Rent*', *Newsweek*, 13 May 1996.
2 E-mail to author from Stephen Schwartz, 2 July 2002.
3 E-mail to author from Stephen Schwartz, 2 July 2002.
4 E-mail to author, 23 September 2003.
5 M. H. Bell, *Whistle Down the Wind*, London: Sceptre, 1997, p. 99.
6 *Daily Telegraph*, 3 July 1998; Coveney, *Cats on a Chandelier*, p. 273.
7 Coveney, *Cats on a Chandelier*, p. 261.
8 Coveney, *Cats on a Chandelier*, p. 274.
9 I. Bradley, *God Save the Queen*, London: Darton, Longman & Todd, 2002, pp. xix–xx.
10 *Daily Telegraph*, 15 October 1999.
11 'Nature in the roar', *The Times*, 18 December 1999.
12 *Independent*, 4 August 1999.
13 *Sunday Times*, 12 September 1999.
14 Theatregoers Programme, 'The Beautiful Game' (2000).
15 *Daily Telegraph*, 16 September 2000.
16 Theatregoers Programme.
17 *Daily Telegraph*, 12 January 2002.
18 *Hotstuff* (Virgin Voyager Train Magazine), Autumn 2002, p. 13.
19 *Daily Telegraph Magazine*, 18 May 2002, p. 37.

7 Catching God's dream – the message for the church

1 V. Turner, *The Anthropology of Performance*, New York: PAJ Publications, 1986, p. 48.
2 'Heart and Soul' (BBC World Service programme broadcast 10 April 2001).
3 Lectures delivered at St Mary's College, St Andrews, 12 April 1999.
4 *Epworth Review*, April 2001, pp. 12–13.
5 *Church Times*, 14 May 1999.
6 T. Sample, *The Spectacle of Worship in a Wired World*, Nashville: Abingdon Press, 1998, p. 104.
7 Sample, *The Spectacle of Worship in a Wired World*, p. 108.
8 Sample, *The Spectacle of Worship in a Wired World*, p. 109.
9 Sample, *The Spectacle of Worship in a Wired World*, pp. 109–10.
10 Sample, *The Spectacle of Worship in a Wired World*, p. 112.
11 Sample, *The Spectacle of Worship in a Wired World*, pp. 115–16.
12 Sample, *The Spectacle of Worship in a Wired World*, p. 119.
13 Sample, *The Spectacle of Worship in a Wired World*, pp. 119–20.

14 Sample, *The Spectacle of Worship in a Wired World*, p. 116.

15 'From Les Miserables to Miracle Moments', *Cathedral of Hope Weekly News*, 15.36, 9 September 2001, p. 7.

16 Sermon by the Revd Michael Piazza, 28 October 2001.

17 *Religion and Ethics Newsweekly*, 1 August 2003.

18 E-mail to author from Paul Hughes, 17 March 2003.

19 O. Willmott, *The Vicar Calls*, Shrewsbury: Bishop Street Press, 2001, p. 58.

20 T. Gieschen, 'Contemporary Christian Music – Problems and Possibilities', lecture given at Concordia University, Forest River, 6 November 1986 and quoted in M. Dawn, *Reaching out without Dumbing Down*, Grand Rapids: Eerdmans, 1995, p. 167.

21 J. Frame, *Contemporary Worship Music*, Phillipsburg, NJ: P&R Publishing, 1997.

22 B. Wren, *Praying Twice: The Music and Words of Congregational Song*, Louisville, KY: Westminster John Knox Press, 2000, p. 53.

23 R. Gawronski, 'Why Orthodox Catholics Look to Zen', *New Oxford Review*, 60.6, July–August 1993, p. 14.

24 'Blatant Bernstein', *Church Times*, 2 June 2000, p. 28.

25 Coveney, *Cats on a Chandelier*, p. 116.

26 Citron, *Sondheim & Lloyd Webber*, p. 327.

27 Coveney, *Cats on a Chandelier*, p. 261.

28 *Church Times*, 31 August 2001.

29 *The Herald*, 10 January 2000; *Dundee Courier and Advertiser*, 10 January 2000; *Scotland on Sunday*, 9 January 2000; *Sunday Times*, 12 September 1999.

30 *Scotland on Sunday*, 9 January 2000.

31 *Scotland on Sunday*, 9 January 2000.

32 *Scotland on Sunday*, 16 January 2000.

33 'Follow the yellow-brick code', *Daily Telegraph*, 11 October 2003.

34 Quoted in B. Wren, *Praying Twice*, p. 160.

35 *Church Times*, 14 May 1999.

36 Wren, *Praying Twice*, p. 382.

37 Wren, *Praying Twice*, p. 158.

38 *Church Times*, 7 January 2000.

39 M. Neary, 'From Hymns to Hollywood', *The Times*, 20 November 1999, p. 22.

40 I. Bradley, *Colonies of Heaven*, London: Darton, Longman & Todd, 2000, pp. 152–3.

41 P. Brook, *The Empty Space*, McGibbon & Kee, 1968, pp. 140–1.

Sources and Acknowledgements

Every effort has been made to trace the owners or administrators of the copyright in the songs and dialogue quoted in this book. If there are any omissions or errors in the following list, the publisher would be grateful to be informed for correcting in future editions.

'At the Basilica of St. Anne,' by Sheldon Harnick. Copyright © 1977 Sheldon Harnick. Publication and allied rights owned by Mayerling Productions, Ltd. (Administered by R&H Music) throughout the world. Used by permission. All rights reserved.

Extracts from *The Beautiful Game*. Lyrics by Ben Elton. Music by Andrew Lloyd Webber. Copyright © 2000 The Really Useful Group Ltd., London. All rights reserved. International copyright secured. Used by permission.

Extracts from *Camelot*. Words by Alan Lerner. Music by Frederick Loewe. Copyright © 1960 Alan Lerner and Frederick Loewe, Alfred Productions Inc., Chappell & Co. Inc., USA. Warner/Chappell North America, London W6 8BS. Reproduced by permission of International Music Publications Ltd. All rights reserved.

'The Highest Judge of All', 'When the Children Are Asleep', 'You'll Never Walk Alone', and dialogue from *Carousel*. Copyright © 1945 Williamson Music. Copyright renewed. International copyright secured. All rights reserved. Used by permission.

Lyrics from *Celebration*. Copyright © Tom Jones. All rights reserved. Quoted by kind permission of the author.

Extracts from *Children of Eden*. Lyrics copyright © Stephen Schwartz. Quoted by kind permission of the author.

Sources and Acknowledgements

Extracts from *Merrily We Roll Along*. Words and music by Stephen Sondheim. Copyright © 1981 Rilting Music Inc., USA. Warner/Chappell North America, London W6 8BS. Reproduced by permission of International Music Publications Ltd. All rights reserved.

'Wishing You Were Somehow Here Again' from *The Phantom of the Opera*. Lyrics by Charles Hart. Additional lyrics by Richard Stilgoe. Music by Andrew Lloyd Webber. Copyright © 1986 The Really Useful Group Ltd., London. All rights reserved. International copyright secured. Used by permission.

'I'm on My Way' and 'Oh the Train Is at the Station' from *Porgy and Bess*. Music and lyrics by George Gershwin, Du Bose and Dorothy Heyward, and Ira Gershwin. Copyright © 1935 (Renewed 1962) George Gershwin Music, Ira Gershwin Music, and Du Bose and Dorothy Heyward Memorial Fund. Warner/Chappell Music Ltd., London W6 8BS. Reproduced by permission of International Music Publications Ltd. All rights reserved.

Extracts from *Prince of Egypt*. Lyrics copyright © Stephen Schwartz. Quoted by kind permission of the author.

'One Song Glory', 'Another Day', and 'I'll Cover You' from *Rent*. Words and music by Jonathan Larson. Copyright © 1996 Finster & Lucy Music Ltd. Co. All rights controlled and administered by EMI April Music Inc. All rights reserved. International copyright secured. Used by permission.

Extracts from *Sabina* reproduced by kind permission of the author, Willy Holtzman, and the lyricist, Darrah Cloud.

Extracts from *Sophie's World: The Musical*. Based on the novel by Jostein Gaarder. Lyrics by Øystein Wiik and copyright © by Øystein Wiik. Used by kind permission of Øystein Wiik.

'Climb Ev'ry Mountain' and 'Sixteen Going on Seventeen' from *The Sound of Music*. Lyrics by Richard Rodgers and Oscar Hammerstein II. Copyright © 1959 Richard Rodgers and Oscar Hammerstein II. Copyright renewed. Williamson Music owner of publication and allied rights throughout the world. International copyright secured. All rights reserved. Used by permission.

'Bali Ha'i', 'Happy Talk', and 'A Cock-Eyed Optimist' from *South Pacific*. Lyrics by Richard Rodgers and Oscar Hammerstein II. Copyright © 1949 Richard Rodgers and Oscar Hammerstein II. Copyright renewed. Williamson Music owner of publication and allied rights throughout the world. International copyright secured. All rights reserved. Used by permission.

Sources and Acknowledgements

Extracts from *Whistle Down the Wind* (Jim Steinman/Andrew Lloyd Webber). Copyright © 1998. Used by kind permission of Universal Music Publishing.